Critical Voices in Library and Information Work

Critical Voices in Library and Information Work presents 25 profiles of notable, transformational library and information science (LIS) workers in the United States, Canada, and the UK, all of whom are involved in progressive library and information work projects or research endeavors.

Discussing a piece of literature, art, or music that helped direct their path into socially conscious library work and that continues to inspire them, interviewees provide insights into their work and the current state of critical librarianship. They also reflect upon the current state of institutions, including academic, public, and school libraries, as well as special libraries. The authors of the book present these conversations in a narrative form that situates their subjects' professional work within their broader historical and cultural milieu, while carefully supplementing the conversations with real-world information and context. The resulting collection gives insight into what grounds and inspires influential LIS professionals and highlights the diversity found in critical librarianship as one of its greatest strengths. Together, the professionals' voices provide the reader with a better understanding of what drives their peers' transformational LIS work.

Critical Voices in Library and Information Work presents the voices of professionals who hail from traditional and non-traditional information environments and who have varying levels of experience. The book will appeal to practicing library workers and information professionals, as well as students and academics engaged in the study of LIS.

Stephen Bales is a Professor in Global Languages and Cultures at Texas A&M University.

Tina Budzise-Weaver is an Associate Professor in the College of Performance, Visualization and Fine Arts at Texas A&M University.

Routledge Guides to Practice in Libraries, Archives and Information Science

This series provides essential practical guides for those working in libraries, archives, and a variety of other information science professions around the globe.

Including authored and edited volumes, the series will help to enhance practitioners' and students' professional knowledge and will also encourage sharing of best practices between different countries, as well as between different types and sizes of organisations.

Assessment as Information Practice
Evaluating Collections and Services
Edited by Gaby Haddow and Hollie White

A Guide to Using the Anonymous Web in Libraries and Information Organizations
Enhancing Patron Privacy and Information Access
Brady D. Lund and Matthew A. Beckstrom

Practicing Social Justice in Libraries
Edited by Alyssa Brissett and Diana Moronta

Discoverability in Digital Repositories
Systems, Perspectives, and User Studies
Edited by Liz Woolcott and Ali Shiri

Digital Libraries Across Continents
Edited by Le Yang and Alicia Salaz

Artificial Intelligence for Academic Libraries
Clifford B. Anderson, Douglas H. Fisher

For more information about this series, please visit: https://www.routledge.com/Routledge-Guides-to-Practice-in-Libraries-Archives-and-Information-Science/book-series/RGPLAIS

Critical Voices in Library and Information Work
Voices and Inspiration from the Discipline

Stephen Bales and Tina Budzise-Weaver

LONDON AND NEW YORK

First published 2026
by Routledge
4 Park Square, Milton Park, Abingdon, Oxon OX14 4RN

and by Routledge
605 Third Avenue, New York, NY 10158

Routledge is an imprint of the Taylor & Francis Group, an informa business

© 2026 Stephen Bales and Tina Budzise-Weaver

The right of Stephen Bales and Tina Budzise-Weaver to be identified as authors of this work has been asserted in accordance with sections 77 and 78 of the Copyright, Designs and Patents Act 1988.

All rights reserved. No part of this book may be reprinted or reproduced or utilised in any form or by any electronic, mechanical, or other means, now known or hereafter invented, including photocopying and recording, or in any information storage or retrieval system, without permission in writing from the publishers.

For Product Safety Concerns and Information please contact our EU representative GPSR@taylorandfrancis.com. Taylor & Francis Verlag GmbH, Kaufingerstraße 24, 80331 München, Germany.

Trademark notice: Product or corporate names may be trademarks or registered trademarks, and are used only for identification and explanation without intent to infringe.

British Library Cataloguing-in-Publication Data
A catalogue record for this book is available from the British Library

ISBN: 978-1-032-75358-4 (hbk)
ISBN: 978-1-032-69658-4 (pbk)
ISBN: 978-1-003-47364-0 (ebk)

DOI: 10.4324/9781003473640

Typeset in Times New Roman
by SPi Technologies India Pvt Ltd (Straive)

Contents

Author Biographies vii
Acknowledgments viii

Prologue 1

1 Maria Accardi 6

2 Liam Adler 12

3 Melissa Adler 17

4 Alex Brown 24

5 Becky Calzada and Carolyn Foote 30

6 Ione Damasco 36

7 Emily Drabinski 43

8 Fobazi Ettarh 48

9 Lia Friedman 55

10 Kelly Jensen 61

11 Amanda Jones 70

12 Alfred Kagan 77

13	Stuart Lawson	81
14	Jessie Loyer	87
15	Annie Pho	93
16	Sam Popowich	99
17	Douglas Raber	105
18	Toni Samek	114
19	Gina Schlesselman-Tarango	120
20	April Sheppard	126
21	Naomi Smith	132
22	Raegan Swanson	138
23	Eamon Tewell	144
24	Jessamyn West	150
25	Baharak Yousefi	156
	Epilogue	*162*
	Index	*170*

Author Biographies

Stephen Bales is a Professor in Global Languages and Cultures at Texas A&M University. He has a master's degree in Information Science, a PhD. in Communication and Information from the University of Tennessee-Knoxville, and a graduate certificate in Buddhist Studies from the Institute of Buddhist Studies. He sole-authored two books, *The Dialect of Academic Librarianship: A Critical Approach* and *Social Justice and Library Work: A Guide to Theory and Practice*, and has co-authored two books, *Transformative Library and Information Work: Profiles in Social Justice* and *Serapis: The Sacred Library and Its Declericalization*. He is General Editor of the *Journal of Radical Librarianship*.

Tina Budzise-Weaver is an Associate Professor in the College of Performance, Visualization and Fine Arts at Texas A&M University. She has a master's degree in library and information science from the University of North Texas and is pursuing a PhD in Sociology at Texas A&M University. She co-authored the book, *Transformative Library and Information Work: Profiles in Social Justice*. Her research explores multiple avenues, including information literacy and social media as forms of performance and the intersections of community art and society.

Acknowledgments

Stephen Bales: I would like to thank my wife Mitzi, the Reds, Mom, Tina, and everyone we interviewed for this project.

Tina Budzise-Weaver: I would like to thank my family for their support. I am especially thankful to the interviewees, who generously shared their origin stories and personal journeys into librarianship. Collaborating with Dr. Stephen Bales has been a true pleasure.

Prologue

The landmark 1972 book *Revolting Librarians*, edited by Celeste West and Elizabeth Katz, is a brief but remarkably loud existential shout to the world by library workers fed up with the status quo. In the book's introduction, West proclaims:

> The Good News is Advocacy! Participation! Librarians can generate information. Why watch it congeal in a 3X5 world? [...] A lovely thing about freedom of expression is that it's contagious [sic]. More and more librarians realize that they too can defy the *CREEPING MEATBALL*. (I think this is a Merry Prankster expression, akin to cartoonist Dan O'Neill's *POOPADOODLE*: a mocking refusal to dignify the big bumtripping forces of evil, which flourish on reeespect.)
>
> (pp. 1–2)

West was correct that members of the 1960s and early 1970s counterculture stood up against the "Creeping Meatball" (Yippie!), i.e., the invasive conformity imposed by the dominant culture. The term, however, was first used a decade earlier by radio personality, raconteur, and humorist Jean Shepherd in his 1957 satirical essay for MAD Magazine, "The Night People vs. 'Creeping Meatballism'" (Shepherd, 1957). The "Day People," Shepherd writes, are the conformists stultified by the day-to-day realities of life as consumers, i.e., they are the average squares who think "in certain prescribed patterns. People today have a genuine fear of stepping out and thinking on their own. 'Creeping Meatballism' is this rejection of individuality. It's conformity" (p. 41). Shepherd's "Night People" were the "'soreheads', wise-guys', 'eggheads', long-hairs', 'outsiders', etc." (p. 41). *Revolting Libraries* was written by Night People for Night People, even if these particular Night People typically worked 9–5 shifts at the library and looked like squares. *Revolting Librarians* collects rabble-rousing essays and poems like Bianca Guttag's "Homophobia in Library School," Sanford Berman's "Libraries to the People," and Kathleen Glab's "The Sensuous Librarian." It indicts the library as a conservative institution and apparatus of the capitalist state and dominant culture. At the same time, it also sees the institution's potential as a force for radical change within this same milieu.

Shepherd's 1950s America reeked of conformity and manifested the unfortunate epiphenomena attendant to late-stage capitalism: homophobia, racism, sexism, and anti-communism (or anything sufficiently egalitarian and supportive of collectivism to get the communist label foisted on it). It is nearly 70 years later, and the Meatball still creeps. Capitalism's byproducts are all still there too, this time supported by Make America Great Again (MAGA) tribalism, neo-fascism, white supremacy, and the re-emergence of far-right political movements around the world. Current scapegoats include undocumented immigrants, members of the transgender community, and "woke" left-wing activists. The library world has encountered a recent surge in censorship attempts and book banning, and library workers have become the targets of reactionary ire. On the other side of the coin, questions have been raised about the complicity of the library in maintaining the dominant culture and the repressive structures inherent in it. Amazingly, defenses of library neutrality still show up in the library and information science professional literature.

The term "critical librarianship" came into vogue in the first decade of the 21st century, and, for a time at least, the hashtag #critlib became a frequently used tool for initiating discussion on Twitter (now X). Toni Samek described critical librarianship as "an international movement of library and information workers that consider the human condition and human rights above other professional concerns" (Robertson, 2007). But, besides the use of the word "critical," there is nothing particularly new about critical library and information work; its "historical roots are firmly planted in the 1930s US progressive library movement" (Robertson, 2007). Library workers of all types (public, academic, school, and government) have been raising their voices and engaging in transformative practices for decades, whether they are identified by themselves or by others as progressive, radical, critical, Marxist, communist, or anarchist. And, like any movement, critical librarianship, as a more or less coherent movement, will eventually end (see Chapter 18's interview with Toni Samek for more on "post-critical librarianship"). There will, however, always be *critical voices* within library work. The word *critical* used here may be seen to have two meanings. In one sense, the critical voice brings critical theory, i.e., theory constructed for the purpose of transforming society through challenging power structures with the aim of dismantling them, into direct conversation with library work. In the second sense, *critical* may be seen as going beyond static theorizing and entering into the world of action and practice. The critical library worker does not only theorize; they may not theorize in the former sense at all. They are *critical* in that their actions constitute *progressive societal transformation* in process. In this capacity, they are *critical* to material change. When the two "criticals" work together, i.e., the actualization of critical processes complements a critical consciousness, the potential for substantive change via dialectical processes becomes greatly amplified.

This book collects profiles of 26 professionals in 25 chapters (we decided to combine Becky Calzada and Carolyn Foote, the Texas FReadom fighters, into one chapter) in the field of library and information science. The profiles are ordered alphabetically by participant last name. Some of the participants might not consider themselves "critical library workers," but all of them are seen by the present authors as *critical voices* in the field. It was our intention to better understand why and how they became *critical voices*, their philosophies, and their motivations. Participants were drawn from various points in their professional careers in an effort to capture the stories of a wide range of people. Some of the participants are relatively new to the profession and not long out of graduate school. Others are mid-career professionals. At the time of the interviews, a few participants were thinking about retirement or had been enjoying their retirement for several years (this does not mean, however, that they do not continue their activism). Doug Raber (see Chapter 17), for instance, had recently retired after spending decades working both in public libraries and as a library school professor, historian, and critical theorist. Al Kagan (see Chapter 12), another participant who had also recently retired after a long career in academic libraries, spent many years weaving social activism into his work as an academic librarian. Some participants had even left the library altogether. Kelly Jensen (see Chapter 10), for example, is a former children's and teen librarian who now champions anti-censorship efforts in libraries through her work as an editor and columnist for the popular book review website Book Riot. Fobazi Ettarh (see Chapter 8), a former academic librarian well-known for her research surrounding "vocational awe," recently left the profession to work on a Library and Information Science PhD full-time. Naomi Smith (see Chapter 21) also left academic librarianship to focus on her own activist projects, one being Black and Gold Education ("Black Librarian Addressing Critical Knowledge gaps Aiming to start discussions & New ways of thinking for disadvantaged people").

When selecting participants for this project, we attempted to recruit from a variety of different types of institutions, including academic libraries, public libraries, school libraries, media centers, and archives. Of the 26 participants, 14 worked or had worked in academic libraries, three in public libraries, four in school libraries, four as library school professors, and one as an archivist. We recognize that our pool of participants was heavily weighted toward academic librarians and the limitations that this imposes on achieving the fullest possible picture of activist library work. It became apparent early in the project that it would be difficult to enlist public and school library workers to take part in interviews, which is unfortunate because of those library workers' long association with social justice issues. This reticence on the part of public and school library workers to participate may be a result of the current political climate and the tenuous nature of many public and school library professionals' job statuses—they do not benefit from the tenure protections afforded to many teaching professors and some academic librarians. At the time of this writing, US President Donald Trump had signed an executive order to dismantle the Institute of Museum and Library Services, a government organization that supports public library services across the United States. Even more dispiriting was the fact that we were not able to recruit any government library workers for the project. This does not mean that there are no *critical voices* employed by the government; we attribute their hesitation to take part largely to the chilling effect of being government workers (Librarian of Congress Carla Hayden, one must remember, was fired in May 2025). Nonetheless, government librarians are working to make change, even if under the radar.

At the time the interviews were conducted, 18 of the participants worked in the United States, six in Canada, and two were working in the United Kingdom. Although there is great work being done by critical library workers outside of these three nations, the authors were limited by both practical restrictions and barriers resulting from institutional review board requirements. While this is a shame—for instance, Mexico and Central and South America are hot-beds for critical librarianship—the authors hope to expand their future research to more international locations.

The interviews themselves were conducted between 2023 and 2025 by means of Zoom videotelephony software. They were open-ended and used only a skeletal interview guide. The participants were encouraged to talk about what was important to them as both library and information workers, and involved citizens and activists. The free-flowing conversation facilitated by the (largely) unstructured long-form interview allowed the interviewers to follow leads to further understand how participants make meaning in their role as library workers qua activists. Sometimes this approach led to interesting digressions. One detour, for example, revolved around the merits of zombie movies. Nonetheless, nearly everything that was said in these exchanges gave some insight into the personalities and motivations of the person being interviewed, as well as their remarkable depth of character, passion for their work, and compassion for others. The primary focus of the interview process was the discussion of work of scholarship, art, music, literature, or other creative output that the participant found particularly impactful in their work as a *critical voice* or in the development of their critical consciousness. All the participants identified something that radically affected their orientation toward critical library work. While some of these works were expected, such as Marxist theorist Sam Popowich's (see Chapter 16) choice of Karl Marx's monumental *Capital Volume 1* or Fobazi Ettarh's (see Chapter 8) choice of an article written by Kimberlé Crenshaw introducing the concept of intersectionality, there were also surprises. Academic librarian, April Sheppard (Chapter 20), selected two things: a soul record by Solomon Burke and the television series *Impractical Jokers*. Academic librarian Lia Friedman (see Chapter 9) would pick an activist organization. Library school professor Melissa Adler (see Chapter 3) picked Canadian author Marian Engel's controversial novel *Bear*. The researchers, however, allowed the sky to be the limit when making selections. We also quickly learned that some participants had difficulty picking just one influence; in those cases, we chose not to limit them and just let the conversations go where they went.

We would like to thank the 26 participants that took part in this project, all of whom are legit Night People: Maria Accardi, Liam Adler, Melissa Adler,

Alex Brown, Becky Calzada, Ione Damasco, Emily Drabinski, Fobazi Ettarh, Carolyn Foote, Lia Friedman, Kelly Jensen, Amanda Jones, Al Kagan, Stuart Lawson, Jessie Loyer, Annie Pho, Sam Popowich, Doug Raber, Toni Samek, Gina Schlesselman-Tarango, April Sheppard, Naomi Smith, Raegan Swanson, Eamon Tewell, Jessamyn West, and Baharak Yousefi.

In solidarity,

Stephen Bales and Tina Budzise-Weaver, July 2025

References

Shepherd, J. (1957, April). The night people vs. "creeping meatballism". *MAD Magazine*, *32*, 41–44. https://madcoversite.com/missing_night.html

Robertson, T. (2007, November 13). Critical librarianship: An interview with Toni Samek. *The (Unofficial) BCLA Intellectual Freedom Committee Blog*. https://bclaifc.wordpress.com/2007/11/13/critical-librarianship-an-interview-with-toni-samek/

West, C., & Katz, E. (Eds.). (1972). *Revolting librarians*. Booklegger Press.

1 Maria Accardi

Maria Accardi is the Coordinator of Instruction and Assessment at the Indiana University Southeast Library. Accardi is an important voice in the development and application of critical and feminist pedagogies in library work.

Accardi has always been a "library kind of person." She was an early reader; her parents said that she started reading at age two, although her older sister "claimed that I just had the book memorized. I am not sure who is right." The first place that Accardi was allowed to go by herself as a child was the local public library:

> I would ride my bike there. It was also the 1980s and no one cared much about kids going places by themselves. Yes, I was going to the library alone as a kid and filling up my little basket of books. I volunteered in the summer reading program one year. Basically, you would just listen to the kids talk about the books they read for the program and give them a stamp or a sticker, a pencil or whatever. And you got to sit at the librarian's desk in the children's section to talk to the kids. It was like readers advisory. I just love that—talking to people about reading in the library.

Even though Accardi said that she has always gravitated to the library and had library work "in the back of my mind as a thing I could do," librarianship was not her first career path. One reason for this was that most professional librarian jobs in the United States require a graduate degree, and Accardi was intimidated by the prospect of having to take the Graduate Record Examination placement test. Then, when she did take the plunge and go to graduate school, Accardi had decided to pursue an English degree instead with the goal of becoming a literature professor. However, working for a year indexing newspapers for ProQuest after graduation led Accardi to reconsider library work. From her experience earning her master's in English, Accardi knew that she liked working with college students, especially teaching them how to research and write papers. She also remembers taking the English classes she taught to the library for bibliographic instruction sessions led by library staff, realizing that this "was something that librarians do." Because of these experiences, academic librarianship just made sense. In 2006, Accardi received her master's in

LIS from the University of Pittsburgh, worked for a year at Sarah Lawrence College, NY, and then started at IU Southeast, where she has been ever since.

Accardi said that there was no critical moment in her development as a social justice-oriented librarian, but an intersection of different threads from her life that came together. Even as a child, she felt strongly that part of her role in the world is to make a difference, to "see where things are wrong and try to make them right." She first learned about social justice and put a name to the feeling while attending Catholic school. The timing for being in Catholic school, Accardi said, was perfect:

> This is like the late 80s, early 90's. I have talked to people about their college or their Catholic school experiences, and they are like, 'We did not learn about social justice and liberation theology.' I just happened to have these nuns who were interested and wanted to raise our consciousness [...] This was at two different Catholic schools in different regions of the country. But Sister Stacy, which is not a very 'nun' name, and she had braces, which is not relevant, but these are the details that stand out. I remember her writing the term 'liberation theology' on the chalkboard, talking to us about the Salvadoran Civil War. We watched a TV movie about the three nuns and lay missionary women that were abducted, raped, and murdered in El Salvador. And we watched the movie *Romero*, about Archbishop Óscar Romero, and it really made a strong impression on me that the Catholic Church and ordinary individuals brought about change in ways that are very brave, literally risking their lives to right grave injustices that were being done to other people.

Even though Accardi considers herself to be a "book person," music has always been a major influence on her development. In eighth-grade music class, another teacher, Sister Mary Carol, passed around images of murdered Jesuit priests in El Salvador. After learning about the murders, the class learned the Peter, Paul, and Mary protest song "El Salvador" (Stookey, 1986). The song's lyrics made a deep impression on Accardi: "There was a part in the song where it says, 'Just like Poland is protected by her Russian friends/The junta is assisted by Americans.'" Hearing these words, Accardi was haunted by the fact that her country was responsible for horrible things happening to regular people for no discernible reason.

Another early influence on Accardi was the soundtrack to the musical *Jesus Christ Superstar* (Webber & Rice, 1970). Her parents had seen the stage production in the 1970s, and Accardi heard the soundtrack frequently as a kid. Sister Mary Carol showed Accardi's class the movie version (Jewison, 1973), and she was struck by the very different depiction of Jesus than she was used to, i.e., the table-flipping Jesus from the scene where he confronts the money changers in the Temple of Jerusalem. For Accardi, this was a Jesus who cared about the poor, marginalized, and oppressed. In the Temple scene, Jesus takes on the establishment through direct action, and this underscored for Accardi the idea that this is what you should care about: helping and serving those who are powerless:

> So here we have this very cool movie. It was 70s cool with bellbottoms and a hippie looking Jesus, and the music was catchy. […] It was a lens through which to see Jesus as a justice-oriented figure in a cool way, and it made a deep impression on me.

Accardi also gives Roman Catholic nuns like Sister Stacy and Sister Mary Carol some credit for her introduction to feminism and strong women:

> Given the whole Catholic Church hierarchy, you do not really think of Catholic nuns—on the surface at least—as being feminist. But even though there is a kind of messed up gender dynamics in the Church, the nuns, in my experience, were powerful. They are the teachers. They are the ones who were bosses of things and, as a kid, that was something that I looked up to. And there is something about a community of women bringing about social change that feels feminist to me, even if the Pope would not describe it that way. There are some nuns that are real badass feminists, real activist nuns. The nuns who are very contrary to Catholic teaching, who speak out against the anti-choice rhetoric of the Church and do work along those lines.

Accardi first encountered the *theory* behind justice-directed *action* upon reading Paolo Freire's *Pedagogy of the Oppressed* (1970) as a graduate student in English:

> I am like, that is what Sister Stacy and Sister Mary Carol were talking about […] This makes sense to me. If you look at my own personal views about what is right and wrong in the world, it was a puzzle piece that just made sense.

During her first professional librarian job at Sarah Lawrence College, Accardi shared an office with fellow reference librarian Emily Drabinski (see Chapter 7 for a profile of Drabinski). Through long conversations with Drabinski, Accardi realized that she could take some of her exposure to critical theory as a graduate student and explore its possible intersections with library work in ways that made sense to her. After moving to her current position at IU Southeast—and being faced with publication requirements as part of the tenure process—Accardi started putting things together and developing a professional praxis and research agenda around feminist pedagogy.

Accardi locates feminist pedagogy at the nexus of feminist theory, teaching, and learning that is primarily concerned with consciousness raising and centering the voice of the learner. This approach harnesses the power of participatory learning to dismantle the hierarchical power structures existing between teacher and student in a way that also pays attention to how gender dynamics govern the classroom, either explicitly or implicitly, both in terms of the content that is taught and the way that content is taught. Accardi's daily work is informed by various threads of critical thought, and she said she cannot imagine approaching it in any other way than she does, seeing praxis as a spiritual, moral calling and something that she is supposed to do with her gifts and talents for writing and teaching.

In 2010, Accardi co-edited an influential book with Emily Drabinski and Alana Kumbier, *Critical Library Instruction: Theories and Methods* (Accardi, Drabinski, & Kumbier, 2010). This collection brings together chapters authored by influential scholars of critical pedagogy in library work, like Maura Seale, John S. Riddle, and Heidi L. M. Jacobs, and provides readers with an array of theoretical and practical tools for their reflective instruction practices. Accardi found one of the book's chapters, Sharon Ladenson's (2010) "Critical Feminist Pedagogy in Library Instruction," particularly interesting and, reading more on the topic, found a gap in the literature concerning feminist pedagogy that invited a fuller, lengthier examination of the topic. This led to Accardi's (2013) monograph *Feminist Pedagogy for Library Instruction*, published by Library Juice Press:

> By then Emily Drabinski was an editor for Litwin Books/Library Juice Press. I told her I had this idea for a book, so we started this conversation. Then I had a contract. I worked on the book for two years. I was looking at questions like what is feminist pedagogy? How do you define it? Who are the major theorists in the field? What does it look like in action? Then I brought feminist pedagogy into conversation with library instruction and information literacy, looking at how we teach and learn in libraries and describing ways of doing those things based on what I was reading and what I had done in my own experience.

Accardi described *Feminist Pedagogy* as a "weird little book" in which she works out her feelings in public. That, however, is how she writes, and it is effective. For example, from the book's introduction:

> There was the time I tried decentering myself in the classroom for the first time, refusing to stand in the front of the room, and requiring students to conduct the demonstrations of databases—and found that it successfully facilitated learning in the classroom. There was the first time I conducted research consultations with students that not only dealt with the practical matters of library research but also addressed the affective dimension of research, how students *felt* about the research process— and found that it transformed my relationships with students. There was the first time that I deliberatively chose to use a feminist-related topic as a sample search to a class full of students—and found that it awakened my students to a new way of thinking about sexism.
>
> (Accardi, 2013, p. 3)

Both the book's style and content resonated with readers, and it was subsequently awarded the 2014 ACRL WGSS Significant Achievement Award. Accardi followed *Feminist Pedagogy* with an edited collection, *The Feminist Reference Desk: Concepts, Critiques, and Conversations* (2017), which took the conversation started in *Feminist Pedagogy* and applied it to reference work more broadly construed. With its more than 20 chapters written by 34 authors, as well as its vibrant range of styles and approaches to theory and practice, the book demonstrates just how fast critical approaches to library work can capture imaginations and gain traction within the profession, confirming Accardi's status as a trailblazer in the area.

Although Accardi described the status of her research agenda as currently "dormant," she remains heavily engaged in activist work outside of the library. She founded the non-profit organization Bringing Justice Home (https://www.bringingjusticehomelou.org/) early in the COVID-19 pandemic with her wife, Constance Merritt. Bringing Justice Home delivers groceries and household supplies to people in Louisville, Kentucky, who are medically vulnerable and experiencing food insecurity. The project started because Accardi and Merritt had previously been involved in food pantries and food ministries, and, early in the pandemic, many food pantries were simply closed or used a car-based, drive-through model that excluded those people who did not have an automobile and could not afford grocery delivery.

When asked if she ever sees herself taking on activist work, such as her non-profit, as a full-time endeavor, Accardi is realistic:

> No, I like a paycheck. I like health insurance. I must pay the mortgage. So, it is hard to see me doing this full time. The other thing that keeps me at the library and not being a corporate trainer for like Humana or one of the big corporations here in Louisville is that I have an economically stable job. I am a tenured full professor. […] It keeps me hooked. It is the velvet handcuffs.

Although the pandemic is over, Bringing Justice Home is still at it, delivering necessities to 50 households a month:

> So, no wonder I am not doing any writing. When I am not at the library, when I am not working at my pay job, I am helping to run a nonprofit. Sometimes I feel like that is the most important work I do.

Nevertheless, Accardi has recently been identifying potential areas of research within library work for future exploration. She is considering revising both *Feminist Pedagogy* and *The Feminist Reference Desk* to address questions like what was missing? And how have things advanced since the book's publication? Accardi would also like to study how people like her—people who have training in areas like writing, rhetoric, and composition, in addition to librarianship—formed as librarians. She would do this with hopes of identifying what these professionals bring into librarianship from this other training and to pinpoint what library schools could be doing better to incorporate such training into their curricula. Accardi also sees a potential line of research inquiry arising from the intersection of her professional work and non-profit activist work. That is, she would like to look at those library workers who are inclined toward some sort of social activism outside of their professional work:

> I know there are other people like me. So, what motivates them? [...] I just feel that there is something about the librarians who are critical—in whatever way that looks like—and the way they engage in activism outside of the library sphere. And these two spheres might intersect or not. Maybe they are inextricable, but I just feel that there is something there.

Accardi feels like she is in academic librarianship for the long haul (or at least the indefinite future) because "it just feels like all the stars and planets are in alignment." She is connecting with students, and students are learning.

References

Accardi, M. T. (2013). *Feminist pedagogy for library instruction*. Library Juice Press.
Accardi, M. T. (Ed.). (2017). *The feminist reference desk: Concepts, critiques, and conversations*. Library Juice Press.
Accardi, M. T., Drabinski, E., & Kumbier, A. (Eds.). (2010). *Critical library instruction: Theories and methods*. Library Juice Press.
Freire, P. (1970). *Pedagogy of the oppressed*. Continuum.
Jewison, N. (Director). (1973). *Jesus Christ superstar* [Film]. Norman Jewison; Robert Stigwood [Executive Producers]. Universal Pictures.
Ladenson, S. (2010). Critical feminist pedagogy in library instruction. In M. T. Accardi, E. Drabinski, & A. Kumbier (Eds.), *Critical library instruction: Theories and methods* (pp. 105–112). Library Juice Press.
Stookey, N. P. (1986). El Salvador. On *No easy walk to freedom*. WEA.
Webber, A. L., & Rice, T. (1970). *Jesus Christ superstar*. Decca.

2 Liam Adler

Liam Adler is currently the Director of Collection Strategy, Access, and Engagement at Barnard College Library, New York, where he also serves as librarian for Women's and Gender and Sexuality Studies. Adler's practice and research focus on critical reference work in libraries and library history. He has always been interested in counterculture and things in conversation with critical theory. This affinity developed in high school when he first encountered subjects like Marxism, deepened in college through in-depth reading, and refined through his early professional library work. Before taking his present position at Barnard College, Adler was Director of the Library at Metropolitan College of New York. Now a private college, Metropolitan College of New York was founded in 1964 as the Women's Talent Corp., a job training and employment agency started by activist Audrey Cohen for the purpose of educating low-income women for jobs. Over the years, the organization sought to fill a deeper pedagogical need based on Cohen's philosophy of Purpose Centered Education, i.e., to "provide a superior, experientially based education that fosters personal and professional development, promotes social justice, and encourages positive change in workplaces and communities" (Metropolitan College of New York, n.d.). Changing its name to Audrey Cohen College in 1992 and then to Metropolitan College of New York in 2002, the institution is now a progressive, experimental college geared to low-income adults with programs in education, business, and public affairs and administration. Adler sees working at Metropolitan College of New York as an important part of his story in terms of critical library work. He spent about 11 years there, and:

> It was a place where I came of age professionally and was exploring things that were interesting and felt simpatico to me in terms of my philosophical outlook. [...] Critical librarianship emerged out of a critique of the neoliberal university. This place was a casualty of the neoliberal university, but a different version of that, I think. So, thinking about criticality when it comes in the context of working with 35-year-olds or 50- or 60-year-old college students who are going to have this kind of

experience for the first time after years and years of working is just a very different way to think about information literacy than the students I am working with now. It is a whole different relationship with what being in college means, what scholarship means.

Working at Metropolitan College of New York, Adler began making connections between theory and practice and asking questions like, how does a particular critical theory apply to a particular work situation? How does theory apply to understanding the sociocultural systems that we live in? How can one implement theory in terms of making positive material changes in their own lives and the lives of others? Adler sees library work as aligned with a criticality that, while not overtly anti-capitalist in the sense that it intervenes with certain kinds of capitalist and corporate logics, prefigures a space that is not completely dominated by such logics. The ability of libraries to allow one to imagine other worlds guides his practice through considering questions like, what does it mean to share resources? Or what does it mean to have a sort of anarchistic relationship with intellectual discovery?

Adler described critical reference work as being closely related to the concept of critical pedagogy. The latter developed as a reaction to what radical educational theorist Paolo Freire referred to as the "banking" concept of education, where people are treated like empty vessels for a teacher to pour knowledge into (Freire, 1970). In contrast, critical pedagogy sees the education process as a *conversation* between the instructor and students that effectively blurs the line between the two parties. Applying this to library reference work, Adler said that the reference process should not be conducted as a "reference interview" but as a discussion where the student or patron likely knows more about any given subject than the library worker, and one in which the reference worker collaborates with them in a utilitarian way that takes in some kind of criticality. Critical reference considers the learner's needs in the moment and holds that how the library worker speaks to those needs should not be based on their own pedagogical agenda. Adler said that the process overlaps with critical library instruction in that both interactions help people to think critically about systems and to consider the way knowledge is structured for economic reasons, asking questions like, why does one have to search a database for information in the first place? Or why is certain information hard to find?

Adler pointed to the law professor and transgender activist Dean Spade's (2022) book *Normal Life: Administrative Violence, Critical Trans Politics, and the Limits of Life* as an inspiration for his work. What intrigued Adler about *Normal Life* is how Spade looks specifically at the law to consider the limits of a reform-based approach to transgender legal rights. In the process, he considers the limits of legal language, a language that turns on the internal logics of a system that impedes transformative change. Spade is interested in both looking at the limitations of a legal rights-based approach to the law and examples of critical resistance to or abolition of that system (i.e., tearing it down and starting again). Adler was struck by Spade's elegant choreography of abstract but consequential concepts:

> It does not seem to me like he started something like [Spade's] Sylvia Rivera Law Project, which concentrates on increasing the life chances of trans people in the prison system. He does not dismiss the importance of the material needs of people for the cause of something that is some kind of idealism but considers the other ways in which we can think about deeper, more transformative change. In founding the Sylvia Rivera Law Project, he centered the material needs of trans people who are caught up in draconian administrative systems (prisons, shelters, etc.), but he connects this concrete work to a theoretical interrogation of the mechanics of systematic injustice, and to larger concepts of mutual aid and transformative change.

For Adler, Spade's critique of the legal system is an actualization of Michel Foucault's philosophy of power. In *Normal Life*, Adler said, Spade clearly and compellingly articulates how the legal system limits trans people's life chances. For example, the act of prosecuting hate crimes against trans folks only serves to bolster the system that victimizes the people whom it supposedly protects.

Something that Dean Spade did not propose himself, but that he draws upon in *Normal Life*, is the Miami Workers Center's (MWC) Four Pillars of Social Justice Infrastructure:

> The Four Pillars that MWC describe are the Pillar of Policy, the Pillar of Consciousness, the Pillar of Service, and the Pillar of Power. The Pillar of Policy includes work that changes policies and institutions using legislative and institutional strategies, with concrete gains and benchmarks for progress. The Pillar of Consciousness includes work that aims to shift political paradigms and alter public opinion and consciousness, including media advocacy work, the creation of independent media, and public education work. The Pillar of Service encompasses work that directly serves vulnerable people and helps stabilize their lives and promote their survival, including work that provides critical services like food, legal help, medical care, and mental health support. Finally the Pillar of Power is about achieving autonomous community power by building a base and developing leadership: building membership organizations of a large scale and influence (quantity) and developing the depth and capacity of grassroots leadership (quality).
>
> (Spade, 2022/2011, p. 102)

While Spade talks specifically about the Four Pillars of Social Justice Infrastructure as they relate to transgender legal issues, what Adler finds great about them is that they are easily transferable to other forms of activism and suggest how one might incorporate theory into grassroots political change through mutual aid:

> Mutual aid is something that I am really excited about in terms of libraries. I think that libraries can learn a lot from what Spade is saying about Mutual Aid. Libraries give people free communal space to work together, they provide for material needs, they provide a sense of place, they can be a space for being together in a community, and at the same time libraries are a place to explore ideas—any ideas really—including political consciousness. It is wild that within capitalism an institutional space like that exists, and I think we can push harder to articulate it and to actualize it.

Adler's first big research project was to co-edit a book for Library Juice Press, *Reference Librarianship & Justice: History, Practice & Praxis* (Adler, Beilin, & Tewell, 2018). The experience led him toward the history of libraries and library work, which has since become the primary focus of their research:

> I felt at the time that I had seen that most of the ways people were talking about criticality and librarianship was either in the context of cataloging or in the context of instruction. I was interested in thinking about reference in a critical way.

Adler is currently writing a book for Library Juice Press entitled *Twisting Spirit: Radical Education, Radical Politics, The War on Poverty & the American Library* (Adler, forthcoming), the inspiration for which grew out of his work at Metropolitan College of New York. The book will focus on the War on Poverty, an anti-poverty initiative started by President Lyndon Johnson in 1964, and will analyze what libraries did with War on Poverty funds to provide outreach services in ways that were deeply engaged with questions concerning how to reach underserved communities. Such questions, he said, had been addressed in the past during the Progressive Era of the late 19th and early 20th centuries. War on Poverty efforts, however, were differently articulated, placing more of a focus on library workers working within their communities. Adler's research for this project has led him to libraries like the Langston Hughes Community Library and Cultural Center in Queens, New York, which was founded with the help of the Black Panther Party and later incorporated into the Queens public library system:

> I looked at a few different such instances and foregrounded it by looking at the Progressive Era and what libraries who were doing also at that time to see the parallels to what they would later be doing with the War on Poverty and grounded both instances to radical free education. In the Progressive Era, there was a startup of anarchist schools, Emma Goldman's labor schools, and there was communist political education

that was happening. Then in the 1960s and 70s, during the War on Poverty era, there were the Young Lords or the Black Panthers, and other analogous organizations.

Twisting Spirit will document the history of such library outreach efforts and community work that puts that history in conversation with the history of the educational practices of social movements, be it the anarchism of the 1920s and the 1930s or the Young Lords in the 1960s.

Adler believes that interest in critical librarianship has been growing and will continue to do so, pointing to the success of events like the annual Critical Pedagogy Symposium (https://criticalpedagogysymposium.org/) held online since 2021. He has also seen a generational shift happening in which critical approaches to library work are finding their way deeper into the library school curriculum. For example, he has recently been working with library school students on a critical librarianship fellowship that includes a critical reading project:

> The students seem so conversant with the level of critical analysis, regardless of what they are drawing upon, regardless of citing actual theory. Just in terms of praxis, it feels to me like they are much more conversant with thinking about things in a deeply critical way. It seems like that is much more of the norm now. There is just something in the water for them in a way that is different.

Adler sees the practice of critical library work and the institutionalization of critical perspectives as reaching a significant tipping point. This institutionalization also seems somewhat counterintuitive. What happens when critical librarianship gets absorbed and appropriated? People with critical perspectives are now in positions of power. What does it mean for the president of a professional organization, such as Emily Drabinski in the American Library Association, to possess such a genuinely critical kind of perspective? Even though Adler sees such questions as yet to be answered, he sees critical librarianship as currently being in a good place.

References

Adler, L. (forthcoming). *Twisting spirit: Radical education, radical politics, the war on poverty & the American Library*. Library Juice Press.

Adler, L., Beilin, I, & Tewell, E. (2018). *Reference librarianship & justice: History, practice & praxis*. Library Juice Press.

Freire, P. (1970). *Pedagogy of the oppressed*. Continuum.

Metropolitan College of New York. (n.d.). *Mission statement*. Metropolitan College of New York. https://www.gnyha.org/wp-content/uploads/2019/12/6v1.-Admissions-Presentation-to-General-Information-Session-11-8-19-revised-jcolelli-tgeorgiou-4pm.pdf

Spade, D. (2022). *Normal life: Administrative violence, critical trans politics, and the limits of life*. Duke University Press.

3 Melissa Adler

Melissa Adler is an Associate Professor of Media Studies and Library and Information Science (LIS) at the University of Western Ontario (UWO), London, Ontario. A researcher in critical classification studies, Adler investigates the intersection of LIS with gender and sexuality and studies questions surrounding the limits and possibilities of information for democracy, political participation, and equity.

Adler grew up in Wisconsin and was inspired by her grandmother, who had, after taking library courses through correspondence school, become a cataloger. She saw that her grandmother loved her work and "she probably was waiting her whole life to be able to do meaningful work like that." Adler's grandmother's passion and dedication influenced Adler's father, who, when they visited her grandmother, would take her to see her at work. Following her father's death during her teenage years, Adler became even closer to her grandmother:

> She was extremely smart and thoughtful and different from other people her age, as far as I was concerned. She questioned God and she questioned everything. That was unusual for her peers in that very Catholic town. She and I just got each other. We made sense to each other, so we were really close. And then I had gotten a bachelor's degree in English, and I did not know what I was going to do. I had a young baby at home, and my grandmother was like 'you should see if there are any library correspondence courses.' So, I investigated it and then found out that there are actually online courses. I had no idea.

Following in her grandmother's footsteps, Adler attended the University of Wisconsin-Milwaukee's School of Information's then-fledgling distance program. After graduation, she got a job in a small academic library in a small Catholic institution as an archivist—even though she had not been trained as one—requiring her to learn archival work on the job along with cataloging. One part of her work included uploading updated Library of Congress Subject Headings (LCSH) to the local system, a process that introduced her to critical classification:

> Doing that work made me see on a regular basis subject headings that I thought were strange. So, at some point, I realized this was interesting and I started making a list of headings that I thought were problems and I did not know about. So, even though I had [Professor of Information Studies at the University of Wisconsin Milwaukee] Hope Olson as a professor for my introduction to information organization class, I did not know that she was an amazing critical scholar. It was not until after reading her stuff and [critical cataloger] Sandy Berman and [librarian, blogger, and publisher] Rory Litwin and all that material. I also started paying attention to the Progressive Librarian's Guide and American Library Association.

Deciding that she was not happy working where she was, Adler determined to pursue some of her questions surrounding critical classification through the University of Wisconsin, Madison's Library and Information Studies doctoral program. This resulted in a dissertation on the LCSH headings for sexual perversion that would serve as the basis for her first monograph, *Cruising the Library: Perversities in the Organization of Knowledge* (2017). After receiving her PhD, Adler took her first assistant professor job at the University of Kentucky School of Information Science. After four years at Kentucky, she moved to the University of Western Ontario (UWO), where she teaches courses on research methods and information organization and is currently chair of the PhD program in LIS and the master's program in Media Studies. With its strong emphasis on critical theory, Adler considers UWO to be her dream faculty.

Adler sees her research work as a labor of love and feels that the critical examination of libraries is not meant to be destructive, i.e., that libraries are in some sense "bad"; instead, it should identify where libraries can do better. She said that her research has had a clear trajectory since her dissertation:

> I knew I wanted to do something about gender and sexuality for my dissertation, and I knew that I wanted to do something dealing with subject headings. So, I started searching the catalog and used the search heading 'bisexuality.' It had subject headings that were bisexuality, neuroses, and paraphilia, and I did not know what paraphilia meant. That was really confusing to me. And I was like 'Oh well, this must be something that is outdated,' like they just did not update it. So, I looked paraphilia up in the catalog, and I found out that there were hundreds of books with this subject heading. What was going on here? Then I looked it up in the Library of Congress Catalog and in the subject authorities, and it said that it had been authorized in 2007!

The use of this highly technical medical terminology and its recency did not make any sense to Adler, and she determined to understand how things had gotten to this point. *Cruising the Library* developed out of the dissertation and represents the full maturation of this line of research. With *Cruising the Library*, Adler wanted to produce something for people in sexuality studies and American studies in addition to an LIS audience, which she said reflects her drive to spread a better understanding of critical theoretical issues in the library to people in other fields who might take libraries for granted:

> Many researchers in other fields do not see libraries as having a history of themselves, and they do not see the significance in the relations of power in everyday life. They look at how it affects their own research and the disciplines themselves. That to me is a really important piece and I want other disciplines to know about what we do.

Following *Cruising the Library*, Adler's research has shifted its focus to the 19th century and Thomas Jefferson's selling of his personal library to the Library of Congress after the latter was burned to the ground by British forces during the War of 1812. Although historians point to the late 19th century as the time period in which librarianship underwent professionalization, Adler wanted to see if she could find the emergence of the categories of the profession—of ideas of what libraries are—in Jefferson's work and that early version of the Library of Congress:

> So, I started analyzing the classified catalog he created for his collection. The version that I work with the most has 44 chapters that are essentially disciplines. Within those, he had what he called his analytic order where he grouped things into subjects, the chapters being the subjects. So, there is 'History, American,' and so on. And then within history, you see there is 'north' and 'south.' There are various things happening and I wanted to figure out if I could find some other categories, social categories.

Digging deep into Jefferson's classification, Adler made fascinating discoveries. For example, around 1782, Jefferson was writing his notes on the state of Virginia and also classifying his books. In his notes on Virginia, Jefferson wrote about books in his personal collection by the Black authors Phillis Wheatley and Ignatius Sancho. In his analysis of their work, Jefferson wrote that if one were to compare Wheatley and Sancho to other authors in the genre, they should be placed at the bottom of the column. Then, in his catalog, he does indeed put Sancho at the bottom of the "Epistolary" class:

> So, he is writing about it in this political document, and then he catalogs it, and then that catalog is transferred to the Library of Congress. There is this marginalization that is set in motion in a system early on.

What started out as research for a single article turned into a massive undertaking that took seven years to complete. At the time of the present book's writing, Adler had two forthcoming books that came out of the project.

Peculiar Satisfaction: Thomas Jefferson and the Mastery of Subjects (forthcoming-a) examines Jefferson's role in the development of American libraries through his classification system and its impact on the Library of Congress. *Surveillance in the Empire of Liberty: Why Thomas Jefferson Matters in Our Information Age* (forthcoming-b) examines Jefferson's plantation and factories in terms of the surveillance technologies and practices that were employed to manage an enslaved workforce, to consider its impact on the development of American society.

For Adler, encountering Marian Engel's (1976) controversial novel *Bear* was a germinal influence on her development as a researcher and part of her story of becoming a Canadian. Adler relocated from Kentucky to Canada in 2017, where she began reading Canadian literature to get a sense of her adopted home. Some American friends posted something about *Bear* on social media, asking Adler if she had seen it. She had not heard of the book before, but decided to read the novel after learning more about it.

Along with novels like Alice Munro's (1968) *Dance of the Happy Shades* and Margaret Atwood's (1996) *Alias Grace*, *Bear* is representative of the Southern Ontario Gothic genre of literature. In the book, Engel tells the story of Lou, a librarian who is sent to a remote island in northern Ontario to catalog the Pennarth Estate library, which had been bequeathed to the Toronto Historical Institute by the recently deceased Colonel Jocelyn Cary. Lou relocates to the old Cary mansion for the summer, where she becomes deeply consumed with the cataloging work. During her lonely work, she falls in love with and has a sexual relationship with a tame bear that lives in the shed behind the house. The book was shocking upon its initial publication, and it remains a target of book-banning attempts. It is also considered by many to be a literary masterpiece with its lyrical language and its exploration of themes like personal discovery, loneliness, desire, liberation, and nature versus the civilized world. Despite the uproar caused upon its publication, *Bear* was awarded the Governor General's Award for Literature in 1976, one of the most prestigious literary prizes awarded for Canadian literature. *Bear* resonated immediately with Adler:

> The main character is a librarian who goes to spend the summer to catalog the collection, which is something I had just done because I had been doing fellowships at Monticello and living on the plantation. I got to live on the plantation on two different occasions for a month each time to study Thomas Jefferson's catalog and his collection. And that is exactly what this main character is doing. She is a librarian and very mousy who is hoping to find something in this collection which, I get it, that is me. I was still in the early stages of the Jefferson material too. I was pretty sure there was something there, but I did not know what it was yet. And then she encounters this bear that is living there, and it is such a bizarre turn of events. But that turn is so interesting to me because I am into sexuality studies.

Reading *Bear* left Adler fascinated with the book's author:

> I became obsessed with Marian Engel in the same way that I am obsessed with Thomas Jefferson. I needed to find out everything I could about her. Some of her letters were published, and I still have it in mind to go to her archive when I have the opportunity.

Adler said that there is something about Engel that really gets to her, such as how Engel was determined to write from the heart. Adler said that Engel's collected correspondence reveals the frequent rejection letters she received over the years. But Engel presses on, and it is this perseverance while remaining true to oneself that Adler found particularly inspiring and encouraging. Engel's tenacity would ultimately be rewarded with the Governor General's Award. Adler also has great respect for Engel's outspoken advocacy for Canadian writers:

> She was one of the founders of the Writers Guild in Ontario, which was a vocal advocate for making it so that if Canadian libraries acquired a person's books, that the author would get some kind of compensation. Engel helped to make that happen, and it is something that still exists today. She knew about librarianship as a practice because she was involved with the library board. She wrote this amazing letter to the library board because she got fines assessed. So, she wrote this major complaint about how ridiculous this was and how hard it was for her to get to the library because she was a single parent. I am a single parent. I have also been told not to do the research that I wanted to do, and I have had to go with my gut and do it. You cannot not do thing that you love.

Adler sees Engel, who died of cancer in 1985, as someone who was brave and principled and insisted on being heard in different ways—in her literature and her profession, politically, and as a mother. She recommends *Bear* to anyone interested in library history, gender and sexuality, or animal studies because all these areas of inquiry are taking place in LIS, and *Bear* poses interesting questions. Yes, Adler said, Lou comes across as a stereotypical librarian, but her experiences while cataloging the Pennarth books raise interesting questions about why people come to library work:

> I think most of us go into it, not just because we think, 'Oh, this will just be a good job.' For most of us it is not just a job. And when we pursue it, when we start library school, we are not under the illusion that it is just a good job. We go into it because we care about it. So, we have desires of our own, even though we are service professionals.

In addition to considering why librarians do what they do, the book asks important questions, like what counts as knowledge? And why do we become obsessed with something? This last question is something that Adler has asked herself concerning the Jefferson project:

> Sometimes I ask myself why I am so obsessed with this dead white guy? Should I be doing this project? What if I am doing the wrong project? *Bear* resonates with me so much because I identify with the character so much, but also with the author.

Adler sees Engel's bravery, poetic voice, and the way in which she writes herself into her novels as a model for her own approach to professional life. Adler tells her doctoral students to find their own model, to "find a writer. And when they speak to you, immerse yourself in them. Do not be them, but there is a way to engage with them deeply to help find your own voice." One model within LIS that Adler often points out to aspiring librarians is Emily Drabinski, past President of the American Library Association (see Chapter 7 for a profile of Drabinski). Drabinski, she said, is an exemplary model of both a scholar and a practitioner. Adler regularly assigns Drabinski's work as readings for her classes and recently arranged for her to come to UWO to give a talk:

> She is such a good human, and she is a person I look up to because she really knows who she is. I think that is the thing that I am always looking for and that I aspire to because I feel that when you know who you are then you are open to criticism, and you are open to changing your mind. That is a good thing. I love watching her in action.

Adler sees such openness to dialogue about ideas, willingness to ask difficult questions, and knowing who you are as necessary components for critical approaches to library work to be successful in the future. She is concerned that, as with everything that is politically left-leaning, critical librarianship has the potential for imposing limitations on thought. To counter this tendency, the critical library worker must remain steadfastly on the side of expansiveness, generosity, and curiosity rather than shutting ideas down without thinking them through. The critical library worker must also learn to listen to critical feedback or negative responses and be able to figure out the value in this feedback:

> So, if it is negative feedback on an article, like one of the reviews of the recent book proposal I submitted was saying that I make claims that I do not back up and that I say things that are not true, which I do not agree with. I want to be offended. The old me would have been offended, but now I think, 'hold on, so if the reviewer thinks that that means other readers are going to think that, and it means I better really have a solid case and make sure that I am clear and that know I what I am talking about.' If you think someone is saying something negative, you need to slow down and try to figure out what is really being said there. What is useful? It is good advice, but it is hard.

Finally, the critical library worker should also always expect pushbacks but Adler said that if people react strongly to something in a negative way, then you are probably doing that something right.

References

Adler, M. (2017). *Cruising the library: Perversities in the organization of knowledge*. Fordham University Press.

Adler, M. (forthcoming-a). *Peculiar satisfaction: Thomas Jefferson and the mastery of subjects*. Fordham University Press.

Adler, M. (forthcoming-b). *Surveillance in the empire of liberty: Why Thomas Jefferson matters in our information age*. Bloomsbury.

Atwood, M. (1996). *Alias Grace*. Bloomsbury.

Engel, M. (1976). *The Bear*. Atheneum.

Munro, A. (1968). *Dance of the happy shades*. Ryerson Press.

4   Alex Brown

Alex Brown's journey into library work was neither conventional nor planned. What started as a practical decision to pursue a stable career quickly evolved into a deep commitment to school librarianship, the preservation of historical materials, and social justice advocacy. From working in public libraries and archives to shaping the library of an independent school, Brown's story highlights the intersection of education, representation, and resistance to systemic inequities in the library world.

Like several other library workers profiled in this volume, Brown "fell" into library work. In need of a job after earning their bachelor's degree in Anthropology and Sociology, Brown pursued a Master of Library and Information Science degree at San Jose State University. Although Brown's initial intent was to stay in library work for less than a decade, they found their niche at the intersection between their passion for history and their love of archives. Having worked for several years in reference and instruction positions, Brown had the opportunity to volunteer with the Napa County Historical Society (Napa County, CA) before eventually being hired full-time as Head of the Society's Research Library. At one point, they had considered becoming an archaeologist, and this interest aligned with the Historical Society's preservation mission, allowing them to work with the past without having to obtain a Ph.D. or dig in the dirt. Brown, who identifies as a genderqueer biracial Black person, saw firsthand the whitewashing that permeated the community's historical timeline in the process of archiving Napa Valley's diverse history, as the archives at the time focused primarily on Napa's white ancestry. As the only librarian of color working in the archives, Brown took on the challenging task of rectifying this inequity by promoting diversity through the archives.

When interviewing for the Napa County Historical Society archivist position, Brown had made it a point that they preferred not to collect more history on figures like George Yount, one of the area's prominent white settlers, but focus instead on the underrepresented and marginalized people whose contributions were routinely omitted from local histories in favor of the stories of rich white men. For example, Brown discovered and uncovered the lives of people like Nathaniel and Aaron Rice, who were brought to Napa County by slaveholder William Rice in 1860 and eventually freed from slavery, and

Carolina Bale, the Mexican American widow of winery owner Charles Krug and daughter of rancho and grist mill owner Edward Bale. In the process of diversifying the archives, Brown remained committed to engaging the community in a dialogue with its obscured past. For example, they developed a partnership with the local high school in Napa to introduce students of color who had immigrated into the United States as children to history and people that they could relate to:

> [...] I took them into the archives and showed them pictures of these Californios, and they are like, 'wait, there were Mexican people here?' And I tell them that this used to be Mexico, before that it was Spain, and before that it was Indigenous people. But them holding a photograph of a Mexican person [living in] 1850, that was mind blowing for them. Suddenly, they felt like they had a place in Napa, that it was not just the place where they were living. They had a connection to it.

While working at the Historical Society, Brown obtained a master's degree in United States History from Adams State University and began their own publishing career as a historian of the underrepresented and marginalized. Their thesis, "'There are No Black People in Napa': A History of African Americans in Napa County" (Brown, 2015), revealed a much more diverse Napa County than the one portrayed in existing histories. It served as the foundation for Brown's first book, *Hidden History of Napa Valley* (Brown, 2019), which chronicles the lives and work of the African Americans, Chinese Americans, other immigrants, and Indigenous peoples who inhabited the Napa Valley but were largely excluded from its mainstream history. Brown followed *Hidden History* with a second book, *Lost Restaurants of Napa Valley and Their Recipes* (Brown, 2020), which centers on the foodways of people of color and immigrants and their entrepreneurial success as restaurateurs in Napa Valley.

In 2014, Napa was hit by a magnitude 6.0 earthquake that caused significant damage to the community, including the Historical Society building where Brown worked. Experiencing burnout from the emotional and physical labor of putting a building and a collection back together, Brown left to pursue school librarianship at a high school. Today, Brown oversees the campus collection and curriculum needs, including developing the collection development policy.

Roughly 52% of the school's student population is made up of people of color, including a reasonably representative population of Asian international students. When Brown took over the administration of the school library, they were presented with a stagnant, poorly shelved collection that circulated less than 300 books a year and contained titles not particularly suitable for 9th–12th grade students (e.g., the James Joyce behemoth *Ulysses*). Brown determined that a change in collection strategy was necessary to engage students with modern and interesting titles, and they started collecting books and manga with diverse characters, cultures, and themes. After five years, circulation had increased dramatically to over 1,900 books a year, illustrating the positive impact of a diversity of representation on student learning and engagement.

Brown's current employer subscribes to key National Association of Independent Schools (NAIS) Principles of Good Practice for Equity and Justice, and Brown furthers this commitment through a library collection plan based on Rudine Sims Bishop's (1990) essay "Windows, Mirrors, and Sliding Glass Doors." Seeing their own philosophy of library work in "Windows, Mirrors, and Sliding Glass Doors," Brown considers Sims Bishop's essay as integral to the development of their own professional identity and practice.

In "Windows," Sims Bishop, a professor emerita of education at the Ohio State University describes children's books as windows to the world, as sliding glass doors that provide readers access to the histories, traditions, and cultures of non-white peoples, and as mirrors that transform and reflect human experience in a way that allows readers to see their "own lives and experiences as part of the larger human experiences" (1990 p. 1). Good books help children to better understand the experiences of people who look like themselves as well as the experiences of those who do not. Therefore, diversity of representation in collections is of the utmost importance because, if children "see only reflections of themselves, they will grow up with an exaggerated sense of their own importance and value in the world—a dangerous ethnocentrism" that can lead to social isolation and insulation from the larger world (p. 1). Because of this, educators and librarians must embrace books and build collections that venture beyond dominant cultures and norms, and "When there are enough books available that can act as both mirrors and windows for all our children" (p. 2).

"Windows" eloquently encapsulated what Brown had already been doing in their work at the Napa County Historical Society and confirmed their own philosophy of library work—one based on diversity, human rights advocacy, social justice, and the drive to make everyone feel represented in the library collection. Where most librarians will build their collection development policies around the American Library Association (ALA) Bill of Rights and adhere to a policy of "neutrality," Brown (2022) contended that libraries are never neutral:

> We cannot 'both sides' human rights. My identities and rights are not up for debate. Libraries cannot escape responsibility for the harm caused by clinging to a comforting illusion at the expense of the people they are supposed to serve. Our reckoning with this fetishization of neutrality that prevents us from fulfilling our roles as library workers is long overdue.

Library neutrality inevitably prioritizes the majority at the expense of the minority. Defending it will not save libraries from book bans, especially not as bad actors use it as cover for the real purpose behind their attacks: to cement control over information access and erase any visible traces of BIPOC, LGBTQIA2+, and other marginalized people. So, rather than abiding by the ALA's policy of library neutrality, Brown follows Sims Bishop's lead by providing students with books that celebrate diversity, in the hopes that "they will see that we can celebrate both our differences and our similarities, because together they are what makes us all human" (Sims Bishop, 1990, p. 2). Brown explained, "the stuff that I did not get to read as a kid, I feel like it is really important that kids have access to that now, even if they do not check it out." Therefore, a collection development policy centered on social justice ensures that all identities are protected.

For Brown, it is of the utmost importance that everybody using the library sees both themselves *and* other possible identities in the collection, and they work to accomplish this objective through designing a robust collection development policy that embraces diverse voices and experiences. Based on this philosophy of inclusion and representation, Brown has developed collections to ensure that the diversity of languages and dialects is available to students. In addition to developing an inclusive collection, Brown ensures that student access to materials comes in many forms, including traditional print, audiobooks, ebooks, software, and other modes to best support different reading and learning styles and accessibility needs. In fact, Brown prefers to use the acronym IDEA (inclusion, diversity, equity, and access) to DEI (diversity, equity, and inclusion) because "you cannot separate out social justice and access from DEI."

Brown's collection development policy is also designed to outmaneuver the small subset of people currently responsible for approximately 60% of book ban filings (Blair, 2024). The ongoing battle against book bans and censorship remains one of the most pressing issues in Brown's work. In states like Texas and Florida, the erasure of DEI initiatives and the proliferation of restrictive policies around LGBTQIA2+ literature make collection development a tricky task. Brown has taken proactive steps to mitigate such threats, establishing rigorous book challenge procedures that make it difficult for external groups like Moms for Liberty (https://www.momsforliberty.org/), a conservative organization that advocates against curricula and books that acknowledge LGBTQIA2+, race and ethnicity, non-binary gender, and anything inclusive that they deem as "woke" (Southern Poverty Law Center, n.d.), to tamper with the library collection through censorship efforts and book challenges. Much of Moms for Liberty's efforts focuses on book bans in public school districts and strategically electing like-minded suppressors of diversity into school boards or political positions. In anticipation of such challenges, Brown has developed a system to thwart the challenge of even one book in the school's collection:

> I built in roadblocks, anticipating Mom's for Liberty. Our collection development policy for the challenge procedure, for example, says that you have to be a community member to make a challenge. You cannot be an outsider. You can only submit a couple of challenges a year. Whatever decision is made; you cannot appeal. The book cannot be challenged again for another four years. You have to mail the challenge in. You have to read all of these steps and if you do not do this step, then the challenge is thrown out and you have to start all over again.

As a result, even though book-banning attempts have created hoops for librarians and teachers to jump through, Brown has built strong collection development and book challenge policies, reshaping their library's internal policies to safeguard against censorship and effectively champion the books frequently targeted by banners.

In addition to the need to constantly fight for inclusiveness in school library collections, Brown said that they are equally concerned with the rise of generative artificial intelligence (AI) in education. Brown sees generative AI as antithetical to the core values of library work, given the way it devalues critical thinking. They are frustrated that generative AI has entered the workflow for many teachers and librarians, and they fear that such systems will inevitably be programmed to devalue the work of librarians and be used as an argument for their obsolescence. In addition, the potential for AI algorithms to construct results containing gender and racial biases harvested from across the Internet does not lend itself to the creation of a truthful and representative information landscape for students to explore (Gross, 2023; Lippens, 2024). How does one use a system that generates its results from sources like The Onion or Reddit? Brown remains adamant that libraries resist AI-driven models that prioritize automation over meaningful human engagement with literature and research.

In addition to their day job, Brown is also a prominent voice in the larger school library and children's literature community by means of their popular blog, Punk-Ass Book Jockey (https://bookjockeyalex.com/)—named after a term used for librarians in the television sitcom *Parks and Recreation*. On Punk-Ass Book Jockey, Brown draws attention to books that represent people who identify outside the binary cisgender messaging of the dominant culture through book reviews (Brown was awarded the 2024 Ignyte Award for reviews and analysis of the field of speculative literature) and the distribution of a popular summer reading list as well as yearly lists of new young adult science fiction, fantasy, and horror books, resources used by many other public and school librarians for collection development. While this work is supplementary to their full-time vocation in librarianship, Brown finds it critical to their ongoing development as a critical library worker.

Brown's work showcases library work qua activism through their commitment to representation, accessibility, and challenging the status quo in school and public libraries. At their school, Brown has created one of the most progressive spaces on campus by rejecting library neutrality in favor of advocacy as seen through the eyes of a trained historian and archivist. They work to ensure that libraries remain empowering spaces for all users, preserving children's autonomy to select and enjoy literature that interests, informs, and represents them. As the landscape of librarianship continues to shift amid growing censorship battles and challenging technological advancements, Brown's work serves as a model for future library professionals striving to make an impact.

References

Bishop, R. S. (1990). Mirrors, windows, and sliding glass doors. *Perspectives*: *Choosing and Using Books for the Classroom*, *6*(3), 1–2.

Blair, E. (2024, April 16). Report: Last year ended with a surge in book bans. *NPR*. https://www.npr.org/2024/04/16/1245037718/book-bans-2023-pen-america

Brown, A. (2015). "There are no Black people in Napa": A history of African Americans in Napa County [Masters Thesis, Adams State University].

Brown, A. (2019). *Hidden history of Napa Valley*. History Press.

Brown, A. (2020). *Lost restaurants of Napa Valley and their recipes*. History Press.

Brown, A. (2022, July 21). Libraries must stop pretending they can be neutral about human rights. *Prism*. https://prismreports.org/2022/07/21/libraries-cannot-be-neutral-human-rights/; https://adams.marmot.org/Archive/adams%3A65/Pdf

Gross, N. (2023). What ChatGPT tells us about gender: A cautionary tale about performativity and gender biases in AI. *Social Sciences*, *12*(8), 435.

Lippens, L. (2024). Computer says 'no': Exploring systemic bias in ChatGPT using an audit approach. *Computers in Human Behavior: Artificial Humans*, *2*(1), 1–15.

Southern Poverty Law Center. (n.d.). *Moms for liberty*. Southern Poverty Law Center. Retrieved January 2, 2025, from https://www.splcenter.org/fighting-hate/extremist-files/group/moms-liberty

5 Becky Calzada and Carolyn Foote

Fueled by incessant book challenges, loud "parental rights" groups, and right-wing legislative maneuvers, censorship attempts in school libraries have gained new prominence in recent years. Amid this shifting landscape, two school librarians, Becky Calzada and Carolyn Foote, along with other colleagues, launched *Texas FReadom Fighters* (https://www.txfreadomfighters.us/), a grassroots initiative born out of a desire to defend intellectual freedom and resist the suppression of diverse voices in literature. Calzada and Foote shared their experiences navigating the complexities of school librarianship while advocating for the rights of readers and the integrity of school library collections.

Born and raised in Mercedes, Texas, Calzada was a first-generation US citizen and the first in her family to graduate from both high school and college, receiving a bachelor's degree in elementary education. After teaching first-grade students for more than a decade in Leander, Texas, Calzada transitioned into the role of school librarian in 2001 after being introduced to the idea by another school librarian who noticed her interest in literacy and love for books. From her early days as a teacher to her current position as a national anti-censorship advocate, Calzada's career has been defined by a commitment to intellectual freedom, educational equity, and an unwavering commitment to supporting students, empowering educators, and defending diverse collections against censorship.

Similarly, Foote, a retired educator with 40 years of service in Austin, Texas, public schools, moved from teaching high school English, where she discovered a passion for connecting students with powerful literature, to high school librarianship: "I loved being a high school librarian. I loved high school students. I loved working with them because you have meaty conversations about things. You see them progress through their high school years and their intellectual growth and curiosity." Foote's career was shaped by a desire to highlight the importance of libraries as vibrant spaces for learning and discovery, and her professional philosophy centered on elevating librarians as leaders in the educational ecosystem and fostering student engagement and collaboration across educational networks.

In 2021, Calzada and Foote found themselves at the center of the emerging library book-banning maelstrom when Texas legislator Matt Krause distributed a spreadsheet of 850 books that he deemed inappropriate for schools because they addressed issues of race, gender, and sexuality (Chappell, 2021; Ellis, 2021). The Krause list subsequently became chum for organized book-banners and caused alarm among Texas school librarians and educators. As book bans and censorship challenges escalated across the state, Calzada and Foote decided to act. Calzada sent a text message to Foote about the possibility of doing a Twitter "hashtag takeover" of the Texas legislative #txlege—a hashtag used for disseminating state legislative news. A hashtag takeover happens when an individual or group co-opts an existing hashtag to tag their social media posts, effectively repurposing it to distribute their own message. In this case, Calzada and Foote coordinated using #txlege with #FReadom as a means of sharing online how a particular challenged or banned book had impacted their lives for the positive. Calzada said:

> We collaborated on the messaging and who to send it to and kept it secret. And then on that day in November [4, 2021], we launched. I remember scheduling my tweets at 5:30 am because I remember thinking that I cannot do this during the day. So, I scheduled some tweets, and I kept checking in. At first, it was pretty slow, but it was amazing to see through the day that over 16,000 tweets were shared, and we were the sixth largest trending topic on Twitter.

The hashtag takeover amplified voices in support of challenged books and drew attention to the broader implications of censorship on educational equity. It also underscored library workers' urgent need for resources, support, and guidance when facing book challenges—and that a rapid response was needed at the ground level to communicate to stakeholders what librarians do and not let the rhetoric go unanswered. As a result, Calzada, Foote, and other colleagues founded *Texas FReadom Fighters* that same year.

Foote said that Texas FReadom Fighters is not a traditional or formal organization, "just [Calzada] and I using our free time when we can and helping the people." Texas FReadom Fighters strives to share information with library workers, the media, and the community to educate and provide them with resources to oppose book bans and the negative narratives pushed by library censorship groups that portray librarians as "pornographers." To do this, they created a website to distribute talking points and tools like intellectual freedom resources, library selection policies, and contact information for groups fighting censorship and for library workers to use to fight back against banning attempts. They have hosted regular "Friday actions celebrating books and libraries, held monthly actions for followers to participate in, presented workshops and webinars on intellectual freedom, and worked with community members to ward off censorship." In addition, Texas FReadom Fighters actively networks with other anti-censorship advocates, transforming their grassroots effort into a powerful platform for change. Calzada said that many organizations have gotten on board protecting and advocating for books since book bans are not only not going away but increasing. The Texas Library Association, for example, now has an Intellectual Freedom Committee, with an Intellectual Freedom Helpline with the ability to report censorship (Texas Library Association, 2025).

Being retired, Foote leveraged her freedom from institutional constraints to speak more openly about the broader implications of censorship. She became the public face of Texas FReadom Fighters, engaging in media outreach, coordinating social media efforts, and connecting librarians in need of support with relevant resources. Here, her background in journalism and public speaking proved invaluable, enabling her to effectively communicate the stakes of the censorship battle to diverse audiences, including students, educators, and policymakers. To date, *Texas FReadom Fighters* have been interviewed frequently in the press, and they are featured in the new documentary film *The Librarians* (Snyder, 2025).

Foote said that the small but vocal minority pressing for book bans often operates outside of community norms, using inflammatory rhetoric to intimidate educators and library staff, scaring or shaming them into removing books from schools. Nevertheless, both Calzada and Foote believe the local community—not outsiders who flit in and out to push a political agenda—must be *even louder* than these groups when books are considered for a ban. If not, power and control risk becoming rooted in the vocal minority pushing the challenges. Calzada described a 2024 incident when a friend who is a member of the school library board reached out to her and said that the Remnant Alliance (https://www.theremnantalliance.com/), a faith-based group from outside of the community that had been going around the state reading cherry-picked passages from books at school board meetings for the purpose of shaming the school boards into removing the titles, would be coming to their next board meeting. Knowing that the pro-censorship faction weaponizes words and strings together passages outside of context from books that they oppose at school board meetings, Calzada warned the school administrators, superintendent, and school board that they needed to be prepared and, because people can sign up the day before the meeting for the public comment period, there was time to get ready for the book-banners:

> So, we had students come out. Parents came out in favor of supporting school policies. And I think the thing that I was really proud of is that the School Board prepared a statement that because we have out of town guests, they have to say who they are and where they are from because we want to know, are you a resident? A taxpayer? Or are you from out of town? It makes a difference because anybody can speak […] but if our Board is going to listen to the people invested in the community, which is the people that live there, they need to know who they are.

Foote said that, while many censorship attempts come from "outside the house," there are some attempts coming from inside and that "those are harder to unearth, because [library workers] are scared to talk about it." In the last few years, Texas school boards have become increasingly partisan due to the election of single-issue—i.e., "parental rights"—board members. In one bizarre case, a Granbury, Texas, school board member entered a library in the dark of the night with a flashlight to remove books from the shelves (Butcher, 2023), violating specific protocols that school board members are expected to abide by.

Throughout their careers, Calzada and Foote have advised fellow library workers to engage with policymakers and school board members, encouraging them to prepare for potential challenges by updating policies and establishing transparent review processes. The two Texas FReadom Fighters, however, have been particularly inspired by the bravery of student activist responses to the increasing number of book challenges. In Leander, students formed banned book clubs and advocated for intellectual freedom, even demanding seats at the table during policy discussions. Calzada sees such student-led initiatives as powerful reminders of the impact that libraries and librarians can have in fostering critical thinking and civic engagement. Agreeing, Foote said that the awareness of high school students has evolved remarkably over the past few decades because of their access to new technologies and many forms of media and information:

> The openness of our students compared to when I started years ago is just like a 180-degree shift. They are not embarrassed to talk about things that I would have been embarrassed about in high school. […] They have dealt with COVID. They have dealt with political craziness. And they have access to their phones and the internet. So suddenly, this idea that they are somehow these protected innocents in high school… What is happening?

Both Calzada and Foote see further empowering youth as a central goal of school library work because student agency is critical to preserving intellectual freedom. Because of this, librarians and educators need to be trusted.

When asked to name works that have impacted them professionally, Calzada and Foote identified two very different books. For Calzada, renowned Indian librarian and philosopher S. R. Ranganathan's *Five Laws of Library Science* (1931) have been particularly inspirational to her professional development and anti-censorship advocacy. And even though the *Five Laws* is over 90 years old, Calzada said that they still resonate and are applicable to libraries and library work:

> In the *Five Laws of Librarianship*, he talks about [1] books are for use, and that [2] every reader has a book, his or her book; I think that that is one that addresses the whole line of misinformation/disinformation that kids are going to have access to these books. We never said that we wanted every kid to read every book, We just said that one book might be good for a reader, right? Then [3] every book has its reader and [4] save the time

of the reader. And then [5] the library being a living organism. I think about how libraries have changed. It used to be that people came, got their books, and left. Now you go to a school library and kids are using the 3D printer. They can reserve a space and record a podcast because we have all of the equipment right there. Those things are exciting, and I think that [Law 5] would be the biggest one that resonates with me.

Foote said that she has long drawn inspiration from Louisa May Alcott's coming-of-age novel *Little Women* (1869), which she read "a million times when I was a kid." Foote found *Little Women* empowering because of its imagery of a powerful woman bucking the society of the time, and she said that much of her own tenacity as a librarian can be traced back to her love of the novel. Foote was particularly drawn to Alcott's depiction of the book's protagonist, Jo March, who is outspoken and never afraid to speak her mind. Foote also identified with Jo because the character is a writer, which, considering the book was written at the height of the Victorian Age, made her ahead of her time. The character's ability to speak truth to power has fueled Foote's continued energy to do so herself for the causes she believes in:

> My philosophy has been that, whenever anyone asks me for an interview, whether it is a student, a high school student, or a reporter from another country, we say yes to as many as we can do, because there are still a lot of people that do not realize what is going on and, to be honest, they do not realize how bad it is, or they do not realize the harassment. Those interviews are an important part of getting that information out there, especially when individual librarians do not feel like they can speak about it. And there really are not that many librarians who are speaking publicly about it still, because people are just scared.

Through their work, Calzada and Foote continue to be leaders at the forefront of the anti-censorship fight. Calzada was recently elected as president of the American Association of School Libraries and said that the position,

> [...] gives me an opportunity to pour back into the profession that has really done a lot for me. And I want to help with the next generation, because I will retire someday. I think pouring into that next group, people that are maybe in the pipeline in school, it behooves me to do that, because I do not want to see school librarians go away.

Calzada has also recently co-authored a book, *Prepared Libraries, Empowered Teams: A Workbook for Navigating Intellectual Freedom Challenges Together* 2024, which prepares librarians for book challenges (Calzada et al., 2024), and she is interested in potentially publishing a solo work that looks deeper into her experiences as an anti-censorship advocate. Foote remains committed to researching the landscape of school librarianship, including examining state policies, tracking job losses, and analyzing the intersection between administrative decisions and censorship efforts. Her work with ongoing media engagements reflects a sustained commitment to protecting intellectual freedom and amplifying the voices of marginalized communities. Foote is also deeply interested in exploring the historical context of censorship, identifying parallels between the current political climate and past movements like the Red Scare and Prohibition. Both the Red Scare and Prohibition were eventually stopped, and she hopes to use such historical lessons to inform how Texas FReadom Fighters can contribute to the demise of school censorship. But for now, Foote said, the fight against censorship in school libraries is far from over:

> Even though we have been in this fight three years already, there are still people that say: 'I did not think this is going to happen here,' or 'I do not know what you are talking about.' It is just crazy to me that there is still not an understanding, or there is not that proactive planning of updating your school policy, even though this has been happening for several years now. So that propels us.

For the Texas FReadom Fighters, protecting student access to diverse literature is not just a matter of policy; it is a moral imperative that reflects their commitment to educational equity and intellectual freedom. Calzada and Foote continue to leverage their networks, resources, and personal experiences to mentor emerging leaders, connect community members, and safeguard intellectual freedom. As the political and educational landscape continues to shift, their work serves as a testament to the enduring power of library advocacy and the critical role of school libraries in preserving access to diverse and inclusive literature.

References

Alcott, L. M. (1869). *Little women*. Roberts Brothers.
Butcher, R. (2023, August 23). Granbury ISD trustee accused of unauthorized library visit to go through books. FOX 4 Dallas-Fort Worth. https://www.fox4news.com/news/granbury-isd-trustee-accused-of-unauthorized-library-visit-to-go-through-books
Calzada, B., Edwards, V., & Heindel, M. C. (2024). *Prepared libraries, empowered teams: A workbook for navigating intellectual freedom challenges together*. ALA Editions.
Chappell, B. (2021, October 28). A Texas lawmaker is targeting 850 books that he says could make students feel uneasy. *NPR*. https://www.npr.org/2021/10/28/1050013664/texas-lawmaker-matt-krause-launches-inquiry-into-850-books
Ellis, D. (2021, November 5). All 850 books Texas lawmaker Matt Krause wants to ban: An analysis. *Book Riot*. https://bookriot.com/texas-book-ban-list/
Ranganathan, S. R. (1931). *The five laws of library science*. Madras Library Association.
Snyder, K. (Director). (2025). *The Librarians* [Film]. K.A. Snyder Productions; Cuomo Cole Productions; ITVS; Ideal Partners; World of HA Productions; Artemis Rising Foundation; Pretty Matches Productions.
Texas Library Association. (2025). Intellectual Freedom Committee. Txla.org. https://txla.org/tools-resources/intellectual-freedom/tla-intellectual-freedom-committee/about/

6 Ione Damasco

Ione Damasco is a tenured professor and Associate Dean for Inclusive Excellence and Organizational Development at the University of Dayton Libraries. Damasco seeks to understand the lived experiences of others (particularly those of members of marginalized groups) for the purpose of transforming the academic library into a more inclusive institution. Their professional work illustrates the efficacy of critical library work as the intersection of socially conscious theory and practice.

A person of Filipino descent and a child of immigrants, Damasco grew up in predominantly white communities where they attended schools alongside mostly white kids in a higher income bracket than their own family. Because of this, Damasco soon became aware of their own racialized identity. Even in junior high, they remember classroom discussions about racism and becoming really upset at other kids' comments. As an undergraduate college student at the Ohio State University, they began developing this basic awareness of being "othered" into a burgeoning critical consciousness. Enrolling in several feminist literature classes, Damasco was introduced to Judith Butler's (1990) performative theory of gender as well as Kimberlé Crenshaw's (1989) theory of intersectionality. It was exposure to ideas like these that allowed them to develop the mindset to not take things for granted, to ask questions, and to challenge power structures.

After receiving their bachelor's degree in English, Damasco went to library school at Kent State University with the objective of becoming an adult services librarian at a public library. They soon discovered, however, that they were "one of like four people who actually liked learning about MARC [machine readable cataloging] records." Damasco found it fascinating to learn how people categorize information and why people choose to put things in the categories that they do, and this led them to start thinking about critical theory and practice qua library work:

> In the early 2000s, critical library work was not a huge thing yet in the library school curriculum, but I did read about it in a few places. I started to explore the systems that are in place to categorize information, what bias shows up, and who is making those decisions. How these systems continue to reinforce biases.

Today, after having been a professional librarian for over two decades, Damasco views critically conscious praxis as a simple cycle revolving around personal reflection. The library worker begins with a foundation of values and theoretical frameworks, i.e., a mindset that informs their work actions. They then reflect upon these actions concerning their impacts, considering what they could have done differently and identifying the gaps that exist in their practice. For example, the critically conscious librarian should consider if there are places where they might be leaving somebody out and not realizing it, what lacuna they might still have concerning patrons' and colleagues' lived experiences, or where they might have made a different decision that would have resulted in a different outcome. Speaking from personal experience, Damasco said that the ability to engage in such critical reflection, coupled with the COVID-19 pandemic and the fact that their partner was recently diagnosed with Parkinson's disease, elevated their understanding of disability both in personal life and in the workplace. In turn, this process of reflection has impacted them in their role as a library administrator:

> We are living with what it means to become disabled in a culture where there are so many things that are not designed in an inclusive way. So that is an area where I am really trying to work on expanding my understanding of physical disabilities, neurodiversity, you know, the many ways that we do not design things to be truly inclusive, everything from pedagogy to physical spaces. How we interview people, how we onboard people, all kinds of things.

As a result of this understanding of praxis, Damasco said, it is not enough to simply be familiar with different critical frameworks like feminism, queer theory, critical race theory, or critical disability studies—no matter how well versed one may be—if one does not put these frameworks to transformative use.

This view of the intertwined nature of theory and practice led Damasco to explore intergroup dialogue as a communication framework for direct application in the library. Intergroup dialogue works under the premise that it is not enough to just be in conversation with one another around a topic; one must be aware of one's own social identities as well as those of the people that they are engaging with and how those experiences impact and affect how one communicates with one another. There are many narratives we are told in our culture that some people accept as the objective truth through the lens of their identity, but there are others with counter-narratives because of their own lived experience and their own identities. Those counter-narratives, Damasco said, need a space to be surfaced to show that what is sometimes perceived as the objective truth is just a perspective.

For many years, the University of Michigan has been one of the institutions at the forefront of developing the framework and has hosted the National Intergroup Dialogue Institute (https://igr.umich.edu/institute). Damasco visited the Institute in 2016 with a group of University of Dayton colleagues to learn more about the communication framework and bring it back to their campus community as a form of social justice education. For Damasco, to effect institutional change, you must work with other people on an individual and interpersonal level, because systemic change cannot happen without genuine, deep, authentic relationship building. When you develop those relationships, you build community and gain an understanding of how to care for both one another and yourself when working with challenges:

> We need new ways of thinking, and we must develop new ways of collective learning. Many library workers still think of themselves as repositories of specific kinds of information that we just make available to people. Sometimes we push information to people. But what would it mean for us to co-create knowledge with the communities that we serve?

Within that process there will be shifting dynamics around when and where change happens and who contributes to it. As a result, a critical praxis requires recognition of other people's experiences through the practice of deep learning.

In terms of their own program of research and publication, Damasco draws on lived experience to illuminate the obstacles faced by librarians who are intentionally marginalized for the purpose of propping up existing power structures. Their first major article, co-authored with Dracine Hodges (Damasco & Hodges, 2012), dealt with the tenure and promotion (T&P) experiences of academic librarians of color. There are many places throughout the T&P process where librarians of color face bias, lack of support, lack of clarity, and hidden expectations. All those things, Damasco said, feed into a culture that maintains a particular status quo: i.e., a profession that remains overwhelmingly white and cisgendered and, even though it has become increasingly feminized, entrenched in patriarchal institutions. The article resonated with library workers and continues to be cited in the library and information science literature, and Damasco was encouraged to see similar research being published in its wake that was also informed by lived experience.

The success of the P&T article propelled this research interest in surfacing people's experiences that are not always made visible, heard, or taken seriously. Damasco's intention is not to take a Pollyanna approach to their research but to use it to envision better outcomes for library professionals. In 2019, Damasco published an article in *Library Trends* with Kaetrena D. Kendrick that looked at the issue of low morale among academic librarians of color, identifying things in place in library organizations that continue to not only result in recruitment issues but also retention and advancement issues in the field (Kendrick & Damasco, 2019). Kendrick and Damasco investigated markers of low morale in organizations to see if there are consistent practices, managerial styles, and organizational structures that lead to librarians of color experiencing low morale in the workplace. Damasco said that an increasing number of library professionals are suffering low morale, but for librarians of color, the issue is compounded: "Add the pandemic and budget pressures, add all that on top of the experiences that they were already having that were racialized, all of that contributed to them having low morale."

Regarding their own professional reinvigoration, Damasco pointed to Kari Grain's (2022) book *Critical Hope: How to Grapple with Complexity, Lead with Purpose, and Cultivate Transformative Social Change* as a work that is particularly inspiring. Damasco first encountered the book after being recommended it by a web algorithm. They said that the title of the book spoke to them right away because "hope is in short supply these days," and they were intrigued by the pairing of the words "critical" and "hope." In the book, Grain draws upon Brazilian philosopher of education Paolo Freire's conceptualization of hope as being rooted in critical consciousness and liberation as being rooted in action to present a collection of stories, biographies, and theoretical frameworks to:

> [...] illuminate that everybody has a role to play in working for more justice, love, and liberation, and less suffering, hatred and inequity. I realized these ideas are vague in their enormity, are variable in their interpretation, and can be read as lofty platitudes, but they are precisely the values that drove Freire to conceive of the notion of critical hope, and they are worthy of attention and labor.
>
> (p. 17)

Damasco said that the book was appealing because when marginalized library workers talk about the issues and challenges that they face around equity, racism, transphobia, patriarchy, classism, and imperialism, they get caught up in deficit thinking:

> That wears down on you. I needed something that was realistic but that gave me a framework for figuring out how I might incorporate hopeful visions for the future while addressing the things that feel bad. Basically, the world is burning around us politically. There is legislation in place that is trying to further marginalize particular folks and hurt people, to directly hurt people. How do you find a path through that that keeps you motivated and invigorated? How do you tap into sources of joy, of love?

With *Critical Hope*, Grain does a phenomenal job of talking about hope not as something *felt* but as something *practiced*. This means recognizing that one cannot just wish for something to be better; they must dream something better and then work toward that dream's realization. For Damasco, reading this was an "aha!" moment.

Damasco has made good use of Grain's source material to further explore critical theory, developing their own critical consciousness and praxis. For instance, the book led them to Paolo Freire's (1970) *Pedagogy of the Oppressed* as well as the work of many scholar-activists of color that preceded Grain. Damasco was impressed that Grain, a white, cisgender woman drawing upon the works of scholars of color, acknowledged her debt to these scholars through a positionality statement in the book. And although Grain does not specifically mention intergroup dialogue in *Critical Hope*, Damasco encountered resonant moments between Grain's writing and some of that framework's practices and principles. Like intergroup dialogue, effective, critically hopeful leaders help team members face "difficult knowledge," as Grain put it (2022, p. 70), to challenge their assumptions while still acknowledging and holding space for their lived experience. Damasco said that human beings possess strength and talents that can lead to thriving, but when humans expend so much energy in a negative place, they lose sight of the things that they do have the capacity to build upon, to do more with, and to do better with. Reading *Critical Hope* also led Damasco to consider the applicability of appreciative inquiry, a model of inquiry first presented by David Cooperrider and Suresh Srivastva (1987), as applicable to their own library work. Instead of focusing on the problems of an organization, appreciative inquiry involves asking "generative questions" to stimulate new thinking about how a particular project is going well, i.e., to uncover what has been successful in an organization to build and expand upon it.

Finally, reading *Critical Hope* proved important to Damasco during a time when they were trying to balance work responsibilities, their commitment to their institution, their commitment to their colleagues, and assuming their new role as a caregiver to their partner. The book encouraged them to think deeply about hope in both their personal and professional lives, and Damasco sees the book as an excellent primer for both new library workers and seasoned administrators:

> We are all facing serious challenges to the work that we are doing. And those challenges are not just small day-to-day obstacles that you might encounter. But there are structural and systemic issues that undergird the daily operational issues that we face. So, having a framework to guide our approaches to addressing systemic issues as well as the day-to-day operational piece. What I really like about *Critical Hope* is this recognition of relationship and community building. When we talk about oppression, people have used models like individual, interpersonal, institutional, three levels of oppression that occur. They are the one-on-one negative experiences that people have where somebody says something openly hurtful. Then there is little bit broader than that, and then you have institutional policies that can be exclusive and marginalizing.

The only critique Damasco had of the book is that it could have benefited from an active partnership with a co-author from a marginalized identity or intersectional identities to bring that perspective directly into the work.

Damasco is optimistic about the state of critical librarianship. They pointed to one recent work that does an excellent job of bringing in a variety of diverse experiences to LIS, Sophia Y. Leung and Jorge R. Lopez-McKnight's (2021)

Knowledge Justice: Disrupting Library and Information Studies through Critical Race Theory. This edited collection brings together pieces from many different authors of color:

> I think that this book, which specifically leans into library and information science, gets us to question our practice. It looks at our history, which I think is important. It asks questions about the history of the field and how it came up. It closes with a section which I love on the idea of putting radical collective imaginations toward liberation. And that gets back to what I was saying about how do we envision and dream something beyond the status quo? How do we envision a world where these oppressive systems really have been dismantled? What does librarianship look like?

Damasco sees the next generation of library workers, i.e., those that have been coming up in the last five to ten years, and particularly those who come from multiple marginalized identities in our culture—e.g., queer library workers, library workers of color, queer library workers of color—as particularly courageous. Such new professionals, they said, are creating supportive communities, doing research, and sharing ideas and scholarship:

> In terms of the state of critical librarianship, there is a group of people who are really trying hard to make critical librarianship *become librarianship*, but it is small numbers. There are still a lot of people who do not even know what, if you use that phrase [critical librarianship], what it means, you know, if you just go to your day-to-day library, whether it is a public or academic library. So, while I am encouraged by this collective effort that is starting to happen, it is still so small in terms of the sheer number of practitioners in our field. But I see more presentations and things where there is an exploration of critical ideas and practitioners actually using them in their practices. I would say that we are in the early stages of embedding it into our field. We still have a long way to go.

As an administrator, Damasco will continue to work to provide opportunities for other people and advocate for the resources needed for them to be successful. In the process, they intend to keep pushing back against policies and practices that are harmful to particular groups at their university and its libraries. Damasco said that this is a necessary task, but it is by no means an easy task: they are a non-binary Asian American working at a Catholic institution where the faculty, administrative leadership, and student body remain predominantly white. And even though Damasco does sometimes feel vulnerable,

> I am also tenured, I am a full professor. I recognize that that has with it power and some privileges that I should be leveraging that to advocate to help those around me be successful and be their full selves.

References

Butler, J. (1990). *Gender trouble: Feminism and the subversion of identity*. Routledge.
Cooperrider, D., & Srivastva, S. (1987). Appreciative inquiry in organizational life. In R. W. Woodman & W. A. Pasmore (Eds.), *Research in organizational change and development* (pp. 129–169). JAI Press.
Crenshaw, K. (1989). Demarginalizing the intersection of race and sex: A Black feminist critique of antidiscrimination doctrine, feminist theory and antiracist politics. *University of Chicago Legal Forum*, *1989*(1), 139–167. http://chicagounbound.uchicago.edu/uclf/vol1989/iss1/8
Damasco, I. T., & Hodges, D. (2012). Tenure and promotion experiences of academic librarians of color. *College & Research Libraries*, *73*(3), 279–301.
Freire, P. (1970). *Pedagogy of the oppressed*. Continuum.
Grain, K. (2022). *Critical hope: How to grapple with complexity, lead with purpose, and cultivate transformative social change*. North Atlantic Books.
Kendrick, K. D., & Damasco, I. T. (2019). Low morale in ethnic and racial minority academic librarians: An experiential study. *Library Trends*, *68*(2), 174–212.
Leung, S. Y., & Lopez-McKnight, J. R. (2021). *Knowledge justice: Disrupting library and information studies through critical race theory*. MIT Press.

7 Emily Drabinski

Emily Drabinski is currently an associate professor at Queens College, City University of New York (CUNY) Graduate School of Library and Information Studies. She is also a past president of the American Library Association (ALA), serving from 2023 to 2024 at the height of book-banning efforts in the US. In addition to her many years of professional service at a national level, Drabinski is well-known throughout the profession for her research in critical librarianship as well as her packed schedule as a presenter and guest speaker.

Before becoming a librarian, Drabinski considered becoming a magazine writer in the vein of the *New Yorker's* David Foster Wallace but found out that "the best way to be a writer was to be wealthy and have writers in your family, and I did not have either." Library work, however, offered economic stability and the possibility of a pension. Taking her first course at Syracuse University's School of Library and Information Science, Drabinski said her "mind was blown": "I thought, 'this is awesome, what a cool field and an amazing project.' Yeah, I am one of those people who felt like librarianship was what I was meant to do really immediately."

Working at the New York Public Library while attending Syracuse, Drabinski appreciated the high-impact nature of frontline public library work but found the intensity of the job less than appealing. After graduating with her master's degree, she worked for a brief period indexing area studies journals for the HW Wilson Publishing Company. Following this, she moved into her first academic library position as a reference librarian at Sarah Lawrence College before spending the next 10 years as a faculty member at Long Island University, Brooklyn. Drabinski then worked for four years as a Critical Pedagogy Librarian at The Graduate Center, CUNY, before taking her current teaching position at Queens College in 2023.

Drabinski was introduced to Bowker and Star's (1999) *Sorting Things Out: Classification and Its Consequences* while earning her library and information science (LIS) master's:

> I was assigned to read that book in my knowledge organization core class at Syracuse with Professor Barbara Kwasnik. I was just a student in her

class, but I have had an opportunity since then to be able to tell her how consequential that class was for me and how consequential reading that book was for me.

In *Sorting Things Out*, Bowker and Star examine the ways in which classification systems construct human realities and prejudiced thinking by enforcing artificial category boundaries. These hidden categorical structures serve to scaffold society and influence how people view one another in terms of constructs like race, workplace, and medical diagnoses. Through examination of various modern classification systems (e.g., the International Classification of Diseases), Bowker and Star argue that political and social agendas become embedded into societal infrastructure so profoundly that they effectively become invisible, but that these information structures retain the power to advantage or disadvantage one group of people over another.

Drabinski found the book consequential due to its recognition of the human labor that goes into creating infrastructure and information systems, with humans enforcing boundaries and borders through classification schemes. She pointed to Bowker and Star's analysis of the Nursing Interventions Classification (NIC) as being particularly impactful on developing her critical thought concerning library and information science due to the similarities between Bowker and Star's analysis of nursing and what Drabinski saw happening in library work. The NIC is a massive undertaking that attempts to classify all possible activities nurses perform on the job and, like the Library of Congress Classification system (LCC), was developed around, and consequently embodies, dominant "political, cultural, ethical, social, religious, economical, and institutional factors" (Bowker & Star, 1999, p. 239). Bowker and Star argued that through its implementation of language, the NIC created a curricular program and structure to control and professionalize nursing. Drabinski said that, in a similar way, the LCC created a structure for the professionalization of cataloging work, one that has proven difficult to modify, with many dated (and sometimes offensive) headings still being used. It also raises questions about how classification and categorization systems like Library of Congress Subject Headings (LCSH) affect the efforts and professional *weltanschauung* of library workers struggling for social, economic, and distributive justice: "I think that sometimes we get away from the core work that we do, which is to build and maintain these invisible systems and structures that govern life in ways that other people do not see or understand." Drabinski said that although updates should be made to the LCC and LCSH, the legacy of outdated classification should not be erased; instead, the problematic past should be acknowledged and documented.

Drabinski recommends *Sorting Things Out* to all progressive librarians. She said that what the book does well is talk about how real, material things come into being through people working together and making decisions. It is a document of how the work that people imagine is different from the actual worldmaking, that the work that a librarian may see as rote and boring—the "day job"—is in fact the consequential work of building the world. Because of this,

> Rather than social justice being like an add-on thing that we do, it is embedded in the daily work that we do. Every single decision that we make in the library that is consequential to our users is actually the work of social justice. For example, here is my stapler. If I put it on the reference desk, someone might steal it, so let us chain it to the desk. But if I chain it to the desk, does that send a message to the students that they are criminals and being scrutinized inside the library? And so, do we lock everything down and is it worth it? Or is it worthwhile just simply investing in more staplers and assuming that stapler loss is part of the cost of doing business of a library? Or do we chain it because we do not have the budget for that? So, the question is, are we going to chain the library to the desk or not? Everybody in a library has had to make decisions like that and, for me, I began to see those decisions about enacting the world that we want or not.

The stapler example may seem trivial, but deciding on how to provide a piece of office equipment or classify a book is one of the many decisions that construct the public's relationship to libraries and vice versa.

Because of her training under teachers like Barbara Kwasnik, who "changed my life, changed my brain," and the impact of books like *Sorting Things Out*, Drabinski said that she now thinks in terms of categorization: "Once you start to see the world as a classification problem, you never unsee it. It is a threshold concept for me—everything is an ordering problem." She recalled that when she worked for HW Wilson indexing area studies journals, she would consistently use the same 10–15 keywords when indexing articles, barely representing their rich content and demonstrating the limits of language when classifying and the way in which such systems impact scholarly communication. Later, when perusing the shelves at Sarah Lawrence College, Drabinski discovered the memoir *Christine Jorgensen: A Personal Autobiography* (1967)—written by a transgender World War II veteran and early recipient of gender reassignment surgery—cataloged under the LC call number range R (medicine) for mental problems. That same memoir would be re-cataloged under HQ (societal problems). Although many libraries have since updated the book's classification to HQ77.8 (the family > marriage > women > sexual life > transsexuals), basic cataloging tools like WorldCat still use the original classification of RC560 (medicine and personality disorders > behavior problems). When asked about recent book-banning efforts, she approached it also from the perspective of information organization:

> I really believe in infrastructure as a way of thinking about book banning because it is infrastructures that are the systems that we operate in or where power resides and accumulates, where resources accumulate.

> Even in a classification cataloging scheme, that is where the power resides, the power to make decisions about what we are going to call something - what we are going to say. That is power at work.

Such observations have sensitized Drabinski to how classification systems bias thinking, reify power structures, and produce and reproduce powerful ideologies that define society:

> The power that we possess to reproduce dominant ways of understanding the world through our classification systems, which are material, right? I have got the scheme, the scheme puts books on shelves in a certain order, and that is the story that the shelves tell you about the world – that is consequential work. We make it happen, and we could make it different.

Drabinski's own research agenda has developed out of both her keen classifier's eye and her drive to "make it different" through researching information organization from the critical perspective of "that queer identified person shelving books in the library of Sarah Lawrence College and finding the shelving order to be rather curious." She recognizes how essential technical services like cataloging and classification are to libraries, and she is interested in their relationships with the people who make, maintain, and use the systems.

Drabinski has focused her advocacy through her research on LGBTQIA2+ and the classification and cataloging systems found in most North American academic libraries—LCC and LCSH. In her *Library Quarterly* article, "Queering the Catalog: Queer Theory and the Politics of Correction" (2013), she calls for not only critically thinking about how knowledge systems are formed and frame social structures but also invites catalogers to consider classification through the "shifting and contextual" lens of queer theory (p. 96), a post-structuralist approach that McCann and Monaghan (2020) said allows activists and scholars to "challenge, interrogate, destabilize, and subvert" (p. 1). Drabinski said that a queer theory-oriented analysis would invite users to engage with the cataloging of materials through dialogue to better understand the invisibility of this knowledge organization.

Most recently, Drabinski completed a book project with Amanda Belantara that documents the history of alternative classification and cataloging systems: *Ways of Knowing: Oral Histories on the Worlds We Create* (Belantara & Drabinski, 2025). A collection of oral histories, *Ways of Knowing* documents the development of the *Homosaurus* (https://homosaurus.org/), an international linked data vocabulary of LGBTQIA2+ terms, *A Women's Thesaurus*, and the *Chicano Thesaurus*:

> We are trying to do further documentation of the *Chicano Thesaurus* as an example of the kind of important work that often is invisible, we do not look at how communities outside the mainstream of American

librarianship have developed their own forms of librarianship to account for their particular communities and ways of knowing.

Drabinski sees this vein of work as both inexhaustible and critical to exploring the alternative classification systems coming from non-dominant and marginalized groups.

Drabinski's term as ALA president ended in summer 2024, and she said that she finds hope in the infrastructure, committees, and tools that the ALA can now activate to address social justice-related issues. Although she is no longer working in a library, she finds real satisfaction in teaching information organization skills to budding LIS professionals from a critical pedagogical perspective—sensitizing them to the classifications and categories that undergird our realities: "I really love students. I love talking to them about their ideas. I am very happy in my career."

References

Belantara, A., & Drabinski, E. (Eds.). (2025). *Ways of knowing: Oral histories on the worlds words create*. Litwin Books.

Bowker, G. C., & Star, S. L. (1999). *Sorting things out: Classification and its consequences*. MIT Press.

Drabinski, E. (2013). Queering the catalog: Queer theory and the politics of correction. *The Library Quarterly, 83*(2), 94–111.

Jorgensen, C. (1967). *Christine Jorgenson: A personal autobiography*. Paul S. Eriksson.

McCann, H., & Monaghan, W. (2020). *Queer theory now: From foundations to futures*. Macmillan Education UK.

8 Fobazi Ettarh

Formerly a school librarian turned academic librarian and currently a Doctoral student at the University of Illinois at Champaign-Urbana's School of Information Science, Fobazi Ettarh made a big splash with her 2018 *In the Library with the Lead Pipe* article "Vocational Awe and Librarianship: The Lies We Tell Ourselves." With this article, Ettarh introduced library workers to the concept of "vocational awe," a term that she coined to refer to "the set of ideas, values, and assumptions librarians have about themselves and the profession that result in beliefs that libraries as institutions are inherently good and sacred, and therefore beyond critique" (Ettarh, 2018). At first look, vocational awe may appear to be a benign and even appealing concept, e.g., as a badge of honor for library workers that elevates professional identity. Ettarh pointed to the modern library's and library workers' roots in religious culture and history, and she sees vocational awe as a consequence of this ongoing association. Ettarh argued, however, that vocational awe leads to negative consequences for library workers and users, critiquing it as a tool for maintaining institutional oppression by which "the efficacy of one's work is directly tied to their amount of passion (or lack thereof), rather than fulfillment of core job duties" (Ettarh, 2018). The institution's and profession's ongoing association with the sacred has led to the poor treatment of library workers who are routinely overworked and undercompensated while being sold on the notion that they should be comfortable with their exploitation because of the inherent nobility of the work. Since its publication, this highly cited and influential article has raised eyebrows and some hackles within the library and information professions. More importantly, it has piqued and informed the critical consciousness of many library workers.

Ettarh was born and raised in the small town of Fort Lee, New Jersey, where she grew up in a conservative family. Her mother is a Christian pastor and educator, and her father, who has since passed away, was an accountant. As a result, Ettarh spent her early years in the church. She gravitated to her public library at an early age for what she described as "the stereotypical reason in that I really like to read." Her reasoning changed, however, when she hit high school and began to question her sexuality:

DOI: 10.4324/9781003473640-9

Up until that point, any sort of problem or question I had in my life, I would just go to the Bible. I would look in the concordance and read about whatever the issue was and feel better through reading the Word and discussion with other teens in the teen group. As you might imagine, when I looked up homosexuality in the Bible, that was not the experience that I had. So, I was terrified of telling anyone or even acknowledging it really to myself because I knew that it was bad and that it would never be accepted by my parents, by my mom especially, being a conservative Christian household.

Ettarh's plan was to remain quiet about her sexuality until leaving home, at which time she would have either resolved the issue or, at the very least, be away from home, where she "could pretend that nothing was happening to me."

Having landed a job in her high school media center, Ettarh came across a copy of *Chicken Soup for the Teenage Soul*. Although popular self-help books are typically not the kind of literature that she gravitates toward, Ettarh perused *Chicken Soup* and was surprised to find a short story by Bruce Coville (1994), an author she recognized and enjoyed. "Am I Blue" tells the story of Vince, a bullied teen questioning their sexuality, who is granted three wishes by their "Fairy Godfather." Vince asks to be able to see all gay people in the world tinted in shades of blue (what the Fairy Godfather calls "gaydar"). To their surprise, Vince sees blue people of different hues everywhere. Next, Vince wishes that everyone else could, for a short time, also have the same gaydar (i.e., "Blueday"). Vince's final wish is to turn their bully blue, but the Fairy Godfather tells the teen that there is no need to spend his wish on a *fait accompli*. Vince decides to save the final wish "for when I really need it—maybe when I meet the girl of my dreams. Or Prince Charming" (Coville, 1994, p. 16). Ettarh said reading "Am I Blue" was a pivotal moment in her life:

I still to this day say that there was the time before I read that story, and the time afterward. It was that much of a catalyst for everything that came next in my life. I really thought that I was the only one and the world that was dealing with this. [...] reading this and understanding that someone else had felt this way, and that maybe it was not necessarily a bad thing was life changing. I immediately started looking up all the books in the school library that dealt with this issue—fiction, and nonfiction. When I finished all the books in the school library, I went to the public library and did the same thing. When I finished all the ones in our small public library, I used interlibrary loan and got all the books from like the county, basically, and just felt consumed with this need, this desire to understand what other people, and especially other teens, did when they went through this.

Even though she was exhilarated by the discovery that she was not alone, Ettarh remained terrified by the prospect of having to face library workers when checking out books on the topic. This fear turned out to be misplaced; the library workers proved to be nonjudgmental and supportive, even helping her find additional books on the LGBTQIA2+ topics:

> If any of those librarians had said anything negative, even as joke, I do not think I would have come out for years. [...] they were so encouraging that it changed my reason for wanting to be a librarian. I was like, 'I want to be this person for other people. Look how much the right book can really change someone's life like it did mine. I want to make sure that I continue to be that safe space for other people who may be going through this.' And yes, that is what I did.

After high school, Ettarh went to the University of Delaware, where she got a degree in English with a minor in sociology. Upon receiving her bachelor's degree, she went straight to graduate school at Rutgers University with the intention of becoming a school librarian. Being in the school librarianship program, most of Ettarh's classes dealt with trends among children and young adults. Many of her teachers would break down issues related to children and teens into different weeks for discussion, with one week focusing on programming for gay teens, the next on programming for Black teens, etc. This format proved frustrating for Ettarh, who, being gay *and* Black, did not consider herself to be just the former one week and the latter the next. When she did bring up that confusion in class, she felt that her feelings were either ignored or minimized. This weekly compartmentalization of identity also begged the question: What happens when your patrons are also dealing with multiple issues concerning identity? This was when Ettarh decided to research the issue on her own, and this was when she discovered the work of Kimberlé Crenshaw, professor of law at Columbia University and a pioneering scholar on the issue of intersectionality.

Specifically, Ettarh discovered Crenshaw's (1989) paper "Demarginalizing the Intersection of Race and Sex: A Black Feminist Critique of Antidiscrimination Doctrine, Feminist Theory, and Antiracist Politics," published in the *University of Chicago Legal Forum*. This article—which, according to Google Scholar, has been cited over 36,000 times across many disciplines—explores the complex constitution of personal identity and the ham-fisted tendency of the legal field (and by extension, many other societal institutions, including higher education) to essentialize identity and neglect the consideration of overlapping social identities. For example, a person may be simultaneously female, African American, and gay, and such overlapping identities deserve careful attention for discourse, scholarly or otherwise, to be truly productive in their examination.

Ettarh said that she was impressed by Crenshaw's novel and powerful argument for the concurrent analysis of sexism, racism, and patriarchy:

> Intersectionality had not become the big sort of cultural moment that it is now. This was before [political commentator] Ben Shapiro and the right got a hold of it. And so, it was still a very new concept, this idea that

identity is not discreet things that happen to you or are a part of you, but something that is constantly changing constantly creating unique experiences within someone's life. The example that she uses [in 'Demarginalizing the Intersection'] is being a Black woman working in the legal field—she was originally a legal scholar—and how as a Black woman, the history of trying to get rights specifically as a Black woman meant that her feelings as a Black person were minimized in the suffrage movement and feminist movements and scholarship. [...] The laws were written such that either you as a woman you have rights or as a Black person you have rights, and the sort of unique experiences that Black women faced because they were Black women were not being recognized by the courts at all.

This situation, Ettarh said, extends well beyond the judicial system. Academia, for instance, is largely complicit in this sort of essentializing and identity siloing. While women are typically stereotyped as soft, overemotional, and caring, Black people are stereotyped as intimidating and angry. Because of this, Ettarh said female Black academics are put in a sort of double bind:

[...] in our Blackness we are excluded from those narratives of softness, of delicacy, that white women are automatically afforded. How do you bring that kind of experience to your Equal Opportunity Commission officer when the standard is to do discrimination as a racial thing or discrimination as a gendered thing?

Ettarh saw Crenshaw's acknowledgment of such gaps and the need for intersectionality as profoundly groundbreaking.

Having become sensitized to Crenshaw's articulation of the concept of intersectionality, and particularly the concept's relationship to library work, Ettarh began presenting on the topic at library science conferences. Because of this exposure through presentations and lightning talks, the library and information science journal *In the Library with Lead Pipe* invited her to submit an article on intersectionality and library work, resulting in the piece "Making a New Table: Intersectional Librarianship" (Ettarh, 2014). In this essay, she considers library work through Crenshaw's theoretical lens, putting forward the argument that library work must stop being viewed as what Ettarh termed a "single-axis" phenomenon. Single-axis thinking, according to Ettarh, represents the dominant narrative in both library work and society at large and has resulted in the normalization of values and practices like individualism:

An example of single-axis thinking is saying that sexism causes the lack of women [in technology and digital librarianship] without considering that women of colour, queer women, and trans women might have a different experience. Any work done that seeks to solve the issue along only one axis leaves behind these women. No one lives a single-axis life. We all embody multiple axes of identity and oppression throughout our lives that often affect us simultaneously. As Flavia Dzodan (2011) said, 'My feminism will be intersectional or it will be bullshit.' To treat librarianship and its communities as a single-axis phenomenon renders those who occupy the intersections invisible and therefore ignored.

"Making a New Table" was followed by more presentations on the topic as well as forays into other aspects of library work and the construction of identity. In 2016, for example, Ettarh created a "Choose your own adventure" style computer game, *Killing Me Softly*, that demonstrates "how it feels to suffer microaggressions and acculturative stress day after day," two phenomena that library workers belonging to minority groups are intimately familiar with (Ettarh, 2016).

Ettarh coined the term "vocational awe" while preparing to be on a panel for the 2017 Identity, Agency, and Culture in Academic Libraries conference, and wrote about it soon after in her blog, "WTF is a Radical Librarian, Anyway?" (Ettarh, 2017). Next, she published a detailed treatment of vocational awe qua library work in *In the Library with Lead Pipe*, "Vocational Awe and Librarianship" (Ettarh, 2018). She had started to notice how library workers talked about their jobs using the "language of the sacred" in similar ways to how her mother and other pastors talked about religion. Even though she had been around this sort of religious discourse most of her life, Ettarh's developing critical consciousness, aided through her exposure to the writings of Crenshaw and others, allowed her to see it clearly being used in the workplace and professional discourse:

> I do not remember the exact year or conference I was at [...] maybe it was someone asking a question during the Q&A, but they said it was a 'sacred duty' to work with children and teens, and that just really took me by surprise. To talk about a secular job and to say literally that it's a sacred duty. It seems to me almost sacrilegious in a way. After that, I really started to pay attention to the ways that libraries and library accounts talked about their work and their job duties. I found that there was a sense of cognitive dissonance there because the language around library work was always 'it's my calling to be a librarian' or 'I'm grateful to be within the field,' or 'I consider myself almost like a spiritual advisor for my patrons,' and so on.

Ettarh also found inspiration in *Jacobin* contributor Miya Tokumitsu's (2014) classic blog post "In the Name of Love." In her essay, Tokumitsu interrogates the old aphorism that one should "do what you love" as an elitist attitude and one that results in the exploitation of workers through encouraging things like unpaid, off-the-clock labor, even in what she calls the "lovable professions" (e.g., librarianship). Such ideology-laden discourse about work, Ettarh said, left scant space for constructive talk about the ways that the library as an institution harmed patrons or library workers—crowding out room for critical discussion. In fact, when the possibility was brought up that libraries might not always be anodyne institutions and that equating library work with the concept of the sacred might not necessarily be a good thing, offenders were muzzled under the idea that they should be grateful to be a part of the profession, what they do is a common good, and that libraries are, according to the old saw, the "last bastions of democracy."

Although Ettarh was pleasantly surprised by how her analysis of vocational awe was received by practitioners, she also encountered backlash from some library workers. Such a negative reaction to criticism of the library and librarianship as sacred institutions was not completely unexpected, and Ettarh encountered it both on the job and during or following conference presentations on vocational awe, when attendees would provide retorts like, "Are you telling me I am not allowed to love my job?" Ettarh understands where her detractors came from. Of course, she said, one should hopefully feel positive about their job. What she disagreed with, however, is that love and passion should be a metric used as a standard for being an effective library worker. You can love your job and still critique it. You can love your job and understand that it is not a perfect thing. Why is it, she asked,

> that when we talk about institutions like policing or medicine, we understand that it is not a perfect thing? Sometimes bad things happen, and it does not mean that it necessarily says something about the institution, but saying something bad about libraries automatically means that you hate the field and do not want it to succeed?

By the time of the second *In the Library with the Lead Pipe* article, Ettarh had left school library work to accept a two-year Diversity Residency at Temple University Libraries. Her time at Temple did much to reinforce her developing ideas concerning professional identity and marginalization. One older library worker at Temple, for example, referred to Ettarh as "the Black one." Ettarh said that this aggression may be because there was a sense among library staff at Temple that the diversity residents would only be around for two years, and, since the positions were likely, in the older library worker's mind, based on identity and not anything "real," they did not have to learn the residents' names or anything about them.

Library workers should not be treated as simple abstractions. They should not be reduced to false essential categories like functionaries of the religious and the sacred—that way leads to their exploitation. It is Ettarh's objective to get this point across to the profession, a profession with a storied history that is also mired by its own hagiography. Like Kimberlé Crenshaw, she offers a sober look at the ways in which professional identity is a dynamic and constructed phenomenon.

Currently, Ettarh has left academic librarianship to pursue a PhD in information science at the University of Illinois, Champaign-Urbana. Her dissertation topic considers vocational awe in tech and startup cultures in addition to librarianship. She has made a strong case for vocational awe in women-centered fields like librarianship, education, and social work, where women of color are expected to perform emotional labor on top of their job duties and face job creep, invisible labor, and the white savior narratives of a field that is primarily composed of white women, and now she is expanding to consider the culture of Silicon Valley. In addition, she is currently under contract with Seven Stories Press to write a book on vocational awe.

References

Coville, B. (1994). Am I blue? In M. D. Bauer (Ed.), *Am I blue?: Coming out from the silence* (pp. 1–16). Harper Collins.

Crenshaw, K. (1989). Demarginalizing the intersection of race and sex: A Black feminist critique of antidiscrimination doctrine, feminist theory and antiracist politics. *University of Chicago Legal Forum, 1989*(1), 139–167. http://chicagounbound.uchicago.edu/uclf/vol1989/iss1/8

Dzodan, F. (2011, October 10). My feminism will be intersectional or it will be bullshit! *Tiger Beatdown*. http://tigerbeatdown.com/2011/10/10/my-feminism-will-be-intersectional-or-it-will-be-bullshit/

Ettarh, F. (2014, July 2). Making a new table: Intersectional librarianship. *In the Library with the Lead Pipe*. https://www.inthelibrarywiththeleadpipe.org/2014/making-a-new-table-intersectional-librarianship-3/

Ettarh, F. (2016). *Killing Me Softly: A Game about Microaggressions*. https://fobettarh.github.io/Killing-Me-Softly/

Ettarh, F. (2017, May 30). Vocational awe? WTF is a radical librarian, anyway? https://fobaziettarh.com/2017/05/30/vocational-awe/

Ettarh, F. (2018, January 10). Vocational awe and librarianship: The lies we tell ourselves. *In the Library with the Lead Pipe*. https://www.inthelibrarywiththeleadpipe.org/2018/vocational-awe/

Tokumitsu, M. (2014, January 12). In the name of love. *Jacobin*. https://jacobin.com/2014/01/in-the-name-of-love/

9 Lia Friedman

Lia Friedman took an unconventional route to academic librarianship and critically engaged library work, weaving together a tapestry of activism, music, punk collectivism, and a commitment to democratizing information access. From a non-traditional academic background to collective activism in Radical Reference, Friedman exemplifies how lived experiences can profoundly shape professional practice.

Growing up in California, Friedman dropped out of high school at 15. She spent a decade at community college before transferring to The Evergreen State College, a four-year public university in Olympia, Washington, which does not offer traditional majors nor assign grades. Later, Friedman attended library school at New York's Pratt Institute, drawn by the university's willingness to admit students without standardized test scores, a crucial detail for someone with her non-traditional background. Friedman graduated from Pratt with her master of science in library and information science (MSLIS) in 2004.

Friedman had never planned to become a librarian. Her passion lay in behind-the-scenes research work, and at one time she had imagined a future as a media researcher. She had previously worked in public radio, and while in library school, she interned at *The New Yorker Magazine* Library as a project assistant. Financial realities after library school, however, led Friedman to a research and music librarian position at NBC/Universal—a role she described as a poor fit but a critical learning experience. After one year at NBC/Universal, she left the corporate world, moving back to California, where she has worked at the University of California, San Diego, Libraries for the past two decades. She is currently the subject librarian for critical gender studies, visual arts, architecture, film, and communication.

Friedman comes from a background of consensus collectives and punk rock, informing her perspective of the world. When asked to discuss a germinal influence on her development as a socially conscious librarian, Friedman selected Radical Reference (RR) (http://radicalreference.info/), a library- and information-centered activist organization that she encountered in 2004 while a student at Pratt. New York-based academic librarian Jenna Freedman began to craft RR after attending a clearinghouse meeting to organize

DOI: 10.4324/9781003473640-10

protests during the 2004 Republican National Convention (RNC) because of the RNC's perceived exploitation of the 9/11 memorial site (Friedman, 2014). Drawing inspiration from the activist work of Jessamyn West (see Chapter 24 for a profile of West)—a former public librarian who organized protests in Seattle in 1999 against the World Trade Organization and initiated mobile reference at the annual Burning Man arts and music festival—Freedman proposed a web-based and street-level reference service to support the RNC demonstrators. After receiving positive feedback from groups like the Progressive Librarians Guild (PLG) and the American Library Association (ALA) Social Responsibilities Round Table (SRRT), Freedman and a group of librarians, including James Jacobs, Chuck Munson, and Shinjoung Yeo, built RR as an independent grassroots effort. With technical support from the InterActivist Network (https://interactivist.net/), they launched a website and began recruiting volunteers. In the weeks leading up to the RNC protests, RR assembled volunteers to provide real-time support to protestors through portable ready-reference kits, phone assistance, and the now-defunct TxTMob text messaging service, giving activists immediate access to information (e.g., maps and legal information) with real-time updates. Before smartphones and widespread mobile internet, this street-level reference work bridged critical information gaps, empowering activists and independent journalists (Friedman, 2014).

Friedman was one of RR's first recruits, joining just before the RNC protests. She was drawn to the organization because of its action-oriented blend of frontline activism and information work. Friedman recalled walking the streets of New York City during the RNC protests with printouts full of critical information on legal rights, protest safety, and basic needs:

> What do you do if you are arrested? How do you get tear gas out of your eyes? Where is the closest bathroom? It was very quaint because it was so long ago, but we put together binders that we had, that we walked around with, and we had people at home in front of computers that we would call if we had questions.

The experience was profoundly positive for Friedman. Working with the collective, Friedman said she realized how library work could intersect with activism, and this offered her a means to complete "the work that I felt was important in the world":

> I am an activist. I could have views that perhaps not everyone shared, but I could still connect people to information that was often behind a paywall, was often challenging to get. That was a large part of the work that we did. The meetings that we held. The unconferences that we held. The papers that we wrote. The articles that we published. All these things worked within the intersection where we were allowed to bring who we were as people, as activists, into the realm of librarianship.

Friedman is proud of RR's efforts as a "conduit or connector":

> There were people who monitored the website for questions that came in, and those would be questions that could be answered. Often it was an independent journalist who was looking for information about something that they were not able to access because it was behind a paywall. We helped people write books. We had lots of thank yous in forwards.

RR formed strong partnerships with activist groups, media collectives, and community organizations to expand its impact beyond traditional library services. For example, the NYC collective worked with groups like the progressive National Lawyers Guild (https://www.nlg.org/) to connect regular people to valuable resources on tenants' rights (a perennial concern in New York City). Members collaborated with the New York City Grassroots Media Coalition (GMC), providing fact-checking and information management workshops. RR also partnered with groups like the New York City Independent Media Center to provide research support for their journalists. It also supported initiatives such as the United States Social Forum in 2007, anarchist book fairs in 2008, and cataloging environmental archives (Morrone & Friedman, 2009). These partnerships allowed RR to embed librarianship into activist movements, offering research expertise and resources to strengthen community access to trustworthy information.

As the organization expanded, local collectives sprang up in multiple cities in the United States and internationally. Friedman estimated that at the height of RR's activity, there were probably up to 20 local collectives outside of NYC. Each collective operated independently, addressing local needs and challenges. Sometimes, they would come together to collaborate on projects and then dissolve afterward. These local RR collectives achieved notable successes. In Portland, volunteers created a lending library for (the now shuttered) *Bitch Magazine*, helping the publication connect with its community. In Boston, the group organized a Critical Library Symposium that sparked rich conversations about librarianship and activism. RR members have also delivered workshops and presentations on radical archives, community documentation, and alternative library practices at conferences across North America (Friedman, 2014).

All the RR collectives operated without formal leadership and traditional organizational structures. Friedman described the organization as "intentionally unorganized," aligning with principles of horizontal organization and consensus:

> We had meetings where we talked about what we wanted to work on and things that we wanted to support. And then after that, there became local collectives. So, because this was in New York, the local collectives would be in Philadelphia or Portland or San Francisco or Texas, and so we had all these different collectives, and they were doing different things. There was no one telling anyone what to do. A local collective could say, 'We are

having problems with white supremacists booking rooms at our local public library and we need to figure out what we can do about that?' Or someone would say, 'We have a large Hmong community, and we need to be able to translate our library information materials into Hmong.' 'How do we source that? How do we find someone who can help us do those translations?' It ran the gamut.

While empowering, this horizontal model also posed challenges. In hindsight, Friedman said that she wished the NYC collective had provided more support for RR's new local groups. Friedman acknowledged that not everyone had the necessary tools to organize effectively:

I wish we had figured out a way to support the local collectives in a different way. Perhaps because people would say, 'I want to start a local collective,' and we would say, 'Okay, go do that.' Not everyone has those tools, and sometimes we would offer to help, but that is a hard thing to do. Let's say in Texas [home state of the interviewers], where you might not have a lot of experience doing something like that and figuring out the best ways to organize and the things that you can do to connect with other librarians who share your views and values. [...] I wish that the local collectives could have been stronger.

This decentralized model of operation had both strengths and weaknesses. While it fostered autonomy and creativity, it also resulted in uneven participation among collective members, with a handful of active members carrying much of the workload. Recruiting and sustaining volunteer engagement remained a challenge, especially when media attention temporarily spiked or faded.

Ultimately, RR became inactive due to a combination of burnout and developments in information technology. As mobile technology became ubiquitous, the model of hitting the streets with physical information in three-ring binders became less essential:

The ways in which we accessed information changed dramatically in those five, ten years, and those binders obviously were not necessary anymore. People had smartphones and Wikipedia and other ways of accessing information. But also, we were tired. That is one of the things that happens to people who are doing activist work. You experience burnout; it is definitely a byproduct.

The spirit of RR, supporting marginalized communities' access to information, lives on. Friedman continues to apply the lessons of collective work in her professional practice. Drawing from her time at a consensus-based food co-op in Olympia, Washington, she incorporates thoughtful, horizontal decision-making whenever possible within the large bureaucratic system of the academic library. Friedman used the metaphor of "carrot circles," taken from her days working at a food co-op, to represent simple, satisfying work free from bureaucratic entanglements and what she aims to accomplish at the academic library.

> At the co-op, I would make these beautiful carrot circles, and then at the end of the day, I would go home, and I would not worry about the carrot circles. The carrot circles were not going to send me an email in the middle of the night, the carrot circles were not going to set off a fire alarm. I did not have to fill out a form for the carrot circles. I did not have to have 18 meetings about the carrot circles. So, there is a longing for that kind of work, and for the simplicity of that kind of work, and my wish to apply that to librarianship, if that makes any sense at all.

Building small collectives committed to equality and critical inquiry is possible even within large institutions. After the George Floyd protests of 2020, Friedman helped establish a Library Community Collective (LCC) at UC San Diego Library. Emerging from a collaboration between the Library Community Building Committee and the Diversity and Inclusion Committee, the LCC is an employee-led, non-hierarchical group that meets monthly to discuss challenging issues while providing a safe space for library staff to process emotions and engage in honest conversations about racism and bias. It provides biweekly discussion forums on anti-Black racism, allyship, anti-Asian violence, microaggressions, workplace inequities, and systemic oppression. The core collective is made up of mostly Black, Indigenous, and People of Color (BIPOC) and Queer staff who engage in the emotional labor of facilitating discussions and highlighting broader issues of labor inequities in Equity, Diversity, and Inclusion (EDI) work (Goodson et al., 2021). The LCC's efforts emphasize the need for authentic, action-driven responses to social justice concerns rather than performative gestures. The organizers aim to broaden participation, reduce the burden on marginalized staff, and implement more structured support systems to sustain the initiative. Having developed a memorandum of understanding on how to engage one another through respecting space, elevating marginalized voices, practicing empathy, and respecting each other's privacy, the group has successfully engaged in fruitful, if at times difficult, conversations (Goodson et al., 2021, Appendix A), and the LCC's work serves as a potential model for other libraries seeking to embed anti-racism and social justice into their institutional culture.

Friedman's own scholarship focuses on the intersection between activism and library work, bringing her lived experience into her research. Her work consistently reflects the idea that librarians are not just information gatekeepers but also agents of change shaped by their own experiences and values. Friedman (2014) wrote about RR in Melissa Morrone's 2014 edited collection, *Informed Agitation: Library and Information Skills in Social Justice Movements and Beyond*, and the LCC's work in an article for *Collaborative Librarianship*

(Goodson et al., 2021). Recently, Friedman has been investigating how activist library workers bring themselves into the profession and how their background affects their professional identity, co-authoring "Integrating Identities: The Intersection of Reluctant Professionals and the Academy," which reflects on collective work and activist librarianship (Friedman & Quiñonez, 2023). In her scholarship and everyday practice, Friedman strives to bring that spirit of community, simplicity, and activist commitment into the often-complex world of academic librarianship.

Friedman's story is a testament to how unconventional paths can lead to transformative professional practices. Embracing her activist roots to approach library work through a critical lens both within and outside of the traditional library itself has helped shape a profoundly human and radically inclusive vision of the work. Friedman's professional journey also demonstrates that meaningful change often takes place outside traditional institutions and that lessons learned from non-traditional organizations, such as collectives, may inform one's work in the traditional ones. Her work with collectives, RR, and the LCC shows how librarians can build flexible, collective models that prioritize collaboration and critical inquiry. Even in large, bureaucratic systems, it is possible to carve out transformative, horizontal spaces where shared values drive action and social responsibility. By weaving activism into the daily practice of librarianship, Friedman positions libraries as sites of empowerment and social transformation. Her work underscores the importance of persistence, coalition-building, and creating opportunities for marginalized voices to be heard and sets an example for future social justice-oriented librarians to bring their full identities to their professional lives as activists, scholars, and community members.

References

Friedman, L. G. (2014). Radical reference: Who cares? In M. Morrone (Ed.), *Informed agitation: Library and information skills in social justice movements and beyond.* Library Juice Press.

Friedman, L. G. & Quiñonez, T. (2023). Integrating identities: The intersection of reluctant professionals and the academy. In A. N. Hess (Ed.), *Instructional identities and information literacy, Volume 2: Transforming our programs, institutions, and profession.* Association of College & Research Libraries. https://escholarship.org/uc/item/0303v3m6

Goodson, L., Moore, A. A., Friedman, L., Robles-Fradet, P., & Almodovar, R. (2021). Library Community Collective: Advocating for social justice through community conversations. *Collaborative Librarianship, 13*(1), 7–22. https://digitalcommons.du.edu/collaborativelibrarianship/vol13/iss1/3

Morrone, M., & Friedman, L. (2009). Radical reference: Socially responsible librarianship collaborating with community. *The Reference Librarian, 50*(4), 371–396.

10 Kelly Jensen

Kelly Jensen is a former public librarian who now works as an editor for Book Riot (http://www.bookriot.com), the largest independent editorial book site in North America. Book Riot has given her the opportunity to both think and write a great deal about libraries and library work while keeping her connected with librarianship as a profession. A staunch advocate for freedom of speech and the freedom to read, Jensen has emerged as a leader and prominent voice in the fight against book censorship in libraries, writing, curating, and editing two newsletters for Book Riot, a young adult literature newsletter and a literary activism newsletter, both of which reach over 100,000 subscribers.

Jensen first encountered book censorship in high school when a teacher confided in her that if the school board found out that he was having Jensen's class read Howard Zinn's (1980) *A People's History of the United States: 1492– Present*, he would " likely get in trouble" (see Chapter 12, for more on Zinn's book). Jensen's first substantive encounter with censorship, however, took place during her undergraduate years at Cornell College, Iowa, where she pursued a dual major in English and Psychology. Working as a student library intern at the college library (which also doubled as the town's public library), Jensen was tasked with researching books that had been censored or challenged in libraries (one of which was Laurie Halse Anderson's 1999 young adult novel *Speak*, which will factor in later in this chapter). The experience of investigating the history of the censorship efforts targeting these books really "cracked something open" in Jensen, introducing her to just how irate people can become about the contents of books in public and school libraries.

Jensen's first personal encounter with library censorship, i.e., one in which she was directly involved in her capacity as a library worker, happened during her first professional job as a teen services librarian at a public library. Nothing really came of that challenge other than an angry letter from a patron. However, during her next professional position, again at a public library, a book challenge came that was a bit different, this time because of the library administration's response:

> I was a children's librarian for patrons aged from birth through 18 at a small library. The patron with the challenge wrote a letter. She was very angry

DOI: 10.4324/9781003473640-11

about a book she found in the middle grade comics section, an award-winning book. She was angry about it because there was scene in the book where the protagonist, who is like 11, is going through puberty and some of the signs of puberty are there. She wrote this long letter about how inappropriate this material was. I am reading it and completely disagree with this, but I do not know what to do with the challenge. At that time, I worked with a boss who was not great and said, 'Let's just pull the book.' Why would you do that? So, my answer was to hide the letters from there on. This is one of those things where I was like, 'there is no formal challenge, sometimes the parent just needs to be mad and put it out and send a letter.' But that was particularly radicalizing because my boss did not have my back on that and for no good reason.

Jensen refused to either pull the book or review the collection for "inappropriate materials" (Jensen, 2023). Although this was an eye-opening experience concerning the potential lack of institutional support for library workers faced with censorship, Jensen's full dedication to anti-censorship activism would come later. Around 2012, she began writing for Book Riot part-time while working as a public librarian. Her early blog posts address a variety of topics related to young adult reading, such as popular trends in the category. In those days, there was not as strident a push for book censorship as seen now, but Jensen vividly remembers writing about how important it is for librarians and teachers to make accessible the types of books that have been challenged to the readers who need them.

Since 2020, however, Jensen's work for Book Riot has focused increasingly on book censorship and book-banning efforts, with the number of such challenges to libraries having increased considerably. In 2023, the US House Committee on Oversight and Accountability reported an increase of educational gag orders in US states of 250% between 2021 and 2022 (Committee on Oversight, 2023, p. 2). Between January and August 2024, the American Library Association (ALA) documented that there were:

> [...] 414 attempts to censor library materials and services. In those cases, 1,128 unique titles were challenged. In the same reporting period last year [2023], ALA tracked 695 attempts with 1,915 unique titles challenged. Though the number of reports to date has declined in 2024, the number of documented attempts to censor books continues to far exceed the numbers prior to 2020.
> (American Library Association, 2024)

After writing several articles about a specific banning incident during the post-2020 library censorship barrage, Jensen began to collect all weblinks to news concerning library censorship attempts and share them online once a week with her commentary. That project only lasted for a few months before it became untenable due to the massive volume of censorship news; she simply could not keep up with writing about every banned story she found. So instead, she shifted her efforts into collecting as many links as possible, and sharing them would do a lot of good for archiving the moment in censorship as well as acknowledging the stories she could not write herself. During her undergraduate internship project at Cornell College, Jensen had relied on the book *Banned Books: 2007 Resource Book*, by Robert Doyle (2007), to find information on banned and challenged books, and she decided that an archive of challenged and banned books was necessary to maintain a historical record of this new spate of censorship efforts, to call out the institutions that engaged in such censorship, and to support the library workers on the ground doing their best to keep good books on shelves.

Jensen found that book-banning efforts had become increasingly more sophisticated and conducted on a larger scale, likely due to advances in communication and networking technologies. She pointed to the group Moms for Liberty (https://www.momsforliberty.org/) as an example of a particularly vocal activist group at the forefront of this new wave of book censorship organizations. Founded in Florida in 2021, Moms has grown rapidly, and the organization currently claims to have more than 300 chapters in 48 US states (although a chapter only needs ten members to be enrolled as such). The Southern Poverty Law Center maintains a page dedicated to Moms that labels it as an "extremist group" and describes it as an "anti-government" organization that originated as a response to COVID-19 safety measures in schools that has expanded to promote an "anti-inclusive curriculum" in schools as "strong supporters of the wave of anti-CRT [critical race theory] bills sweeping the country and key actors in the sharp increase in book bans occurring in schools and libraries" (Southern Poverty Law Center, n.d.). Moms also produces weekly episodes of its Joyful Warriors podcast with episodes bearing titles like "How This Dad Saved His Son From Transgenderism," "Understanding the LGBTQ's Push Toward Children, with Chad Felix Greene," "The Marxification of Education," and "Combatting Woke Education and School Unions" (https://portal.momsforliberty.org/podcast/) (Moms for Liberty, n.d.).

Moms for Liberty was connected to the now inactive BookLooks (https://www.booklooks.org) (Jensen, May 16, 2022), a site that identifies books they deem inappropriate for children and teenagers. Jensen explained that BookLooks solicits volunteers to review books that might be read by children or young adults and then posts a "book report" about that book on their site. These reports, she said, are not professional reviews like those that appear in professional legacy publications like *School Library Journal* or *CHOICE Magazine*, and BookLooks reviewers typically had no background in librarianship or education or child development. The review process included counting words in the book in question (detailed for readers in a table at the end of each report), looking for ideas that went against the organization's moral beliefs on issues, and creating a label or rating for that book. For example, the BookLooks report for the graphic novel adaptation of Margaret Atwood's (2019) *The Handmaid's Tale*, which received a 4 out of 5 "Not For Minors" rating (the higher the rating being considered more problematic), provides a one-sentence summary of the plot, a brief "Summary of Concerns," and a list of content deemed concerning by the anonymous reviewer. Concerning passages are excerpted from the book text and presented without context. Problematic illustrations are summarized, again with no context. For example, from *The Handmaid's Tale* graphic novel: "p. 85. The illustrations on the bottom of the page depict a man and a woman kissing. One illustration is a zoomed in view and the other is a zoomed out view of the couple" (BookLooks, n.d.). Scores with high ratings would often then be challenged in school districts across the United States by groups like Moms. Although BookLooks has recently shut down—evidencing how quickly things change in the world of pro-censorship groups—RatedBooks (https://www.ratedbooks.org/), a project of another "parental rights" group, subsumed all the BookLooks reviews.

The small minority of people who advocate for banning books is disproportionately loud and has developed effective techniques for getting into the ears of state legislators sympathetic to their moral panic. The problem, Jensen said, goes beyond just book censorship and banning. Yes, the pro-censorship groups find the books objectionable, but their attempts to remove material also work as a convenient way to sow confusion and discord in what she described as an attempt to convince politicians to pass items like school voucher bills, which may lead to the defunding of public schools or to getting rid of taxpayer-funded libraries altogether. One much-publicized example of such efforts coming to fruition is the Trump administration's 2025 executive order to eliminate the Institute of Museum and Library Services "to the maximum extent consistent with applicable law" (White House, 2025). Another example of such defunding, this time on a much smaller scale, is the defunding of Fairhope Public Library (AL) at the behest of the state because they did not ban a number of LGBTQIA2+ books (Jensen, 2025).

In many cases, libraries are so overwhelmed by book challenges that they would rather give in to them than fight back, the easiest response being to comply, i.e., to voluntarily remove the targeted books from circulation. One example of this conceding to the demands of book banners, Jensen said, came from a banning effort led by Vicki Baggett, a public-school English teacher in Escambia County, Florida. Baggett presented Escambia County Public Schools with a list of over 100 elementary, middle, and high school books that she considered to contain inappropriate sexual content, including award-winning novels like Atwood's *The Handmaid's Tale* (an evergreen target of censorship efforts), *Speak* by Laurie Halse Anderson, *Forever* by Judie Blume, and *The God of Small Things* by Arundhati Roy (Baggett's list is available online at https://www.wkrg.com/wp-content/uploads/sites/49/2022/09/Vicki-Baggett-Book-List.pdf). The library board caved to the pressure and took the books off the shelf or restricted access to many of them (Pendharkar, 2023). A recent spate of red state legislative measures that threaten library workers with possible jail time has also made librarians more likely to fold in the face of outside pressure and intimidation. In a Book Riot article, Jenson wrote about York County public libraries in South Carolina, where library materials had been challenged. In response to the challenge, the County Library Board of Trustees winnowed their library board from ten people to seven people and appointed three new board members who were sympathetic to the book banners (Jensen, 2024).

Nonetheless, despite the aggressive tactics on the part of the pro-censorship activists and the failure of some libraries to fight back against challenges, members of the communities affected, including parents, students, and other educators, have not remained silent. The increase in book censorship efforts has resulted in a valiant response on the part of both individual citizens as well as anti-censorship groups. Groups like Moms for Liberty, Jensen said, do not represent the majority opinion concerning attempts at library censorship, and book-banning efforts in the US remain unpopular among most of the wider public. Media coverage has led to public outcries, and there have been successful lawsuits filed against First Amendment violations. Jensen has witnessed an increasing number of people who may not have thought often about their libraries realize that they cannot take them for granted any longer, and they are stepping up to defend them. The visibility that Jensen has achieved from her writing has led to her receiving an increasing number of messages from concerned people, including anonymous whistleblowers, many of whom are library workers who have felt unable to speak up on their patrons' behalf out of fear of retribution and a lack of support from their employers. People want to share their stories, and Jensen learns a lot from frontline library workers concerning challenges and bans that she brings to light in her columns. Jensen's columns also connect people with others who have been in similar situations, allowing them to talk through what to do in a particular situation or how to engage in effective messaging when challenged.

There are, as a result, reasons to be optimistic in this fight. Anti-censorship efforts have increased in response to the uptick in book-banning attempts, with grassroots organizations doing brave work. Such groups, Jensen said,

> Parents and community members are learning how to organize and engage with others around the issue of book banning and the importance of public libraries and schools from one another. Most have no previous experience doing this, and most have no relationships with affinity organizations or political groups. Most also have no funding to do their work, other than what they personally bring to the table. That stands in contrast to these large groups contributing to book censorship, like Moms for Liberty and No Left Turn in Education.

Although there is no real central authority for anti-censorship efforts, startup groups may look to more established groups for help and inspiration. There are big tent organizations like the American Library Association's Unite Against Book Bans (https://uniteagainstbookbans.org/) and PEN America (https://pen.org/) that advocate and educate around book bans. There are also ground-level, grassroots organizations like Texas FReadom Fighters (https://www.txfreadomfighters.us/) (see Chapter 5 for more information on this group) and Florida Freedom to Read Project (https://www.fftrp.org/), which are spearheaded by parents, librarians, educators, and other concerned citizens doing advocacy and activism independently for both inspiration and strategies on how to best operate, and these larger, more established groups have been happy to share information and advice. And, despite the censorship onslaught, resistance works and successes are coming. In 2023, PEN America, an organization that advocates for freedom of expression, filed suit against Escambia County schools—which had folded under the pressure of Vicki Baggett's efforts with the publisher Random House (Girod, 2023)—and recent victories for the plaintiffs include the court-ordered return of over 24 of the banned books to Escambia County shelves (PEN America, 2024).

When asked about a particular work that inspired her in her professional career and fight against library censorship, Jensen pointed to Laurie Halse Anderson's (2011/1999) young adult novel *Speak*, a favorite target for the book banners and one of the books she was tasked with researching during her college internship. *Speak* tells the story of Melinda Sorino, a high school freshman and rape victim who, at the book's beginning, is unable to communicate the violence that has happened to her but finds her voice and personal agency by the story's end. Jensen first read *Speak* as a teenager in 1999. Her local public library had just created a young adult section, and *Speak* was one of the few books they had on the shelf at that time: "I must have been 17, something like that. It knocked the wind out of me because there really were not a lot of YA books at that time." Jensen was struck by the power of the story and has reread the book several times. Each time she reads *Speak*, she connects with something new:

> This time as I read it, I read it this weekend. I had not realized how much of a story it is about depression. I always read it as a story about rape and sexual assault, which it is, but I had never seen the depression throughline until this last time when I read it. As somebody who writes about mental health, but also as someone who struggled with depression in her teen years but did not have the language or words to talk about it… reflecting on it now, it is no wonder that book struck me at that point and stuck with me.

Jensen describes *Speak* as timeless, as something that teens still connect with 25 years after its initial publication. This timelessness, she said, is because Melinda's voice registers as authentic in its portrayal of teenage frustration and anger. Not only did Jensen find the novel to be incredibly powerful, but she was also particularly affected by Anderson's postscript in the 2006 edition (and subsequently reprinted in later editions), where the author responds to the multiple attempts to get the book removed from school and public library shelves:

Because most of the censorship I see is fear driven. I respect that the world is a very scary place. It is a terrifying place in which to raise children and in particular, teenagers. It is human nature to nurture and protect children as they grow into adulthood. But censoring books that deal with difficult adolescent issues does not protect anybody. Quite the opposite. It leaves kids in the darkness and makes them vulnerable. Censorship is the child of fear and the father of ignorance. Our children cannot afford to have the truth of the world withheld from them. They need us to be brave enough to give them great books to they can learn how to grow up into the men and women we want them to be.

(Anderson, 2011/1999, p. 199)

Speak has been with Jensen through many stages of her life and career, and after having worked as a librarian, reading Anderson's postscript recontextualized the novel for her. She sees Anderson as a role model who has been a fierce advocate for library workers and teen readers since the beginning of her career.

It is this sort of authenticity that Jensen found in Anderson's work that she aims to bring to her own writing. In addition to her editing work for Book Riot, Jensen has authored a book, edited three anthologies, contributed her own work to edited collections, and had her articles published in periodicals including *Ms. Magazine* and *Library Journal*. Jensen's anthologies deal with issues familiar to teenagers' daily lives, including their developing bodies and mental health, through chapters written by public figures and young adult authors. She is drawn to the anthology format for two reasons. The first reason is her love of editing, and she finds it fun and fulfilling to work with both writers and people who have never written before but have an interesting story to tell. The second reason is that Jensen's work deals with weighty topics like mental health, teenage perceptions of the human body, and feminism. Being a white woman and occupying a position of privilege, she recognizes the need to access a diversity of voices and realizes that it would not be fair for her to have the final say on subjects like the political meaning of the body or mental health. The anthology format presents readers with many different voices, engages them with critical thought on difficult topics, and, because the authors do not always agree on issues, leads to fruitful conversations.

Jensen's (2018) second anthology, *(Don't) Call me Crazy: 33 Voices Start the Conversation About Mental Health*, was named a Washington Post Best Book of 2018 and a Schneider Family Book Award Honor Winner. Her third, *Body Talk: 37 Voices Explore Our Radical Anatomy* (Jensen, 2020), was named by *School Library Journal* as a "Best Book" of 2020. Despite these accolades, and somewhat unsurprisingly, the books have also been the target of the censorship crowd because of their sensitive subject matter, and quite possibly as retaliation for Jensen's Book Riot columns. *Body Talk* was banned in Clay County, Florida, schools and has also been pulled from the collections of several other Florida school libraries, as well as school libraries in Tennessee,

Missouri, and New Hampshire (the ONLY documented book ban in the state), likely because of recent laws passed at the state level concerning visual depictions:

> In *Body Talk* there are some images of people without clothes on—joyful illustrations of nude humans depicting a wide range of physical characteristics, all of which are tasteful, artistic, and that was over the line, even though they are perfectly appropriate for teen readers.

Having faced book challenges as both a library worker and as an author, Jensen knows how scary they can be and has advice for the library professional who may be up against a censorship attempt for the first time. First, it is always best to be prepared. One should anticipate the potential for challenges and take the opportunity to see if there are any holes in institutional policies and procedures and fix those holes:

> I think immediately of the libraries that have very broad collection development policies or big challenge policies. Those [types of] policies are very easy to exploit. And I think particularly in public libraries they have learned this over the last few years. I have seen many better collection development policies recently than I have in the past. […] [Dealing with collection development policy issues] can be annoying and boring, but yet so important because it is going to help you down the line.

Second, when a public or school librarian faces a book challenge for the first time, they should keep in mind that nothing requires an immediate response. It can be easy, especially if somebody is in your space complaining about a book, to enter fight or flight mode or just freeze up; one needs to remember not to respond from that place. Instead, thank them for their concerns and let them know that you will be in touch. This should provide you with an opportunity to step away, gather necessary information, and do the things you need to do to address the challenge: "This is not a fire. This is something you want to talk to your colleagues about." Follow all policies and then respond through whatever protocol the library has set in place.

While book challenges may feel like personal attacks on the library worker in the crosshairs, and library administrations and boards may not always be supportive, with anti-censorship advocates like Jensen out there, you are not alone.

References

American Library Association. (2024, September 23). *American Library Association reveals preliminary data on 2024 book challenges*. American Library Association. https://www.ala.org/news/2024/09/american-library-association-reveals-preliminary-data-2024-book-challenges

Anderson, L. H. (2011/1999). *Speak*. Farrar Straus Giroux.
Atwood, M. (2019). *The handmaid's tale* [graphic novel] (R. Nault, Illus.). Nan A. Talese.
BookLooks. (n.d.). The handmaid's tale: The graphic novel. Booklooks.org. https://web.archive.org/web/20250313214803/https://booklooks.org/data/files/Book%20Looks%20Reports/H/The%20Handmaids%20Tale%20The%20Graphic%20Novel.pdf
Committee on Oversight and Accountability, US House of Representatives. (2023, October 5). House oversight report. https://www.govinfo.gov/content/pkg/GOVPUB-Y4_OV2-PURL-gpo219516.pdf/GOVPUB-Y4_OV2-PURL-gpo219516.pdf
Doyle, R. (2007). *Banned books: 2007 resource book*. American Library Association.
Girod, B. (2023, May 17). PEN America, Penguin Random House sue Florida school district over book ban. What we know. *Pensacola News Journal*. https://www.pnj.com/story/news/crime/2023/05/17/florida-book-ban-lawsuit-pen-america-penguin-random-house-unconstitutional-what-we-know/70226457007/
Jensen, K. (2018). *(Don't) call me crazy: 33 voices start the conversation about mental health*. Little, Brown Books for Young Readers.
Jensen, K. (2020). *Body talk: 37 voices explore our radical anatomy*. Little, Brown Books for Young Readers.
Jensen, K. (2022, May 16). BookLooks, framed as "objective" book rating resource, a Moms for Liberty joint. *Book Riot*. https://bookriot.com/moms-for-liberty-booklooks/
Jensen, K. (2023, July 2). My own book censorship story: Or the time I had a very toxic boss. *Book Riot*. https://buttondown.com/wellsourced/archive/my-own-book-censorship-story/
Jensen, K. (2024, October 22). What's happening in York County Library (SC) should be a wakeup call. *Book Riot*. https://bookriot.com/whats-happening-in-york-county-library-sc-should-be-a-wakeup-call/
Jensen, K. (2025, March 25). Alabama Public Library Service defunds Fairhope Public Library; City Council will not follow suit. *Book Riot*. https://bookriot.com/fairhope-public-library/
Moms for Liberty. (n.d.). The fire of liberty show. *Moms for Liberty*. https://portal.momsforliberty.org/podcast/
PEN America. (2024, October 7). Victory for Freedom to Read, as Escambia County returns 24 restricted books to school library shelves. *PEN America*. https://pen.org/press-release/victory-for-freedom-to-read-as-escambia-county-returns-24-restricted-books-to-school-library-shelves/
Pendharkar, E. (2023, May 17). District that restricted access to over 100 books sued by publisher, free speech group. *Education Week*. https://www.edweek.org/politics-policy/district-that-restricted-access-to-over-100-books-sued-by-publisher-free-speech-group/2023/05
Southern Poverty Law Center (n.d.). Moms for Liberty. *Southern Poverty Law Center*. https://www.splcenter.org/resources/extremist-files/moms-liberty/
White House. Presidential Actions. (2025, March 14). Continuing the reduction of the federal bureaucracy. *White House*. https://www.whitehouse.gov/presidential-actions/2025/03/continuing-the-reduction-of-the-federal-bureaucracy/
Zinn, H. (1980). *A people's history of the United States: 1492-present*. Routledge.

11 Amanda Jones

A lifelong educator in the small town of Watson, Louisiana, Amanda Jones's career journey reflects a powerful commitment to student-centered learning. Dedicated to serving the community where she grew up, Jones has worked at Live Oak Middle School for 23 years—the same school that she attended as a middle school student—first as a seventh and eighth grade English language arts teacher and then, since 2015, as school librarian. This may sound like noble if not particularly unusual work; there are thousands of school librarians working in small towns across the United States. What sets Jones apart, however, is her remarkable transformation over the past few years into a fierce anti-censorship activist and a defender of intellectual freedom in school and public libraries. In 2022, Jones received national media attention after being aggressively targeted and harassed by book banners—even receiving death threats—for speaking out against censorship in her school district. But it is not just the vehement response of extremists to a librarian doing what a librarian should be doing that is extraordinary; it is how Jones responded in the face of this harassment that makes her story so compelling.

Even before receiving national attention for speaking out against library censorship (and suffering the consequences), Jones enjoyed a distinguished career as a school librarian. As the only librarian for a school of around 700 students, she transformed her school library into a dynamic environment that encourages reading and exploration. Jones said that she is "a teacher *and* a librarian" that centers her practice on student development through instructing teens on things like library skills and digital citizenship: "I want to be the best I can be for our community, because I live in a small town, every child in my community will have me as a school librarian, and we are the only middle school." For Jones, being an effective librarian means embodying best practices, adapting to meet students' evolving needs, and continually educating herself. Jones's approach is collaborative and responsive, based on the latest educational research and paying close attention to student feedback. For example, when Jones taught a lesson on the dangers of social media and the pitfalls of online content, students confided in her about being bullied and harassed online (many, for example, had been told to KYS, "kill yourself," in online messages). Based on their online experiences, Jones initiated a social media safety lesson to teach responsible online behavior. Jones also ensures that students play an active role in selecting titles for the collection, encouraging them to make purchase suggestions through a Google Form as well as informal conversations. She is careful to make sure that book orders reflect both student interests and award-winning literature, with a keen eye on inclusion and cultural relevance. Because of her innovative approach to school librarianship, Jones has received multiple awards, including State Middle School Teacher of the Year in 2019, State School Librarian of the Year in 2020, and School Library Journal National Librarian of the Year in 2021.

Jones's professional work is guided by Martin Luther King Jr.'s (1967) words in his "What Is Your Life's Blueprint?" speech, which King delivered to students at Barrett Junior High School in Philadelphia just months before his assassination:

> You're going to be deciding as the days, as the years unfold what you will do in life - what your life's work will be. Set out to do it well. [...] If it falls your lot to be a street sweeper, sweep streets like Leontyne Price sings before the Metropolitan Opera. Sweep streets like Shakespeare wrote poetry. Sweep streets so well that all the hosts of heaven and earth will have to pause and say: Here lives a great street sweeper who swept his job well. If you can't be a pine at the top of the hill, be a shrub in the valley. Be the best little shrub on the side of the hill.
>
> (King, 1967)

For Jones, King's words mean striving for excellence as an educator and community member. Another profound influence on Jones's career as a school librarian was when she heard Samira Ahmed, *New York Times* bestselling author of young adult fiction, including *Internment* (2019a) and *This Book Won't Burn* (2024), implore attendants at a 2019 *Library School Journal* Teen Live! event to use their "power and privilege for purpose" (Ahmed, 2019b). That moment inspired Jones to reflect on her own identity as a white, cisgender, middle-class woman with a platform. Writing about her talk for the *Library School Journal*, Ahmed (2019c) said,

> [...] we must use our power and privilege for a purpose - to make this world better for all our children. It's a lofty goal, but our children deserve no less. I'm asking you to make a choice, to realize there is no room for moral equivalencies when we're faced with hatred that dictates policy.

Encountering the inspirational words of King and Ahmed, as well as being recognized as National School Librarian of the Year, deepened Jones's sense of duty to others, particularly those people who are most vulnerable or at risk of being silenced: "It made me think about everything I do going forward should be with a purpose to make, not just libraries, but the world a better place."

Considering her dedication to advocacy, it is no surprise that Jones has always strongly believed in intellectual freedom and vocally supported it, even taking part in a 2021 webinar panel on the topic with well-known children's and young adult literature author Nikki Grimes. Jones said that she felt prepared for anything that might come her way. However, she did not realize what she was taking on until the targeted harassment started. In July 2022, Jones spoke at a Livingston Parish Public Library Board meeting against book banning. Even though she was one of many people who weighed in against censorship at the meeting, Jones was singled out by the pro-censorship crowd for harassment, likely because of her visibility in her small community and role as a public-school librarian. Facing relentless attacks, Jones was accused of providing middle-schoolers access to pornographic materials, her personal information was doxxed online, and she was even threatened with violence—one meme distributed through social media depicted her with a target on her back. But rather than back down, Jones doubled down:

> They wanted to silence me. I was defamed and harassed, and I still am. I have gotten used to it at this point. They wanted to silence me, so I decided to do the opposite of what they wanted and talk more about it and try to learn everything I could.

Jones educated herself on intellectual freedom and its opponents, reading extensively on the topic, including books like the *American Library Association Intellectual Freedom Manual* (Magi & Garnar, 2021) and Emily Knox's (2022) *Foundations of Intellectual Freedom*. She followed Kelly Jenson's weekly censorship newsletter on Book Riot (see Chapter 10 for a profile of Jensen) and got herself up to date on important court cases and legislative maneuvers having to do with censorship: "I read about every city, every school, every public library, to stay up to date, because [the recent wave of banning attempts] hit us in Louisiana about two years ago. It is still hitting us."

This fast-tracked education quickly came in handy, as the early 2020s saw an onslaught of book challenges and censorship efforts. Through her research, Jones connected the dots between book-banning efforts and politically motivated campaigns led by dark money nonprofits like Citizens for a New Louisiana (https://www.newlouisiana.org/) and Moms for Liberty (https://www.momsforliberty.org/), groups created to wreak havoc on libraries and public schools, exploiting parental fears with the goal of defunding and destabilizing schools and public libraries in favor of privatization, in hopes of replacing them with charter schools and private library systems:

> It is a money racket, but they also use [book banning efforts] to stir up fake controversies. If you watch, it is usually around election times, so these groups, like Citizens for a New Louisiana and Moms for Liberty, come in and they say, 'oh, there's porn in the kids section' so that these people running for office can swoop in and say, 'If you vote for me, I'm going to save us all.' So, it is politically motivated and motivated by money.

Jones sees these movements as deeply interconnected with attacks on LGBTQIA2+ rights, diversity, equity, and inclusion initiatives, and accurate historical education. She recognizes these organizations are attempting to "other" people who are Indigenous and people of color, including folks who identify as LGBTQIA2+. She explained how these groups operate through fear. They photocopy book challenge forms often filled with untruths and disinformation and then ask fearful community members to sign their names without even reading the books. Citing personal experience, Jones recently fought a book ban for the children's book *I'm Not a Girl: A Transgender Story* (Lyons & Verdi, 2020), a book written for four-year-olds to six-year-olds. Jones's Library had 12 book challenges based on the book's supposed "ungodly" and "sexually explicit" content. Jones stood firm, and the book remained on the shelves. Jones said, however, "Even just the challenge on [a book], it sends a message to all of the queer community that they do not belong on a bookshelf, or they need to be relocated to the adult section."

Jones has been at the front lines of resisting anti-library legislation in Louisiana that, if successful, would extend beyond the removal of individual books to the provocation of entire communities, especially marginalized groups. These efforts have included bills seeking to defund libraries, criminalize librarians attending American Library Association (ALA) conferences, and reorganize public library boards for political purposes; the Louisiana legislature recently passed a bill (SB 262) into law that restricts teaching topics like oppression in public schools (Bolden, 2024; Hodges 2024). The state currently has an extremist governor and an extremist supermajority in both its House and Senate, and eight anti-library bills were introduced in the 2024 Regular Session. "It has gone beyond book banning," Jones said, "They are trying to change the shape of public library boards. They are trying to arrest librarians." This last statement is not hyperbole. In 2024, H.B. 777 was introduced by Jones's own state representative and former school board representative into the Louisiana state legislature. If H.B. 777 had become law, it would have made it illegal for a public employee to "request or receive remuneration in any form for continuing education or for attending a conference if the continuing education or conference was sponsored or conducted in, in whole or in part, by the American Library Association or its successor" (H.B. 777, 2024). A Louisiana school or public librarian would have faced up to two years imprisonment and hard labor for attending the ALA Annual Conference. Fortunately, H.B. 777, which became informally known as "the Amanda Jones bill," was defeated. Of the eight anti-library bills introduced in the 2024 session, six were defeated. Only two passed, one of which had so many amendments added to it that it effectively made it null and void: "I think we did pretty well this past legislative session, but it is a full-on assault on our public-school libraries in Louisiana." And Louisiana is not the only state where libraries and library workers are being attacked by the legislature. Missouri and Iowa are also moving to defund public libraries if they are affiliated with the American Library Association (ALA) (DeBerry, 2023; Obradovich, 2025).

Jones said that library workers and concerned community members are not alone in the face of extremists' attempts to control public and school libraries. Although Jones does not always agree with ALA, often being vocal with the organization about the need for them to do more, she campaigned to get a volunteer position as a counselor for the state of Louisiana, representing its ALA members and working from the inside to make change. She said that in the past, ALA has often tried to stay neutral, but they recently offered training on the established laws and librarians' rights to protect themselves and disseminate information back to their constituencies to prepare for book bans and new legislation aimed at defunding public libraries. Jones also reached out to ALA to help her defeat one of the recent anti-library bills in the Louisiana legislature, and they came through with assistance, understanding that some of the work they do remains invisible to the public. In addition to professional organizations like the ALA, Jones pointed to other organizations that library workers can look to for help:

> A lot of hands-on help has been provided by EveryLibrary [https://www.everylibrary.org/], helping build coalitions and providing strategies for even the smallest local meetings all the way to the legislature. They will hop on a Zoom meeting and guide me in the right direction and tell me what I need to do to fight these people at the local level. EveryLibrary [https://www.everylibrary.org/], National Coalition against Censorship [https://ncac.org/] has helped a lot, Comic Book Legal Defense Fund [https://cbldf.org/] has helped, and local help organizations like 10,000 Women Louisiana [https://www.10000womenla.org/], Louisiana League of Women Voters [https://www.lwv.org/local-leagues/lwv-louisiana], things like that. Some nonpartisan people have helped locally. There are people in my community who have been hateful and awful, but many librarians and people outside of my community have been great.

Jones (2024) recently published a book, *That Librarian: The Fight Against Book Banning in America*, which details her resistance to the book banners and library censors. She wants library workers to read the book and to know that they are not alone and that all the feelings that they have are valid:

> I know so many librarians that are being attacked right now across multiple states and in states that I never thought would have those problems, like Maine, New Jersey, New York, and California, I thought, 'Oh, they are safe there.' They are not. I just spoke in New York three days ago to over 100 librarians, and I asked, 'who has had a book challenge?' And over half the room raised their hand, and this is New York.

She also hopes not just library workers read *That Librarian* so that non-librarians might reconsider what they believe about librarians and the role of public institutions:

I want other people to see that you should not believe everything you read on the internet and social media about people. We are all a lot more alike than we are different, and we are all humans and should treat each other a little better.

Finally, Jones hopes that *That Librarian* will inspire community members to take action to defend their local public and school libraries. And Jones knows from experience that this is possible. When the tax millage rate, which funds Jones's public library system, was up for a vote, a campaign was waged against the effort to defund all five branches. The vote to continue funding for the library branches was overwhelming, and the branches remained open. Even though book banners are inordinately loud, they represent only a small fraction of the population. Most people appreciate their public and school libraries and, when mobilized, will fight for them.

Despite the personal cost and continued harassment, Jones remains committed to her mission. She uses her position and visibility to amplify the voices of others. Her strategies are grounded in research and informed by an ethos centered on community care. Her message is clear: libraries are essential, and the people who run them are often the last line of defense in safeguarding democratic access to knowledge. Jones's story is one of courage, and in a time when libraries and library workers are under siege across the United States, her voice is a beacon of resistance and hope.

References

Ahmed, S. (2019a). *Internment*. Little Brown Books for Young Readers.
Ahmed, S. (2019b, August 14). Internment author Samira Ahmed at SLJ Teen Live. *LB School & Library Podcast*. https://podcasts.apple.com/us/podcast/internment-author-samira-ahmed-at-slj-teen-live/id1019181903?i=1000446913428
Ahmed, S. (2019c, November 15). Samira Ahmed challenges librarians: "use your power". *School Library Journal*. https://www.slj.com/story/samira-ahmed-writing-and-reading-in-the-trump-era-opinion
Ahmed, S. (2024). *This book won't burn*. Little, Brown Books for Young Readers.
Bolden, B. (2024, August 27). Louisiana Gov. Jeff Landry signs order to ban critical race theory in schools, duplicates existing law. *Louisianafirstnews.com*. https://www.louisianafirstnews.com/news/louisiana-news/louisiana-gov-jeff-landry-signs-order-to-ban-critical-race-theory-in-schools-duplicates-existing-law/
DeBerry, J. (2023, April 11). GOP book bans reach new level as Missouri lawmakers push to defund libraries. *MSNBC*. https://www.msnbc.com/opinion/msnbc-opinion/missouri-defund-libraries-book-ban-rcna78014
H.B. 777, 2024 Reg. Sess. (LA. 2024). https://legis.la.gov/legis/BillInfo.aspx?i=246874
Hodges, V. (2024, August 1). SB262: Education accountability: Expands the parents' Bill of Rights for Public Schools. *Legis.la.gov*. https://legis.la.gov/legis/BillInfo.aspx?s=24RS&b=ACT326&sbi=y
Jones, A. (2024). *That librarian: The fight against book banning in America*. Bloomsbury Publishing.
King, M. L., Jr. (1967, October 26). What is your life's blueprint. *The Seattle Times*. https://projects.seattletimes.com/mlk/words-blueprint.html
Knox, E. J. (2022). *Foundations of intellectual freedom*. American Library Association.

Lyons, M., & Verdi, J. (2020). *I'm not a girl: A transgender story* (D. Simpson, illus). Roaring Brook Press.

Magi, T., & Garnar, M. (Eds.). (2021). *Intellectual freedom manual*. American Library Association.

Obradovich, K. (2025, February 24). Bill would strip state funds from public libraries based on association membership. *Iowacapitaldispatch.com* https://iowacapitaldispatch.com/2025/02/24/bill-would-strip-state-funds-from-public-libraries-based-on-association-membership/

12 Alfred Kagan

Al Kagan retired in 2013 as African Studies Bibliographer and Professor of Library Administration from the University of Illinois, Champaign-Urbana Libraries. Kagan has been an activist his entire life, beginning with the war in Vietnam, through conflicts and humanitarian crises in South Africa, Iraq, Afghanistan, and now Palestine. He has also been heavily involved with progressive library organizations for decades, including the American Library Association (ALA) Social Responsibilities Round Table (SRRT), of which he has been a member since 1982 and served on its Action Council from 1991 to the present.

Although having long been committed to social and political activism, Kagan struggled to figure out what he wanted to do with his life after receiving his bachelor's degree in Government from Boston University in 1970 and master's degree in International Relations from San Francisco State University in 1972. The results of a career aptitude test, however, suggested librarianship as a possible route. Kagan thought, "why not?" landed a library assistant job at Tufts University—liked it—and next went to library school at Indiana University, Bloomington. After an eight-year stint as a reference librarian at the University of Connecticut, Storrs, Kagan moved to Champaign-Urbana in 1992, where he became active in progressive activities on campus. Having previously done a lot of work on Africa for his International Relations master's degree and having worked on a lot of anti-apartheid work and liberation support work in Africa, he could bring all of that knowledge and experience to campus and the university's Center for African Studies.

Kagan said that the impetus for his life of activism was growing up in the 1960s, a time when it seemed like everybody was getting active in the countercultural movement and anti-imperialist movements. As an undergraduate at Boston University, he would take classes from famed historian and socialist intellectual Howard Zinn, a decision that would lead to particularly formative experiences in Kagan's own development as an activist:

> It was an amazing experience. First of all, Zinn had hundreds of students in his classes. Many hundreds. I remember we used to meet in an old Jewish temple that the university had bought, and it was huge. Howard

would get up and speak for an hour without notes. It was all in his head. And he would describe various people's struggles through the times.

Zinn (2012/1970) advocated for "radical history," i.e., a "value-laden historiography" that rejects the legitimacy of the historian maintaining a neutral position:

> This search for a nonexistent objectivity has led us into a particularly retrogressive subjectivity, that of the bystander. Society has varying and conflicting interests; what is called objectivity is the disguise of one of these interests—that of neutrality. But neutrality is a fiction in an unneutral world. There are victims, there are executioners, and there are bystanders, In the dynamism of our time, when heads roll into the basket every hour, what is 'true' varies according to what happens to your own head—and the 'objectivity' of the bystander calls for inaction while other heads fall.
> (p. 90)

Zinn's approach to history, and particularly his most famous and popular book, *A People's History of the United States: 1492–Present* (1980), made a deep impact on Kagan. While he does not remember the first time that he read the book itself, he vividly remembers Zinn discussing elements of what would be included in it during his Brown University lectures. And then, finally, reading *A People's History* was "a real eye opener." In just over 600 pages, Zinn presents American history from Christopher Columbus's landing in the Bahamas to the conclusion of the Vietnam War (later editions would extend the book by almost 100 pages to include the last two decades of the 20th century and the first decade of the 21st). What makes A *People's History* so groundbreaking is that it is told from the perspective of everyday people rather than elites and "great men." This was a history of the US that privileged the words of the downtrodden and dissenters and addressed issues of classism, sexism, racism, and imperialism. Predictably, both *A People's History* and Zinn himself would become frequent targets of right-wing political ideologues. Neoconservative activist David Horowitz (2006), e.g., would write in *The Professors: The 101 Most Dangerous Academics in America* that the book is "a pedestrian Marxism" and "really not a 'history' of the American people, but an indictment of white people and the capitalist system" (p. 359) (it is interesting to note that in his indictment of Zinn's historiographical acumen and bona fides, Horowitz gets Zinn's age wrong in his profile by a decade) (p. 360). Nevertheless, it is Zinn's refusal to submit to what he saw as the historiographical establishment's false objectivity that likely struck a chord with readers, particularly young readers who had become disillusioned by American ultra-nationalism, capitalism, Vietnam, and Watergate. The book has currently sold over 2.5 million volumes, securing its place among the bestselling American history books of all time. It continues to be taught in US schools, even if sometimes necessarily covertly, and Kagan recommends it as an excellent starting point for anyone to develop a critical understanding of history:

I think everyone needs a good perspective on positioning themselves in the world. I was just having dinner the other day with a retired high school teacher from Urbana [Illinois], and she was telling us about a class that she developed which was based on Howard's book. I think that is indicative of the importance of both.

Following in Zinn's footsteps, Kagan's own research agenda was based basically on two tracks: (1) his work as a bibliographer and (2) documenting the history of progressive library institutions. As a bibliographer, Kagan has published extensively in the area of African Studies, producing multiple reference materials on Africa, including compiling the *Publications List and Comprehensive Indexes* (Kagan, 1983) for the United Nations Centre Against Apartheid.

In addition to this bibliographic work, a major part of Kagan's professional legacy is the documentation of the history of progressive library organizations like SRRT and organizations in countries including Sweden, Germany, South Africa, and the United Kingdom. This work is unique and necessary because it is not only library history, but it can also serve as an inspiration for new generations of progressive library workers. In 2015, Kagan (2015) published his book *Progressive Library Organizations: A Worldwide History* by McFarland & Company. The most comprehensive work of scholarship of its kind, the book documents the history of progressive library organizations in South Africa, Sweden, Germany, Austria, the United Kingdom, and the US through detailed analyses of such organizations as America's SRRT, the UK's Information for Social Change, Germany's Arbeitskreis kritischer BibliothekarInnen, and South Africa's Library and Information Workers Organization. Kagan has since followed *Progressive Library Organizations* with two updates published in the *Journal of Radical Librarianship* (Kagan, 2018, 2024).

In addition to researching and writing about progressive library organizations, Kagan has long been a member of many such organizations, including SRRT (since 1982), the Association of Concerned Africa Scholars (1982–2013), and the Progressive Librarians Guild (PLG) (since 1990), providing frequent news and commentary articles for the PLG's *Journal of Progressive Librarianship*. When asked about the state of progressive librarianship today, Kagan understandably speaks in terms of such organizations:

> The Social Responsibility Round Table of the ALA is still a vibrant organization. We still do a lot. We still influence daily. I think that SRRT is in a position right now with Trump coming in to try to influence ALA to push back against some of the Trump policies that are going to come at us, and I am thinking that SRRT is not, I am sure it is not, as activist as it used to be. It needs a little shot in the arm, so to speak, and I have been trying to do that. But it is still there, and it is quite vibrant and working. Progressive Librarians Guild was also an important organization, but it has really diminished over time.

Kagan said that the international progressive library organizations that he follows in his research are not doing particularly well. The only international organization that he wrote about in *Progressive Library Organizations* that is still really functioning is Sweden's Bibliotek i Samhälle, but they have experienced diminishment as well. Kagan said that the problem might be generational change, with younger librarians in places like Sweden doing other things in an impressive way outside of the larger organization.

Kagan's advice to new librarians engaging in social justice activism is to be cautious:

> I have known a lot of progressive librarians, and the one I am thinking of was never able to get a foothold in the profession because he was too radical. Especially if you are in academia, they do not like that. If you start doing programs that they do not like and you do not have tenure, you can lose your job. My advice to a new librarian is to do a fantastic job at what you are supposed to work on. And, at the same time, do the progressive things but be careful and aware that you need to understand your environment and not alienate people that might want to get rid of you. Academic librarians sometimes can get a tenure track job, but many places do not have a tenure system, so you do not have the protection, and it is much harder. I was lucky. I came in with tenure here, and so I was never restrained and that made all the difference. And there is so much more repression going on today throughout society with book banning, people protesting libraries, state library associations, and ALA. There is just so much going on right now that people do have to figure out what is possible and what they should be careful about.

As for himself, Kagan remains busy with his activism. He is currently working with the organization UC Urbana-Champaign Jews for Ceasefire (https://www.facebook.com/people/U-C-Jews-for-Ceasefire/61559259868923/) to address the ongoing genocide in Gaza. Recently, the group has successfully gotten the Urbana City Council to pass a ceasefire resolution and is providing support to campus protestors targeted by the university.

References

Horowitz, D. (2006). *The professors: The 101 most dangerous academics in America*. Regnery Publishing.

Kagan, A. (1983). Publications list and comprehensive indexes (1967–1982). *United Nations Centre Against Apartheid*. https://digitallibrary.un.org/record/68870

Kagan, A. (2015). *Progressive library organizations: A worldwide history*. McFarland.

Kagan, A. (2018). Progressive library organizations update, 2013–2017. *Journal of Radical Librarianship*, *4*, 20–53.

Kagan, A. (2024). Progressive library organizations, 2018–2023. *Journal of Radical Librarianship*, *10*, 194–222.

Zinn, H. (1980). *A people's history of the United States: 1492–present*. Routledge.

Zinn, H. (2012/1970). What is radical history (1970). In Timothy Patrick McCarthy (Ed.), *The indispensable Zinn: The essential writings of the "People's Historian"* (pp. 85–103). New Press.

13 Stuart Lawson

Stuart Lawson is a Research Repository Advisor at Edinburgh Napier University and an advocate for the open access movement. Lawson is also an anarchist and a musician, elements that factor into a professional career aimed at making information accessible to the masses.

Lawson said that the focus of their life has been music, but that they "eventually decided to get a so-called 'real job' and ended up working in the library and starting an LIS master's program." Although Lawson held anarchist political beliefs long before becoming a library worker, they were not particularly politically involved in organizations. This changed around 2011 after starting their first library job at Anglia Ruskin University. Lawson was drawn to the open access movement because it involved radical politics and had the goal of making all scholarly knowledge available to everyone. Now with a focus for their activism, Lawson made contact through social media with like-minded colleagues interested in the potential of libraries and library work for effecting radical change. In 2012, Lawson became a founding member of the Radical Librarians Collective (RLC), a UK-based organization that was largely born through Twitter.

The RLC's goal was to "offer a space to challenge, to provoke, to improve and develop the communications between like-minded radicals, to galvanise our collective solidarity against the marketisation of libraries and the removal of our agency to our working worlds and beyond" (Radical Librarians Collective, n.d.). Its first steps toward organization began with a couple of annual meetups, first in Bradford, England, in 2013 and then in London in 2014. The initial small group of people slowly grew and began to think of themselves as a collective. Although the annual events continued (the largest of which peaked at about 100 participants) as well as monthly meetups in London, most of the conversation and organizing took place on Twitter.

Lawson said that the RLC never had any official form of membership other than being involved in these meetings and online discussions; no hard and fast organizational affiliation was required. RLC conversations concerned how to translate the left-wing political views that were loosely shared by members into viable actions that people could accomplish through their library work. Because almost everyone taking part in the RLC was a library school student and/or worked in a library, it served as a means for library workers and prospective library workers to figure out what they could do on the ground to make incremental changes to library services and how librarianship is done.

To fully understand the RLC's ethos, one needs to have some understanding of the punk and Do It Yourself (DIY) subcultures. Lawson, as well as many of the other members of the RLC, came out of the UK's anarcho-punk subculture, which, starting with bands like Essex's Crass and Burnley's Chumbawamba, presented a clear anarchist message couched in the punk rock aesthetic and its DIY lifestyle. Dunn (2015) wrote that:

> Rather than debate revolutionary theory, anarcho-punks are primarily interested in engaging in actions that, to them will make a difference in daily life. As one Czech anarcho-punk said to me, 'Anarchism isn't about how to think, it's about how to do. And that means to resist' (interview with CP May 28, 2009).
>
> (p. 205)

Lawson discovered punk when they were 14 years old, and a friend gave them some tapes copied from compact discs. That kicked off an obsession with loud music of all sorts. Lawson said that it is not a coincidence that many of the people who were most heavily involved in the RLC came from punk, DIY backgrounds:

> Probably half of the people in RLC. It makes sense that they would, that radical or critical librarianship would attract people that had come from that kind of ethos, that grew up with that punk message that the world is messed up in these ways, so what can we do about it? Punk is about not accepting that the way things are must stay the same.

One anarcho-punk album that Lawson found to be particularly representative of this ethos to them is the Swedish group Refused's (1998a) fourth long-playing recording, *The Shape of Punk to Come: A Chimerical Bombination in 12 Bursts*. Formed in 1991, Refused:

> [...] became one of the most important punk bands of the 1990s, playing punishing music that was as smart and committed as it was muscular. Purposefully rebellious, Refused took their revolutionary political views seriously, and while the clean lines and precision of their performances helped them win an audience much larger than most punk acts of the time, they did so while presenting a thoroughly uncompromised vision.
>
> (Ankeny, n.d.)

The Shape of Punk to Come is considered by many fans to be the group's magnum opus, and tracks like "The Deadly Rhythm," "Protest Song '68," and "Refused Are Fucking Dead" fuse a hard-edged anti-capitalist message with an innovative approach to song composition that goes well beyond the genre's reputation for simplistic three-chord progressions. The name of the album is a reference to Ornette Coleman's 1959 album, *The Shape of Jazz to Come*, which is widely considered to be the first free jazz album released. With this presentation, Lawson said Refused says that, even though they are a punk band, punk can be done differently. By bringing in as many different perspectives as possible into the progressive thing that they are doing, the group can push boundaries in all sorts of new and interesting ways.

One song on the album that particularly influenced Lawson is "Liberation Frequency" (1998b), with its strident chorus of questions:

What frequency are you getting?
Is it noise or sweet, sweet, sweet, sweet, sweet?
What frequency will liberation be?
What frequency? What frequency? What frequency?

Lawson said that Liberation Frequency:

[...] is about taking control of the narrative - looking at things afresh from alternative points of view. Finding patterns in the noise. We can create freedom for ourselves. The Marxist insight that there is no *outside* of capitalism, so anti-capitalist alternatives must be born from within capitalism. This means we can take what already exists and repurpose it for new ends. But each line is a question - not declaiming a solution, just opening up the options.

The Shape of Punk to Come, Lawson said, is about questioning everything and always questioning authority. But it is not only about questioning *what is* but also about considering *how can we do things differently*?

Although Lawson said they lost touch with the rock music scene when they became fully absorbed with the open access movement, they have recently been getting back into it as an inspiration for their work and activism. They mentioned their interest in a relatively new group, King Gizzard and the Lizard Wizard, a psychedelic garage rock act that, while not explicitly political, reflects an experimental approach to their art that Lawson saw in Refused's work, as well as Lawson's own approach to activism:

Every album is totally different from the one before. They just work in all genres because they like all genres of music. They do everything. So, they release a thrash album and then an electronica album. And they have just done a country rock album. Musically, it is not from the same lineage as the Refused, that kind of hardcore noise stuff. But the way they do things... They have their own record label to release their own stuff. They put their money where their mouth is in terms of making political statements on stage about Palestine or trans rights.

And even though the group is politically aligned with Lawson's politics, the main attraction for Lawson is the group's adventurousness and their willingness to take chances with their art. Both Refused and King Gizzard and the Wizard Lizard exude a sense of curiosity, and Lawson said that for radical library work to be successful, it must likewise embody this intense inquisitiveness. Effective radical library workers are going to be those people who constantly ask themselves when doing their work how they will align how they think the world *should* be with the day-to-day work that needs to be done to get paid.

Anarchist collectives, like punk rock groups, do not tend to last long. Today, the RLC is largely inactive. The mailing list still exists, and the website is still available online, but the annual meetings have not been held in several years. By 2020, Lawson said interpersonal issues, as are often quite common with anarchist political groups, began to dominate, and the group essentially fizzled out. So, much of what made the RLC work relied on the effort being as open and participatory as possible. However, there ended up being a small number of people who were just more dedicated to doing the kind of administrative work to continue the momentum. Lawson thinks that this would have been fine, and RLC could have continued if they had been capable of continuing to bring more people into it. However, they said, the RLC became increasingly perceived as cliquish by other people in library work who were not involved with the collective or did not go to its meetings, and Lawson admitted, by 2020, it sort of was (if not intentionally). After the RLC's peak, meetings in the late 2010s became less well attended, and Lawson said that the collective was less proactive in reaching out to as many people as possible who might be interested in progressive library work. In RLC's attempt to be a national organization for the entire UK, this meant that, by its nature, most people could not go to most meetings. Also, because so much of the RLC organization was done on Twitter (now X), that avenue for communication and organization was effectively cut off because most RLC members left the platform following Elon Musk's takeover in 2022. A lot of organizing, as a result, has gone a bit more "back to the basics," Lawson said, "in terms of who do you know locally."

Even though the RLC is currently inactive, with its website showing no updates for the past several years, the open access *Journal of Radical Librarianship* (JRL) (https://journal.radicallibrarianship.org/index.php/journal), currently in its 11th volume, is a testament to the enduring spirit and lasting impact of the collective and what Lawson considers to be the RLC's most noteworthy achievement. Over the years, JRL has published research articles, reports, and commentary on a range of radical topics relating to library and information work, with such titles as "The Digital Divide in the Post-Snowden Era" (Clark, 2016), "Privatization of Government Information as Primitive Accumulation" (Kunkel, 2020), and "Critical Cataloguing and Contradiction Analysis: Using Mao Zedong's Dialectical Materialism to Address Classificatory Antagonisms" (Burley, 2024). The idea for JRL came out of the 2014 London RLC meeting and was further developed through Twitter conversations about ways in which open access could be done successfully and the fact that, at the time, most of the prominent library journals remained closed access. The policies and processes for operating JRL, Lawson said, were developed to align with the ways that the RLC wanted to do library work. The journal started out with a core of around a dozen interested RLC members. Decision-making was intended to be as participatory as possible, using a consensus model to determine each aspect of journal policy, including elements like what license was used for intellectual property rights and what the peer review policy would be. Lawson became the first JRL general editor essentially by default, considering that they were "the person who kept saying, 'come on, we need to do this.'" Simon Barron, a digital librarian and advocate for open access, worked to set up the journal's website at the start and remains a part of JRL technical support to the present day.

The original model for operating JRL was to spread the editorial responsibilities by having section editors for different subject areas, including Politics and Social Justice; Political Economy of Information and Knowledge; Equity, Diversity, and Inclusion; and Digital Rights, an operational framework loosely based on the University of London's Open Library of the Humanities (https://www.openlibhums.org/), which attempts to cover all areas of the humanities, assigning section editors in charge of each niche area. When asked whether running a journal using a consensus model involved any difficulties, Lawson said that it was difficult maintaining engagement among the section editors. Since everything for the journal was performed on a voluntary basis, some members of the editorial team might be engaged, but some others would essentially drift through, losing interest after a time. The consensus model for decision-making eventually began to veer off course:

> I do not think we ever officially decided to stop trying to have that consensus-based model for future work, but it was really just used for the initial setup of the journal. Consensus-based decision-making is just hard when you do not have formal structures in place. It was so because the general model of the journal was based on the RLC, which was a loosely anarchist collective, but did not have a charter or membership or any kind of organizational structure—it was all who were just available to do the work at the time. That is how RLC was mostly run. Well, RLC did end up being slightly more formal. Because the journal was born out of the same way of thinking, but because it is an academic journal, it had to look and feel enough like an academic journal to be taken seriously as a journal. So there had to be some kind of editorial responsibility, and that ended largely falling on me.

Lawson feels that the radical open access movement has reached an impasse because the money within the system has reorganized itself around open access, with the same big publishing companies, particularly those in North America and Europe, "hoovering up all of the money." That is, open access had been co-opted by capital, so something that Lawson and the RLC argued publishing should try to avoid has, in effect, already happened. Nonetheless, Lawson said that there are still some people working within humanities publishing trying to keep the experimental and oppositional side of open access going. Notably, they said the third Radical Open Access Conference (https://www.lib.cam.ac.uk/research-institute/events/radical-open-access-conference-2025) was held in Cambridge in April 2025. Lawson said that there are other areas outside of the scholarly publishing arena relating to open access that have potential: "There are a lot of radical archives, all types of radical content, and an interest in preserving histories in a way that makes them more readily accessible and changing the *narrative of what is*." Most people, they said, would not associate that archiving work would be a particularly politically radical sort of profession, but that:

> [...] when you are trying to preserve important histories of different communities and populations and make them known and accessible to other people, that is definitely an area with a lot of potential for more radical spaces to make themselves felt in way that does not happen within publishing anymore.

References

Ankeny, J. (n.d.). Refused biography. *Allmusic.com*. https://www.allmusic.com/artist/refused-mn0000885375#biography

Burley, R. (2024). Critical cataloging and contradiction analysis: Using Mao Zedong's dialectical materialism to address classificatory antagonisms. *Journal of Radical Librarianship*, *10*, 91–103. https://journal.radicallibrarianship.org/index.php/journal/article/view/97

Clark, I. (2016). The digital divide in the post-Snowden era. *Journal of Radical Librarianship*, *2*, 1–32. https://journal.radicallibrarianship.org/index.php/journal/article/view/12

Dunn, K. (2015). *Global punk: Resistance and rebellion in everyday life*. Bloomsbury Academic.

Kunkel, R. (2020). Privatization of government information as primitive accumulation. *Journal of Radical Librarianship*, *6*, 1–15. https://journal.radicallibrarianship.org/index.php/journal/article/view/47

Radical Librarians Collective. (n.d.). About. *Radical Librarians Collective*. https://rlc.radicallibrarianship.org/about-2/

Refused. (1998a). *The shape of punk to come: A chimerical bombination in 12 bursts*. Burning Heart Records.

Refused. (1998b). *Liberation frequency. The shape of punk to come: A chimerical bombination in 12 bursts*. Burning Heart Records.

14 Jessie Loyer

Jessie Loyer currently serves as the Indigenous Engagement Librarian at the University of Alberta, Edmonton. As a Cree Métis woman and member of the Michel First Nation, she brings to her academic and professional life a perspective shaped by Indigenous culture, community, language, and history. Through her work, Loyer resists and counters misleading information models that devalue Indigenous realities, in the process redefining academic librarianship through Indigenous frameworks of kinship and care.

Before becoming an academic librarian, Loyer worked as a business analyst and a technical writer, jobs where she condensed complex information and organized it for people for easy access and digestion, aligning with her future career as a librarian. Seeking more personally fulfilling work, Loyer attended library school at the University of British Columbia, Vancouver, where she worked for a time at the Xwi7xwa Library, the only Indigenous branch of an academic library in Canada and a space that actively engages with Indigenous ways of knowing. While in school, Loyer also worked as an archives intern for the Tsawwassen First Nation. These experiences helped affirm her commitment to recovering, protecting, and reclaiming spaces for Indigenous knowledges.

After graduating from library school in 2012, Loyer started her professional career at Calgary's Mount Royal University, a small, teaching-focused institution. It was at Mount Royal that she came into her own as an academic librarian, working as an embedded librarian with teaching and subject liaison responsibilities in a diverse range of areas, including Women and Gender Studies, Mathematics, Physics, Health, and Physical Education. The wide range of experiences that the job provided helped her see how disciplinary norms influence information practices and how library workers are positioned to respond to information needs. In 2023, Loyer accepted her current position as Indigenous Engagement Librarian at the University of Alberta Libraries, where she works with the Native Studies faculty and students. Her role at the University of Alberta continues to center on teaching but also expands into institutional strategy and the creation of welcoming, thoughtful spaces for Indigenous students within the library system. This transition to working with her own community and its cultural traditions resulted in a deep integration of Loyer's personal and professional identities.

DOI: 10.4324/9781003473640-15

Loyer believes that one's work should be challenging, interesting, and worth putting energy into. Nevertheless, she said, "Work does not love you back," and it should not be romanticized. Loyer understands that institutions see people as replaceable and that ultimately, "if I died tomorrow, someone else would be hired to do my job":

> I am very cautious about how the institution sees people as interchangeable. I came up through labor solidarity and where people were like, you take every break. You take your coffee breaks, you take your lunch breaks, because the institution will always ask more of you. That is my personal approach to work itself—the clocking in, clocking out. I love the work that I do. I am very grateful to have work that is exciting and that I love coming to work every day, but I hold it at arm's length.

While Loyer maintains clear boundaries with her institution, she deeply invests herself in her relationships with students and colleagues, her pragmatic work ethic coexisting with a profound commitment to deep care, both of herself and others. While she is candid about the need to resist the institutional tendency to extract emotional energy without reciprocation, Loyer sees her relationships with students and faculty members as inherently reciprocal, ongoing, and a fundamental element of her professional practice. She used the metaphor of "stepping into a stream" to emphasize the continuation of knowledge relationships that both precede and outlast formal academic interactions:

> Librarians step into relationships that are created before we even meet somebody. When I meet my students, they already have a relationship with the concept of a librarian, and so I am stepping into that. And then we have our time together, whether that is in a class or whether that is a one-on-one consultation. Then that relationship continues, whether they see me again, or whether that information that we have talked about kind of just persists in their mind. So, this idea of stepping into a stream that is already running is part of the way I think about my work, that no one is an empty vessel.

A major influence on Loyer's thought concerning the intersection of library work and community is the work of Cree writer and legal scholar Sylvia McAdam. McAdam's (2019) book, *Nationhood Interrupted: Revitalizing nêhiyaw Legal Systems*, describes how *wâhkôhtowin* (kinship) is central to Indigenous social reality. In *Nationhood Interrupted*, Loyer said that *wâhkôhtowin* essentially means "knowing who your relatives are," i.e., participating in distinct kinship relationships full of joy and connecting at all the intersections of one's life in an expansive concept of community.

Through her encounter with *Nationhood Interrupted*, Loyer realized how *wâhkôhtowin* underpins her professional work, and this has allowed her to reframe the librarian-student relationship as one of obligation and continuity. In Cree legal traditions, treaties are formed with distinctive relationships:

It is like treaty making made cousins. Marriage makes cousins, or relationships, which makes kinship, but also processes like business. The fur trade, for example, was a process of creating kinship. So, what does kinship creation look like within education, and even more specifically, within library and information literacy instruction?

Loyer sees kinship relationships as the foundation for teaching and learning, as well as underpinning the ethical responsibilities of library work. Rather than viewing librarianship as neutral service provision, she positions it as a form of care and relational accountability: "We are called to care for people's emotional health." This relational understanding of library work is evident in Loyer's approach to teaching information literacy. Loyer resists deficit-based educational models that treat students as blank slates, an approach that diminishes student background and experience. While she may start with basic information literacy skills, she understands that students come to the library with a variety of lived experiences. A central theme in Loyer's work is reimagining information literacy through Indigenous frameworks:

> One of the things that I have been considering a lot is how I can do this work without commodifying this knowledge. It is not my job to make it consumable. In many ways, it is my job to make it accessible to the people who have lost access to it. There are ways that we are connected to other people who have also experienced oppression, and that is important to me, to share those things so that people can see themselves in this struggle. I am cautious of the way that information can be shared outside of the correct context, because when we talk about outsiders, speaking of indigenous knowledge, it has largely been through that valence.

As a result, Loyer actively creates relationships with students that are interdependent and ongoing, whether engaging them as they navigate their academic careers or advising them after graduation.

This relational/dialectical understanding of Indigenous library work goes beyond the librarian-patron relationship. Loyer sees professional practice as inherently political, i.e., that libraries exist within biased information environments shaped by colonialism, Enlightenment-era ideas, and Western hierarchies. Through interviewing Indigenous students, Deborah Lee (2001), a Cree Métis librarian at the University of Saskatchewan, found that while libraries gave some agency to Indigenous students, they were also extractive entities. While Loyer acknowledged libraries and archives as public goods, she said that they exist within systems that marginalize Indigenous knowledges, resulting in archival representations of Indigenous peoples that reduce them to things to be studied rather than knowledge holders with agency:

> Libraries are a particular concept, they are a public good, and they do wonderful things. If [assuming they did not previously exist] someone tried to pitch the idea of a library today, I am sure it would get shot down

as something ridiculous. But even with their goodness and all the things that they achieve, they come to us from a particular perspective [i.e., one with the desire to 'civilize' societies], and that perspective is very uninterested in Indigenous knowledge and Indigenous people. When we think about Indigenous people appearing in libraries or appearing in records, it is often as subjects, as people who can be studied, researched or collected. For me, practicing in this area means that I give people who have not had access to information a critical lens to think about the way that we consume this information, the way that we forward this information, the way that we use these kinds of information, and how this kind of information is reflective of what people know about indigeneity and how people think about themselves.

To illustrate this point, Loyer pointed to anthropologist David Mandelbaum's (1978) book, *The Plains Cree: An Ethnographic, Historical, and Comparative Study*. While Mandelbaum wrote about Cree people, he was a non-Indigenous American of European descent that almost exclusively interviewed only Cree men in his research. Such routine marginalization of women in academic work by outsiders has prevented the sharing of cultural traditions, ceremonies, songs, and stories that often go unseen. But Mandelbaum is just one example of colonizer distortion of Indigenous realities; there have been hundreds of years of non-Indigenous people writing about Indigenous people, often resulting in gross misrepresentation and romanticization when representing these communities and portraying Indigenous peoples as violent or even non-human. Indigenous peoples have had their stories stolen, twisted into children's storybooks for mass consumption, or used against them to further the land claims of colonizers. Furthermore, these stories get repeated with little regard for the truth and are subsequently passed down from generation to generation *as truth*. Because of such distortions, Loyer said, when Indigenous students come to university, they are often prepared for and expecting their own marginalization:

> We have experienced the way that mainstream society has a particular view of Indigenous people that is violent, that is harmful, that is based in erasure, that is based in stereotype. It is necessary to give the [students] the tools to talk about the way that reality was constructed, like the process that created that, and around interventions in it. So, what are ways that we can intervene in this oppressive weight of history, of the way that people have talked about Indigenous people?

One purpose of Loyer's work is to recover these obscured knowledges and, in the process, question the "concept of ourselves" supported by archives and libraries as apparatuses of the dominant culture. This critique extends to a call for solidarity with other marginalized communities whose stories have been misrepresented by dominant information systems:

For me, professional practice is around making sure that those voices are there and that there is solidarity from the Indigenous perspective. We see these big gaps in our own stories but also understanding the way that those gaps exist for other people's stories too, like the lack of discussion of transgender voices, thinking about how women in general do not show up in archives, including other groups that are marginalized by mainstream society. There is that solidarity within that as well. I think for me, that practice means that I understand. I help people within my own context understand how we have been represented within information, and I also think through in what ways do we have to stand in solidarity with people who have experienced these same kinds of processes of erasure.

One issue that is of particular concern to Loyer is Indigenous language revitalization. She said that this work should be done by people within Indigenous communities to ensure that they maintain the continuity of their knowledge but also because there is a great deal of emotional labor taken on by Indigenous people who are working with their own language. Outside researchers may not grasp the emotional weight of reclaiming their languages after generations of oppression. For Loyer, ensuring that such work remains within Indigenous communities is part of a broader ethic of responsibility. She believes that engaging in closed practices around culture and language can strengthen Indigenous communities, rather than being merely a performance by outsiders with no connection.

Loyer said that the emotional labor of Indigenous librarianship is not incidental but central to practice, and that it informs her critique of outsiders working with Indigenous languages and cultures without understanding the trauma and context embedded in these systems. She spoke openly about the emotional toll of working with Indigenous knowledges and histories, confronting systemic erasure, and supporting students through similar traumas. Loyer emphasized the need for self-care, boundaries, and mutual responsibility, and she makes it a point to remind herself and her students to take care of themselves in the research process because the work "can wreck you." Despite the burden of the task, Loyer is awed by the courage of the students she works with and draws strength from their bravery. Loyer spoke of their efforts with admiration—how they navigate extractive, often alienating institutions while striving to learn, connect, and resist. She is shocked by her students' resiliency but also their creativity in traversing academia, an institution and ideological apparatus that takes so much from Indigenous people.

Loyer found a sense of community working with other Indigenous librarians while earning her master's degree; there are so few Indigenous librarians practicing today that professional isolation is a real risk. Loyer said that she was able to combat such isolation and fulfill a sense of collective purpose through attending the International Indigenous Librarians Forum (IILF). Participating in this biennial gathering, which includes Indigenous librarians from around the world, allowed her to witness the strength of other Indigenous librarians working within colonial institutions:

> There is a sense that you are so isolated and so singular, and then to come into a room where everyone is an Indigenous librarian, and everyone has these same kinds of challenges with interacting and trying to intervene in the way that information manages Indigenous thought, that was powerful to me.

The community fostered by the IILF provided Loyer with the language necessary to address what was happening in academic libraries and archives from a critical perspective. She saw the autonomy these Indigenous librarians had and the impact of their work on maintaining Indigenous knowledge, an impact that will long outlast the libraries and archives in which they are housed. She also learned through the IILF the notion that Indigenous information systems do not have to conform to Western norms to be legitimate, powerful, or real. Loyer recalled the symbolic presence of a Maori carved stone, carved by Maori librarian Bernard Makoare (Shim, 2023). This stone travels with the Forum and symbolizes a living knowledge system and embodies the life force of the Forum. Information that exists on the stone is an oral history; it holds the personal experiences of the attendees who interact with the stone in a non-textual format.

In Cree, Loyer said, the concept of a good life, *miyo-pimâtisiwin*, is not defined by ease or comfort, but by fulfilling one's responsibilities to others. Her work embodies a profound reimagining of Indigenous librarianship as a relational and reciprocal decolonial practice. Loyer's professional praxis is embedded not only in teaching and information management but also in *wâhkôhtowin*, community, and care ethics. When viewing the library through Loyer's eyes, information becomes more than merely a resource to be organized but an integral part of a network of living human relationships and something to be honored and protected. Loyer's work invites us to build information institutions that respect Indigenous knowledge systems and challenge conventional boundaries in librarianship. Through her work, she has developed tools to intervene in oppressive systems, helped students learn about themselves, their people, and their history, and has created something exciting.

References

Lee, D. A. (2001). Aboriginal students in Canada: A case study of their academic information needs and library use. *Journal of Library Administration, 33*(3–4), 259–292.

Mandelbaum, D. (1978). *Plains Cree: An ethnographic, historical, & comparative study*. Canadian Plains Research Center.

McAdam, S. (2019). *Nationhood interrupted: Revitalizing Nêhiyaw legal systems*. Purich Publishing.

Shim, K. (2023). *Research guides: International Indigenous Librarians' Forum (IILF) Guide: Home*. https://guides.library.manoa.hawaii.edu/iilf

15 Annie Pho

Annie Pho, current Head of Instruction and Outreach at the University of San Francisco Libraries, dissects and challenges dated ideas surrounding library workers to shift both public and scholarly discourse and to promote diversity in the profession.

Pho attended community college before taking time off from school to figure out what to do with her life. While living in Savannah, Georgia, she chanced upon a job advertisement for a librarian position. Even though she had grown up in libraries as both a patron and a part-time worker, Pho did not really know what it took to work as a professional librarian and had not realized that a master's degree is typically required for employment. The job notification gave Pho direction, and she was determined to complete her bachelor's degree with the goal of applying for the master's program in library science at Indiana University's Department of Information & Library Science. Intrigued by the idea of working in either an academic library or an art museum, she used her graduate school experience to better understand the differences between the two career paths and, "feeling more aligned with public education, or just with education in general, and with helping people with their research and their academic journey," Pho settled upon academic librarianship as a career path. She also gravitated to academic library work because she saw the academic library as an environment where she could continue to learn and, at the same time, be of service to people doing the same. After graduating from library school, Pho started her first full-time librarian position at the University of Illinois, Chicago, after which she moved to UCLA before landing at the University of San Francisco Libraries.

Pho's work philosophy rests on a foundation of feminist values:

> I think that, as much as possible, I try to provide a space for people to self-actualize and have agency in their work, showing an ethic of care for my colleagues as well as my students, and leaving enough space for people to share their opinions and feelings on things. I think that, at least at my university over the last few years, and especially with the pandemic, there have been some emotionally trying or difficult or stressful times for people. Part of my philosophy is understanding that people are showing up to

work and dealing with their own personal life. I think that it is important to go beyond a focus on return on investment way of thinking, especially with middle management. So, trying to see beyond that. The other aspect of feminist values is advocating for people who are not always able to advocate for themselves—especially in the spaces I have the institutional privilege to be able to do that. I see that as my responsibility.

Pho first encountered critical theory and method as an undergraduate at San Francisco State University while finishing her degree in art history, and it would impact her future scholarship on intersectionality, feminist pedagogy in information literacy, and women of color in library and information science (LIS). At the time she considered the work of theorists like Michel Foucault to be difficult and somewhat obscure. Early in her career as an academic librarian, however, Pho discovered the work of communication scholars Marie L. Radford and Gary P. Radford on the librarian stereotype. Although it was difficult for Pho to commit to any one work that she considered particularly germinal to her professional development as a critical librarian ("it is hard to choose a favorite. I try to be very expansive in the things that inspire me"). One article that she now views with nostalgia is Radford and Radford's (2003) *Library Quarterly* article "Librarians and Party Girls: Cultural Studies and the Meaning of the Librarian," which she happened upon while researching a book chapter she co-authored for the collection *The Librarian Stereotype: Deconstructing Perceptions and Presentations of Information Work* (Pho & Masland, 2014).

The librarian stereotype is a stale formula that shows up repeatedly in popular culture. Cowell (1980) memorably described the pop culture boilerplate librarian as "a fussy old woman of either sex, myopic and repressed, brandishing or perhaps cowering behind a date-stamp and surrounded by an array of notices which forbid virtually every human activity" (p. 167). Pagowsky and Rigby (2014) wrote about stereotypes "still fixed in the public mind," such as "'librarian glasses' 'librarian shoes,' 'hipster librarian style,' and 'sexy librarian.'" (p. 3). Both the "fussy old woman" and the "sexy librarian" stereotypes can be partially accounted for because library work is typically gendered work—it is seen as "women's work." As a result of such stereotypes, library labor is undervalued, leading to things like inequities in pay. Add to this the fact that many higher education administrators do not know what academic librarians really do in the first place, and librarians often end up with relatively little professional capital on campus.

For Pho, "Librarians and Party Girls" presents a sophisticated analysis of how many people view library workers, effectively deconstructing what is communicated via the stereotype through an incisive critique of the 1995 cult classic movie *Party Girl*. In *Party Girl*, Parker Posey portrays Mary, a twenty-something party animal forced to take a desk clerk job at the New York Public Library to repay a debt. Over the course of the film, Mary transforms from a chaotic party girl into a stereotypical staid librarian obsessed with organization, and by the movie's end, we see her "dressed in a black suit with bun and glasses" and determined to pursue an LIS graduate degree (Radford & Radford, 2003, p. 66).

In the process of considering Mary's change from party girl cliché to librarian cliché, Radford and Radford analyze common stereotypes through the theoretical lens developed by cultural studies doyen Stuart Hall. Stereotypes, Hall (1997) wrote, "get hold of the few 'simple, vivid, memorable, easily grasped and widely recognized' characteristics about a person, *reduce* everything about the person to these traits, *exaggerate* and *simplify* them, and *fix* them without change or development to eternity" (p. 258). Adopting a cultural studies approach allows Radford and Radford to accomplish three things. First, they situate the librarian stereotype within the "political rather than aesthetic" (Radford & Radford, 2003, p. 56), demonstrating its ideological nature and functions in modern cultural production. Second, they challenge stereotypical assumptions about library workers and suggest strategies derived from Hall's work that might be used to contest and subvert the stereotype. Finally, they present cultural studies as a viable method of analysis in LIS research, which, considering the discipline's penchant for positivism (Harris, 1986), represented a novel approach to LIS research and analysis. This last point had a particular impact on Pho, and not only do Radford and Radford present cultural studies as a viable approach to LIS, but they do so in a way that demystifies theory that may sometimes be seen as impenetrable or obscure:

> [...] It was interesting how Radford and Radford took theorists like Foucault, who I remember reading and thinking—at least at the time when I was studying art history—as being really dense stuff. I still hear this criticism, even from other librarians, that it is sometimes hard to understand theory and question how it applies practically to our everyday lives. What I appreciated about 'Librarians and Party Girls' is that it breaks these theories down and shows how to apply them.

"Librarians and Party Girls" builds upon Radford and Radford's earlier work like "Power, Knowledge, and Fear: Feminism, Foucault, and the Stereotype of the Female Librarian" (Radford & Radford, 1997), another article that Pho cites as important to her professional development and research agenda. Like "Librarians and Party Girls," "Power, Knowledge, and Fear" takes aim at popular depictions of library workers, drawing on the work of the French postmodernist Foucault as well as feminist scholarship to deconstruct the power relations imbedded in and obscured by the stereotype of the librarian as an outwardly fearsome woman obsessed with order. This article introduced Pho to

> how people set up arguments and how they bring in these different theories and break things down in a way that sets up their arguments. That makes sense to me. I came to the realization that this is why we take popular culture seriously, because we understand the world through it.

While Radford and Radford's work tuned Pho into how cultural studies and feminist approaches to the study of LIS provide new ways to understand the role and function of library workers in society, she acknowledged that both "Librarians and Party Girls" and "Power, Knowledge, and Fear" were written before the social media revolution and that:

> If 'Librarians and Party Girls' were to be written today, it would have to include a different set of media which in some ways has democratized the representation of library workers. There are still going to be issues, but it has really shifted the landscape. I feel like the representation of library workers has changed.

Following Radford and Radford's lead, Pho represents one of the new wave of innovative LIS researchers working in this new cultural landscape that employs cultural studies methodologies to unpack and challenge inherited ideological constructs to promote social justice and diversity within the profession.

As is the case with many early-career academic librarians on the tenure track, Pho initially collaborated with departmental colleagues to work on research projects that focused on information literacy and student success. However, after gaining experience and confidence in doing research, she felt comfortable looking more closely at topics of intersectionality in library work. In doing so, she noticed a gap in the research, a corpus of literature that focused primarily on recruitment numbers and the huge disparity in diversity and representation within librarianship, with the goal of increasing diversity in libraries. There were, however, a few publications that focused on the lived experiences of people of color working in libraries:

> If you look at the statistics, it looks like the demographic composition of librarians has not changed much in the last 50 years. Honestly, probably for even longer than that. The number remains very much the same. And we have all these advancements, these different scholarship programs. We are doing all these different things. Why is it that the numbers are not really increasing? So, I worked with Rose L. Chou on a research project that focused on the experiences of women of color in public services. So again, coming back to the idea of intersectionality, but also to feminist theory.

Chou and Pho (2018) would co-edit the scholarly collection *Pushing the Margins, Women of Color in Librarianship*. The impetus behind that book was to apply the philosophy that "we do not have to lead or do everything. We can also provide a platform or space for other women to share their stories." She is proud of *Pushing the Margins*: the book contributed something to professional literature that was missing by allowing other women of color to offer their personal perspectives and experiences on many different aspects of library work, including emotional labor, activism, scholarly publishing, and tenure.

Pho continues to provide librarians of color a platform through her work as a series editor (with Rose L. Chou) for the Library Juice Press book series Critical Race Studies and Multiculturalism in LIS.

Pho's most recent research project focused on the intersection of artificial intelligence literacy and critical librarianship. Intrigued by the feminist aspects of how the profession looks at libraries and labor as the work sees an influx of new technology tools, Pho set out to identify the unique things that library workers have to offer in the current environment "where everyone is either freaking out about AI or simply adopting it and trying to make it their entire professional brand." She asks critical questions surrounding these issues and looks closely at things like race and gender. "If we are not careful," she said, "we risk leaving people behind in our attempts to advance the culture."

Today's academic librarian faces many obstacles, including the move in higher education to strip tenure and, as a result, place restrictions on academic freedom (which places library workers who are interested in social justice issues in a precarious position in today's political climate). In terms of future research, one area that Pho is interested in exploring more is library leadership:

> Library organizations tend to be flat and provide little opportunity to move up or be promoted. So how do you give people opportunities to grow or feel like they are progressing in their careers if they are not literally progressing into library leadership or something like that?

When asked what she would suggest an academic librarian read to expand their theoretical horizons, Pho suggested, in addition to Radford and Radford, Todd Honma's (2005) "Trippin' Over the Color Line: The Invisibility of Race in Library and Information Studies," which she considers a must-read for all library professionals: "It really changed my life. I do not know if Honma is the first, but he is among the first scholars to really apply and break down how critical race theory applies to information science." But, while Pho said that she could recommend reading after reading for those going down the critical librarianship rabbit hole, she would also encourage new colleagues to seek out communal spaces where people are presenting or talking about the pragmatic issues involved in LIS work. Critical librarians should read about the work that other people have done and seek those people out, particularly if they are interested in similar things. They should find spaces where they can engage in conversations about how library workers are applying scholarship like "Librarians and Party Girls" and "Trippin Over the Color Line" to their everyday jobs with positive results. Pho recommended the Critical Librarianship and Pedagogy Symposium (CLAPS) (https://clps.arizona.edu/), held at the University of Arizona Libraries since 2016, as one such space for fruitful dialogue. Professional library workers of color, she said, should also seek out specific affinity spaces to get support.

Pho considers herself to be on the early side of middle career and, heeding her own advice, plans on spending "the next year or two to keep an open mind and explore what is out there and make more connections with other mid-career librarians or people who are doing fascinating work to hear about their journeys." As she reflects on her time as a librarian, Pho has realized how important it is to keep oneself engaged, to constantly "ask questions about what is going on at your library" and "ask questions about why things are the way that they are, especially if you feel like it might be going against your values or what your library's values are."

References

Chou, R. L., & Pho, A. (Eds.). (2018). *Pushing the margins: Women of color and intersectionality in LIS*. Library Juice Press.

Cowell, P. (1980). Not all in the mind: The virile profession. *Library Review*, *29*(3), 167–175.

Hall, S. (1997). *Representation: Cultural representations and signifying practices*. Sage Publications.

Harris, M. H. (1986). State, class, and cultural reproduction: Toward a theory of library service in the United States. *Advances in Librarianship*, *14* (1986), 211–252.

Honma, T. (2005). Trippin' over the color line: The invisibility of race in library and information studies. *InterActions: UCLA Journal of Education and Information Studies*, *1*(2). https://escholarship.org/content/qt4nj0w1mp/qt4nj0w1mp.pdf

Pagowsky, N., & Rigby, M. (2014). Contextualizing ourselves: The identity politics of the librarian stereotype." In N. Pagowsky & M. Rigby (Eds.), *The Librarian stereotype: deconstructing perceptions & presentations of information work.* (pp. 3–37). Association of College and Research Libraries.

Pho, A., & Masland, T. (2014). The revolution will not be stereotyped: Changing perceptions through diversity, In N. Pagowsky & M. Rigby (Eds.), *The librarian stereotype: deconstructing perceptions & presentations of information work* (pp. 257–282). Association of College and Research Libraries.

Radford, M. L. & Radford, G. P. (1997). Power, knowledge, and fear: Feminism, Foucault, and the stereotype of the female librarian. *Library Quarterly*, *67*(3), 250–266.

Radford, M. L. & Radford, G. P., (2003). Librarians and party girls: Cultural studies and the meaning of the librarian. *Library Quarterly*, *73*(1), 54–69.

16 Sam Popowich

Sam Popowich is the Digital Infrastructure Librarian and Head of Systems at the University of Winnipeg Library. He is at the forefront of the early 21st-century wave of library and information science researchers engaging in Marxian analysis of the library as an institution and librarianship as a profession, a small group tackling exciting questions relating to libraries' role and place within politics, culture, and ideology.

Born in Winnipeg, Canada, Popowich said that he did not do particularly well in either high school or during his undergraduate years at the University of Manitoba. While he was not very interested in academics during this period, he was absorbed in books and reading. During his late teens, Popowich also had his first taste of the corporate world, which he did not find appealing:

> There was a job posting for technical support workers at a call center. This was AT&T, a major corporation, not some little call center. It was a good job on paper and paid well. So, I applied for it and got the job. I was 18 and I went to work for this multinational corporation doing tech support over the phone. I hated it and just could not understand why this good job on paper was not working for me. At the same time, I started my undergrad that fall.

It was then that Popowich found the *Communist Manifesto* on sale for five dollars at a local bookstore:

> And my initial reaction when I saw it was to think, 'Was it legal to sell the *Communist Manifesto* in Canada?' I got it simply because of its reputation. But even though it is an earlier version Marx and Engels's thinking and it is designed as a pamphlet rather than as a fully worked out treatise, there were things there that stuck with me and helped to explain my experience working for the corporation.

Popowich began to read more leftist literature during his undergraduate days as a history and Slavic studies major at the University of Manitoba. By the time that he went into library school at Dalhousie University in 2005, Popowich had read enough on Marxism to see its potential applications to libraries and library work, particularly its use as a means for investigating library history and the role of libraries in politics. Popowich's understanding of critical approaches to analysis, and particularly his understanding of Marxist approaches, matured when he pursued a second master's degree in music and culture at Carleton University, Ottawa. Popowich earned the degree while working as an emerging technologies librarian at the University of Ottawa Libraries, seeing it as a tool to deepen his understanding of critical theory. In 2013, Popowich was invited to give a keynote address for the Association of Academic Librarians in Alberta. After having thought about Marxism and libraries for years, he decided that it was the right time to share his ideas with colleagues through the presentation. Thus started a fruitful research agenda surrounding the academic library's complicity in neoliberal politics.

Since then, Popowich has published multiple articles, chapters, and books that draw on Marxist thought and critical theory. Generally, his research agenda centers on a Marxist analysis of libraries, politics, and culture, with the types of questions asked including:

> What are the politics that play within libraries? What are the class relations found within libraries? But also, what is the political role that libraries play in broader society? What is their ideological role? What is their role in the maintenance of a particular political culture?

For example, his 2019 monograph for Library Juice Press, *Confronting the Democratic Discourse of Librarianship: A Marxist Approach* (Popowich, 2019), thinks through what the history of libraries would look like if you mapped it to transformations in capitalism. In the process, the book "tries to unpin the discursive insistence on libraries both as democratic institutions themselves and as cornerstones of liberal democracy more broadly" from a Marxist perspective. Popowich discovered that those two pieces, the history piece and the discursive piece, fit together quite well.

Popowich (2024b) published a second book with Library Juice Press, *Solving Names: Worldliness and Metaphysics in Librarianship*. He said that when he was writing *Confronting the Democratic Discourse of Librarianship*, one of the big debates in Canadian libraries concerning intellectual freedom centered around issues like "cancel culture" and transphobia. Popowich found himself heavily involved in those debates, particularly the debate over whether Canadian libraries should be platforming transphobic speakers. Because of this, Popowich began thinking extensively about intellectual freedom and asking questions about what the concept means:

> *Solving Names* settled on the idea that, in our culture more broadly—but in librarianship in particular—we try to find what I think of as 'solving names.' We try to come up with rules or terms or concepts which are like master keys which allow us to ground other things that we want to do.

And we spend a lot of time and energy searching for and trying to define these solving names because we think that they will solve all our political problems or ethical problems or social problems. And so, the book takes some of the solving names, 'intellectual freedom' being one of them, 'democracy' being one of them, and sort of unpacks them, criticizing and deconstructing them to a certain extent.

Solving names like "intellectual freedom" and "democracy," Popowich said, effectively place constraints on what is and what is not possible within the library profession.

Not surprisingly, Popowich cited the works of Karl Marx and Friedrich Engels as the most important influence on his evolution as a critical library worker, and particularly Marx's (1990/1867) magnum opus, *Capital, Volume 1*. *Capital* is a massive tome in which Marx presents his most developed exposition of capitalism as an economic mode of production, uncovering its internal processes and relations, identifying and analyzing "an interrelated set of political problems that are either invisible to or wished away by virtually every other book in the canon of great works" (Roberts, 2017, p. 20). Popowich first discovered the book during his undergraduate career:

> I ended up finding books about Marxism in secondhand stores and discovered that *Capital* was Marx's main work. And then again, the university bookstore had a wall of Penguin Classics, and they had the three volumes of *Capital* there. I was probably 19 or 20 at the time and had no background in economics, had no background in political economy, and I just struggled through it. Some chapters are easier than others. They are more narrative and less technical. Some chapters are more Hegelian. So, I worked through it, did not really understand it, but got enough out of it to come away with a better understanding of my own experience and what I was seeing around me. [...] I maintained a what we would call a 'vulgar' Marxist understanding after the reading, very deterministic and not particularly nuanced. But *Capital* was the book that I kept coming back to and understanding in different ways and understanding more and more things.

Popowich was particularly struck by *Capital* Chapter 10: "The Working Day," which he recommended as a starting point to people who want to read the book for the first time. While the first three chapters of *Capital* are very dense, technical examinations of commodities and value that employ an essentially Hegelian analysis (Hegel being a philosopher notorious for his obscure writing style), Chapter 10 is a good introduction to what the stakes of the book are about. *Capital* is a daunting book, but one that Popowich said "teaches you to read it," and one should expect to reread it more than once to come to grips with it.

Now, having read the book multiple times, Popowich said that it has shaped his professional praxis in profound ways, making him conscious of things taken for granted in the day-to-day work of being an academic librarian, and particularly an information technology librarian. Of particular importance is the understanding the book gave him of the way in which labor is a commodity, including cognitive labor and academic labor. *Capital* also provided him with insight into what exchange means in a non-corporate environment, i.e., in a publicly funded organization like academic libraries and public libraries. The way Marx begins with an analysis of the commodity, Popowich said, and then traces the concept through larger and larger social forms through the rest of the book, instilled in him the capacity to intuit and identify commodity relationships in his professional work, like the social relationships between librarians and between librarians, students, and teaching faculty members. On the information technology side, Popowich has become more attuned to identifying the relationships between actual commodities to ask questions like what librarians are selling, buying, and deploying from a critical vantage point.

Capital, Volume 1 is now over 150 years old and has received its fair share of criticism, particularly that its economics of Capital are outdated. Popowich, however, said that it remains a monumental work:

> I still think it is an amazing book. Intellectually, it is probably one of the greatest achievements that I have ever read. *Volume 2* and *3* of *Capital* were pieced together by Engles after Marx's death, so they do not really have this quality. But the first volume of *Capital*... Over the course of a thousand pages, it has an intellectual trajectory that is so detailed and was so well worked out. It is one of those books that teaches you how to read it. So, it is actually difficult to criticize the book.

Popowich said that Marx's analysis of the commodity still works for many of the things that today's Marxian analysts of the library still look at. One of Popowich's recent articles, for example, considers the use of artificial intelligence in the academic context from a Marxist perspective (Popowich, 2024a). The historical chapters, like the chapter on the working day, also remain incredibly relevant in terms of how social struggle works, how "the details of capitalism that we have now like the five-day workweek, eight-hour days, were not decided and implemented by anyone, but were the result of struggle."

In addition to Marx and Engels, Popowich pointed to other important Marxists and Marxism-influenced thinkers as major influences. The Italian Marxist Antonio Gramsci (1891–1937) is one such thinker, and Popowich said that Gramsci's *Prison Notebooks*, with its difficult yet groundbreaking explication of the now-classic Gramscian ideas of hegemony and organic intellectuals, has had a great influence not only on critical librarianship but on many other fields of study as well. He suggested that those new to Gramsci begin with the compiled and more cohesively organized *Selections From the Prison Notebooks* (1971). Stuart Hall, a pioneering cultural studies theorist, is also an important influence on Popowich's work, largely due to Hall's writings being relatively recent (Hall died in 2014) and therefore much closer to the present cultural moment: "All of the 'rise of the right' stuff around Thatcher and Reagan that Hall was writing about in the 70s and 80s is relevant today in the context of Boris Johnson and Donald Trump." Gramsci and Hall, Popowich said, may be read together to get a better understanding of the former, as Hall distills his own reading of Gramsci, providing a useful way to get into his work.

Although Popowich thinks that library school students and new professionals interested in studying critical theory and methods should read *Capital, Volume 1*, he recommended that those interested in approaching library work from a Marxist perspective begin with the secondary literature:

> There is this book that Karen Nicholson and Maura Seale (2018) edited, *The Politics of Theory and the Practice of Critical Librarianship*, that I have a chapter in about Marxism. But their book is about critical librarianship more generally and would recommend that a library student start with that, because it will give critical librarianship context. And then there is some general stuff on Marxism. I tend to recommend a book by Michael Heinrich (2012), *An Introduction to the Three Volumes of Karl Marx's Capital*, which is really just the economics boiled down.

Popowich said, however, that there is no substitute for Marx and Engels and that when one is ready to take on *Capital, Volume 1*, they should start with a good English translation like the Pelican Books edition first published in the 1970s (and last reprinted by Penguin Classics in the 1990s).

Although for a time, Twitter (now X) allowed for the development of a community of people researching similar subjects, Popowich said that recently, critical librarianship has been in flux, and it is his sense that the coherence of a position called "critical librarianship" is probably over. This shift, Popowich said, is expected: something new will come along to take its place (a very dialectical notion). For example, the progressive librarianship that preceded critical librarianship faded away around 2005, possibly because of its traditional views of labor, unions, and activism, positions that those in the emerging critical librarianship of the late 2000s oftentimes did not fully subscribe to:

> [...] seeing unions as in some sense products of capitalism and therefore integral to the function of capitalism rather than something that was anti-capitalist. In the same way that I think critical librarianship took over some of the same space from progressive librarianship, I suspect something else will develop over the next few years from those of us who were working in critical librarianship.

Some of the fracture points that Popowich sees in the critical librarianship that followed the era of progressive librarianship are the same ones seen in broader left politics, such as those around identity. While he thinks that critical librarianship did not necessarily try to steer clear of identity politics, with most critical librarians having a "progressive" but perhaps outdated view of identity—that perspective is being superseded by other viewpoints. The other major splitting point between critical librarianship and what follows, he said, will likely center around the Israel-Palestine conflict and humanitarian crisis. Although Popowich said that he thinks most librarians are also on the same page concerning this issue,

> we can just tell from the debates over Israel and Palestine, even amongst Jewish populations in different places, that there is going to be a fracture point there someplace. So, I suspect those are the two lines where we will see a new coherent leftwing critical librarianship arise, when we take a position on identity politics and Israel-Palestine in a different way than we did.

Having just published his second book and completed his doctorate in 2024, Popowich said that he has taken a step back from research to recharge and see what grabs him in terms of future research projects. While he currently does not yet have a concrete focus in mind for his next project, he said that he would like to do something that is less library-focused and more general interest. Regardless of what topic Popowich settles on, it is sure to be both challenging and transformative. For, as Marx wrote in his *Thesis on Feuerbach*, "The philosophers have only interpreted the world, in various ways; the point is to change it" (Marx, 1888).

References

Gramsci, A. (1971). *Selections from the prison notebooks*. International Publishers.
Heinrich, M. (2012). *An introduction to the three volumes of Karl Marx's Capital*. Monthly Review Press.
Marx, K. (1888). Theses on Feuerbach. *Marx/Engels Internet Archive*. https://www.marxists.org/archive/marx/works/1845/theses/theses.htm
Marx, K. (1990/1867). *Capital volume 1*. (B. Fowkes, Trans.). Penguin Books.
Nicholson, K., & Seale, M. (Eds.). (2018). *The politics of theory and the practice of critical librarianship*. Library Juice Press.
Popowich, S. (2019). *Confronting the democratic discourse of librarianship: A Marxist approach*. Library Juice Press.
Popowich, S. (2024a). ChatGPT and the commodification of knowledge work. *CAUT Journal*, *3*, 1–20.
Popowich, S. (2024b). *Solving names: Worldliness and metaphysics in librarianship*. Library Juice Press.
Roberts, W. C. (2017). *Marx's inferno: The political theory of capital*. Princeton University Press.

17 Douglas Raber

Throughout his long professional career, Doug Raber has been an instrumental figure in the incorporation of critical theory into the examination of the history of libraries and library work, combining his training in political science with his study of the American public library to locate public libraries as pivotal institutions within an industry of cultural production and reproduction.

Raber's career in library and information science (LIS) has taken many twists and turns over the decades. After receiving his undergraduate and master's degrees in political science, Raber was inspired by the example of his father—who was also a librarian—to attend library school at Northern Illinois University. Upon graduating with his master of library and information science (MLS), Raber began his career as an academic librarian. This route, however, was relatively short-lived. After working two years as a subject specialist in political science at the State University of New York, Buffalo, he took a job as public library director in the small town of Harvard, Illinois, in 1979. With this move, Raber had found his professional calling. For Raber, the move to the public library,

> [...] changed everything. My father had been the Assistant Director of the Indianapolis-Marion County public library and in to a great extent I already knew what public librarianship could do, but doing it was a different matter. That's when I realized that public library practice provides a direct connection with a community of people who can be friends as well as patrons, especially when you're in a small town. Being a small-town library director lets you get close to your patrons and understand their needs, and that is when I began to see the possibilities. I began to think of what libraries might be able to do as change agents.

After serving in three public library administrative positions and earning his doctorate in LIS in 1992 from Indiana University while still working part-time as a reference librarian, Raber left working in public libraries to pursue preparing budding public librarians for their careers. He subsequently spent nearly half of his professional career teaching for library school graduate programs, first at the University of Missouri, then at the University of Tennessee School of Information Sciences, capping his tenure there as interim director, and then again at the University of Missouri, School of Information Science and Learning Technologies as a tenured associate professor. After 18 years in the academy teaching public library management, services, and history, Raber left Missouri in 2008 to become the director of the Ferndale Michigan Public Library. While at Missouri, he had become increasingly frustrated by the relative lack of meaningful teacher-student contact in the iSchool's asynchronous distance learning model. In fact, he was left feeling like he was spending more time manipulating classroom technology than he was teaching graduate students. Going back to library practice, on the other hand, would provide a return to the direct community involvement that Raber cherished. While returning to professional practice was in some ways like returning home, it was also a risky move. Raber said that after teaching public librarianship for over 20 years, if he could not go back to work and do it successfully himself, then there must be something wrong with library education and its relation to the profession. His return to public library service was indeed successful, leading him to conclude that the relation between education and practice was, after all, not "structured so badly!" In 2016, Raber retired as Director of the Marion Indiana Public Library, having been involved in library work in some manner for nearly 50 years.

Along with LIS academics like John Budd, Ronald Day, John Buschman, and Lisa Given, Raber has made significant contributions to exploring the intersection of library science and critical theory. As a result, he has influenced the work of critical library workers (the authors of the present volume included) through both his research and his teaching. When asked about his own influences, Raber pointed to Michael H. Harris's (1986) *Advances in Librarianship* article "State, Class, and Cultural Reproduction: Toward a Theory of Library Service in the United States" as a key factor in the development of his own research agenda concerning the public library as an ideological institution as well as his application of the early 20th-century Italian Marxist Antonio Gramsci's thought to the library in his own scholarly work.

In 1987, Raber was working as a full-time librarian in Indiana and taking classes in political science as an outside minor while completing his LIS doctorate. Therefore, prior to reading the Harris article, he had already studied Euro-Communism and thinkers like Gramsci and French Marxist Louis Althusser, building a foundation for his encounter with Harris.

Michael H. Harris (1941–2017), formerly Professor Emeritus at the University of Kentucky School of Information Science, spent his career documenting library history, with his best-known work being the scholarly monograph *History of Libraries in the Western World* (Harris, 1984). In "State, Class, and Reproduction," Harris locates American public libraries as cultural institutions within an industry of cultural production and reproduction, and specifically the production and reproduction of the dominant culture in capitalist society. For Raber, this encounter with Harris's ideas was exciting and thought-provoking. At the time the essay was published, most library workers (or, for that matter, librarianship in general) had not even considered that they simply accepted libraries as more or less given American institutions (a symptom of what Fobazi Ettarh would identify as "vocational awe." See Chapter 8 for more explanation). Furthermore, the role of the public library in the United States, as well as its activities, had not been interrogated thoroughly from the perspective of either critical or cultural theory.

In "State, Class, and Cultural Reproduction," Harris first argues that research in LIS was entrenched in a pluralist, positivist paradigm, resulting in "methodologically primitive" work requiring a theoretical intervention (Harris, 1986, p. 211), which he then provides through the lens of critical theory and particularly the thought of Gramsci. He seems to look at library work as an almost entirely oppressive institution in the sense that libraries, as well as other cultural institutions, serve as parts of an interpretive superstructure that organizes social life to support and reproduce the economic base and class relations of capitalist production. As a result, the "Library use and nonuse is stratified by class" and that libraries, in fact, "reproduce these class relationships" in the larger society (p. 244). He sees the public library's job within the cultural industry, therefore, as a matter of largely passing dominant culture onto the public through its collections. According to Harris,

> What emerges is a sense of the library as an institution embedded in a stratified ensemble of institutions functioning in the high cultural region, an ensemble of institutions dedicated to the creation, transmission and reproduction of the hegemonic ideology. Such an interpretation challenges the 'apolitical' conception of the library held by library professionals, and strips the library of the ethical and political innocence attributed to it by the pluralist social theorists.
>
> (p. 241)

Raber, however, thinks that Harris's pessimism toward the American public library belies the institution's counterhegemonic history and potential:

> There always has been, I think, a socialist aspect to the American public library, more so than probably public libraries anywhere in the world. Clearly, it represents the pooling of a collective resource through taxation to provide individual benefit, a benefit provided without cost to the individual. That is basically a mechanism for sharing capital resources and redistributing wealth [...] transforming private capital into public goods, for example, library materials, buildings, salaries for staff and expertise. But this is also a long-term cultural investment that benefits communities by providing public goods to individuals.

Through his encounter with Harris's investigation into the ideological realities of the modern public library, Raber began to consider the institution as what

Gramsci referred to as a site and a stake of conflict. That is, the public library is a site where class conflict occurs and, at the same time, is a stake in that class conflict. This is because control of the public library as an institution makes a difference in producing and reproducing the superstructure and its material base. Raber explained that the current efforts of the political right to impose restrictions on public libraries reveal a kind of "blockheaded awareness" of this ideological and political reality on their part. The right sees library collections as a stake of ideological conflict, and they want to control publicly funded libraries so that they can make their preferred literature the backbone of the collection or at least eliminate and censor literature that they do not approve of. This ideological conflict, Raber said, also happens within the library itself through a combination of materials that the library buys and the services that it provides. Although library workers may buy progressive materials for their collections and offer progressive services to their patrons, they may also buy materials and provide services that fundamentally reinforce the hegemony of the dominant culture and the exclusion or exploitation of non-dominant cultures.

"State, Class, and Reproduction" is notable for its application of Gramsci's concept of hegemony to the public library as an institution, hegemony meaning the dominant class's ability "to maintain the status quo via consent rather than force by utilizing a myriad of institutions to shape the mental structures within which people recognize, define, and address problems" (Harris, 1986, p. 244). Raber would follow Harris's lead by further exploring hegemony and the public library qua institution in his own work but went further by considering the role of Gramsci's "organic intellectual" in the public library's internal struggle as a site and stake of conflict. For Gramsci (1971), all humans are intellectuals because all humans have the ability for rational thought. Gramsci posited, however, that certain individuals assume the role of organic intellectual because they are attached to a particular social class (e.g., bourgeoisie, proletariat) and, as a result, serve the interests of that social class:

> Every social group, coming into existence on the original terrain of an essential function in the world of economic production, creates together with itself, organically, one or more strata of intellectuals which give it homogeneity and an awareness of its own function not only in the economic but also in the social and political fields.
> (Gramsci, 1971, p. 5)

There are, therefore, those intellectuals who are organic to the capitalist enterprise (including, although they would likely deny it, those "neutral" intellectuals that Gramsci identifies as "traditional" intellectuals), as well as intellectuals who are organic to the laboring classes.

Although he did not write about librarians or library workers per se—in early 20th-century Italy, libraries were not especially prominent institutions—Gramsci wrote extensively about schools, education, and ideology, and about schools and education as mechanisms of cultural production and reproduction. He saw the schools and educational institutions of capitalist societies as apparatuses for reproducing capitalism, and teachers fit into that reproductive apparatus as organic intellectuals (typically as assets of the dominant culture and capitalism, but potentially as counterhegemonic intellectuals). Raber saw that public librarians would also have easily fit into Gramsci's notion of the organic intellectual. As a result, the public librarian's *own mind* becomes a site of ideological conflict. The library workers themselves have a stake in this conflict because, Raber said,

> [...] if they begin to change their minds, they can begin to do things within the system or with the dominant culture that challenge it. Or, if they do not change their minds, they continue to support the dominant culture by serving its knowledge needs.

This personal situation, then, reflects a similar and parallel activity within and throughout librarianship as a profession and gives rise to professional ideologies. Raber would expand upon this idea in essays like "Librarians as Organic Intellectuals: A Gramscian Approach to Blind Spots and Tunnel Vision" (Raber, 2003) and "Gramsci, Hegemony, and Intellectual Freedom" (Raber, 2014).

So, while Harris's critique of the library is still relevant for today's readers, Raber takes him to task for his determinism and particularly the way Harris described the public library as a captive institution. That is, Harris portrays modern libraries as hopelessly locked into the mechanisms of the production and reproduction of the dominant culture, i.e., that they essentially had no choice but to simply carry that mission out. In contrast, Raber does not feel that cultural institutions of any kind, and particularly libraries, have ever been that rigidly locked into their roles or inevitable societal outcomes. One needs to understand that there is more freedom for library workers to move than Harris would imply or admit. Appreciating that the library exists primarily to reproduce a dominant capitalist culture, which is inherently oppressive, is where the critique starts, but theorists should also explore to what extent progressives can capture part of the state and push back against the dominant culture.

Raber has also explored the role of ideology in the history of the American library through his first monograph, *Librarianship and Legitimacy: The Ideology of the Public Library Inquiry* (Raber, 1997). This book takes a close look at the 1947–1950 Public Library Inquiry, a major nationwide study of US public libraries immediately after World War II that was sponsored by the American Library Association (ALA) and was conducted not by library professional researchers but by political scientists and sociologists. The motivation for the study, Raber said, grew out of the post-war cultural movement that was trying to decide "what to do now" since fascism had been defeated (at least it was thought to have been defeated; recent political events suggest otherwise) by asking the question, where do the public institutions go from here? Public libraries were not the only institution dealing with that problem, but they were certainly trying to understand their role in a post-war world, how they fit in the post-war world, what their mission was in this world, and how it must be different from what it was before the war drove the inquiry. Raber's argument was that not only was the profession searching for a purpose after World War II, but it was also searching for a purpose that would secure for it the legitimacy that it needed to continue its funding:

> In other words, as a state institution, the public library has got to be legitimate. Otherwise, its reason for public funding comes open to the question 'why should we put any money in it?' And, of course, people who argue that things like public libraries, museums, anything to do with the arts, the entire National Endowment for the Arts, The Institute of Museum and Library Services, that none of this has any business in their mind being funded for any reason at all because it is a matter of private enjoyment—that is the argument on the other side. So how do you create legitimacy, create an argument that secures legitimacy of the funding that actually allows the library to continue to exist?

This question of securing legitimacy was what the Public Library Inquiry was all about. American public libraries were looking for a purpose for themselves that was existential, as well as a practical way of securing continuing support for the institution and the profession.

Such legitimation, Raber said, goes on in today's libraries. Real legitimacy, however, is not earned so much by arguing that you do good things and people believing you. Real legitimacy is earned by actually doing those good things for enough people so that, if someone tries to take these good things away from them, they complain politically and vote against the people trying to take them away. That means, in effect, that legitimacy is achieved through the services and materials the public library provides. Because of this, many library workers attempt to secure legitimacy in ways that will not challenge anything in fear of losing their audience and funding. This fear has created a sort of demand-driven librarianship where, in the words of Charles R. McClure, the library should "Give them what they want" (McClure, 1993, p. 198). That is a political stance seeking legitimacy. There are, nonetheless, other ways for libraries to justify themselves and, Raber said,

> [...] other services to be provided that could also justify or create the legitimacy for the institution or the profession. [...] This is where again, action can be taken at the site of class conflict that challenges the dominant hegemony, for example, new tools and services for underserved and excluded populations, including youth. Many libraries, for example are pushing and getting out there in response to anti-gay activity, offering more gay and trans-oriented programming. So, they are pushing back against the dominant culture.

In many communities, such an approach will gain the local library credibility, but Raber cautions that library workers must tread carefully. They must carefully consider the decisions that they are making concerning their collections because choosing what services to provide and what books to buy are inherently political decisions. In addition to harassment and/or termination, library workers in some states may be fined, arrested, and even jailed for their collection development decisions. This last statement is by no means an exaggeration. In Granbury, Texas, for example, a local law enforcement officer drafted criminal complaints against three school librarians for allowing students access to such books as Toni Morrison's *The Bluest Eye* (Hixenbaugh et al., 2024), and in Missouri, "legislators passed a law in 2022 subjecting librarians to fines and possible imprisonment for allowing sexually explicit materials on bookshelves" (Hillel & Kruesi, 2024). The counterhegemonic organic intellectual remains perpetually at risk of drawing the ire of the dominant classes, and they should proceed with caution.

Lately, Raber has been thinking about the ways in which late capitalism has moved on in some ways beyond what the nineteenth-century Marxian analysis can cope with. Raber found the line of research coming out of Gramsci's research in the late 20th and early 21st centuries to be the most valuable Marxist contributions to library work, in that they may be used to understand how the state itself is a mechanism of capitalist society. Marxist theory can bring interesting insight into the role of state institutions as sites and stakes of conflicts. By looking at libraries as state institutions, the critical theorist and/or the critical practitioner can ask interesting and significant questions about what they are doing, who they are doing it for, and why they are doing it. "Among other things," he said,

> I think Marxism and librarianship reminds us that the practice of librarianship is not value neutral. It is not value-free, and that ethical and moral and political decisions are baked into what librarians do as professionals. They cannot be avoided.

One obstacle to effective counterhegemonic action, however, is that, while library workers always seem to be telling themselves that they are on the cutting edge, many do not receive adequate training in theoretical thinking in LIS graduate school. Because of this lacuna in training, many LIS professionals do not know how to explicitly think theoretically when they are looking at their communities and when they are looking at their libraries, and engaging in theoretical thinking is necessary to be relevant to the everyday lives of people that they are serving. There are, however, no easy answers to the conundrum due to present trends in LIS education:

> One of the things that you would normally [advocate for] is better communication between—going back to the notion of praxis—the world of academics and the world of librarianship. I do not see that as being a possibility now because as library schools have become increasingly 'information schools' they are focusing more on the behavior of

information than the behavior of people. As a result of that, as the faculty, ~~as~~ the academic part of the profession, becomes more grounded in the study of information than in the study of libraries and their user communities, as they become schools of information science, they actually become more theoretical. But the theory is about information and its behavior, not about library practices. That is one of the reasons that I think it is going to be really difficult to infuse critical theory [through LIS education].

Despite this scarcity of formalized training for future library professionals in areas like critical and cultural theory, Raber sees the current state of critical library work as healthy overall, particularly as it is found in public libraries. Public library workers, however, are largely not self-conscious of their own criticality (although this is changing as libraries and librarians personally come under great threats of defunding and even prosecution). That is, many public library workers offer services and collections that could be regarded as "critical" but, unfortunately, do not know it themselves. Instead, Raber said, public library workers "just think they are doing services that need to be done" and are engaging in critical librarianship on the job, even if they are not fully cognizant of doing so. They just think they are offering services that need to be done. So, while critical librarianship is possibly alive and well in a naïve manner out in the field, if you look at state-level conferences or even the Public Library Association conference programs, "you will not see much on those programs that is going to sound much like critical librarianship."

And for this reason, despite the good work being done by public library workers, there remains a deficit in thinking about that work theoretically. Not only are future librarians not encountering the theory of critical librarianship in school, but critical librarianship also remains undertheorized, resulting in stagnation. There are some beacons out there, he said, for those people who have little experience in critical library work and want to develop a critical consciousness. One such book is the collection *Critical Theory for Library and Information Science: Exploring the Social from Across the Discipline* (Leckie et al., 2010), which includes chapters covering applications of the theories by Roland Barthes, Roy Bhaskar, Michel Foucault, and Pierre Bourdieu. In Raber's own chapter on Gramsci, he summarizes the collection's value:

> This volume of readings represents a more conscious and fully theorized action in another trench, that of LIS education and research located in institutions of higher learning. It is an effort to bring together and present introductions to counter-hegemonic social and political theory with ~~eh~~ the hope that it might inform progressive practices, at least in the realm of LIS teaching and research if not professional practice.
>
> (Raber, 2010, p. 154)

Raber also recommends the Mark Alfino and Laura Coltusky (2014) edited *Library Juice Press Handbook of Academic Freedom*. This book primarily focuses on intellectual freedom but does so from a critical librarianship perspective, covering topics such as hate speech, privacy issues, religion, intellectual freedom, sexual orientation, and gender expression.

References

Alfino, M., & Coltusky, L. (Eds.). (2014). *Library Juice Press handbook of academic freedom*. Library Juice Press.
Gramsci, A. (1971). *Selections from the prison notebooks* (Q Hoare & G. Nowell-Smith, Eds.). International Publishers.
Harris, M. H. (1984). *History of libraries in the western world*. Scarecrow Press.
Harris, M. H. (1986). State, class, and cultural reproduction: Toward a theory of library service in the United States. *Advances in Librarianship, 14*(1986), 211–252.
Hillel, I., & Kruesi, K. (2024). *Librarians fear new penalties, even prison, as activists challenge books*. Associated Press. https://apnews.com/article/book-bans-libraries-lawsuits-fines-prison-0914fa6cbb2a99b540cbbd28a38179b4
Hixenbaugh, M., Kingkade, T., Friedman, S., & Parks, E. (2024, July 25). Inside the two-year fight to bring charges against school librarians in Granbury, Texas. *NBC News*. https://www.nbcnews.com/news/us-news/school-librarians-banned-books-investigation-texas-rcna161444
Leckie, G. J., Given, L. M., & Buschman, J. E. (Eds.). (2010). *Critical theory for library and information science: Exploring the social from across the discipline*. Bloomsbury.
McClure, C. R. (1993). Updating planning and role setting for public libraries: A manual of options and procedures. *Public Libraries, 32*(4), 198–199.
Raber, D. (1997). *Librarianship and legitimacy: The ideology of the public library inquiry*. Praeger.
Raber, D. (2003). Librarians as organic intellectuals: A Gramscian approach to blind spots and tunnel vision. *Library Quarterly, 73*(1), 33–53.
Raber, D. (2010). Hegemony, historic blocs, and capitalism: Antonio Gramsci in library and information science. In G. Leckie, L. M. Given, & J. E. Buschman (Eds.), *Critical theory for library and information science: Exploring the social from across the discipline* (pp. 143–160). Bloomsbury Publishing.
Raber, D. (2014). Gramsci, hegemony, and intellectual freedom. In M. Alfino & L. Coltusky (Eds.), *Library Juice Press handbook of academic freedom* (pp. 41–70). Library Juice Press.

18 Toni Samek

Toni Samek is a Professor and Former Chair at the University of Alberta's School of Library and Information Studies. Samek's research focuses on information ethics and the ethos of intellectual freedom and social responsibility of librarianship. The first recipient of the Library Journal Teaching Award in 2007, she teaches courses in the foundations of library and information studies, intellectual freedom, and social responsibility in librarianship.

Samek began studying critical librarianship when earning her PhD at the University of Wisconsin-Madison Information School, where, as part of her dissertation under the supervision of Professor Wayne A. Wiegand, she documented the history of the alternative library press. As part of her program of study, Wiegand advised Samek to take a course in mass communication with the renowned history of communication Professor James L. Baughman, who tasked the class with writing a historical study using primary resources. Discovering that the State Historical Society of Wisconsin was on campus, Samek scoured the institution's access drawers, eventually coming across a listing for an organization founded in 1969 called the Radical Research Center (RRC), predecessor to the Alternative Press Center:

> I needed primary sources for this assignment for Baughman. I got into that file and low and behold, this was the crew of folks, young liberal arts students at Carleton College, that created the Alternative Press Index [(API), an index of progressive literature created in 1969 by the RRC]. And, in reading these documents in the State Historical Society of Wisconsin, there were also letters from Celeste West, Jackie Eubanks, Sanford Berman—the librarian-folk. I thought 'this is interesting,' but what really engaged me was trying to understand why non-library and undergraduate students created the API.

Samek's exposure to the API files as well as other primary source materials got her interested in understanding the alternative press through the lens of librarianship. In the process, she uncovered some of activist reference librarian Jackie Eubanks' letters to the American Library Association (ALA) Social Responsibilities Roundtable (SRRT) Alternatives in Print Task Force.

DOI: 10.4324/9781003473640-19

As Samek searched through the ALA Archives' SRRT material, she repeatedly encountered Eubanks' distinctive peach-colored felt tip and her memorable signoff, "struggle and giggle." Eubanks, Samek said, "was just always so outspoken and radical, a 'positive troublemaker.'" Light bulbs went off for Samek, and she formulated her dissertation topic on intellectual freedom and social responsibility in American librarianship during the late Vietnam era, which would later become the book *Intellectual Freedom and Social Responsibility in American librarianship, 1967–1974* (2001). If it had not been for the Baughman assignment, Samek said, she might not have gotten to the State Historical Society:

> It is just a collision of circumstances and my own instincts, I suppose. And then I just lucked out again because the ALA records were just a four-hour drive down the road. [...] And at Madison, Wisconsin at the time there was collision of people that I learned just as much from as from my professors at the school. I hit the jackpot.

During her dissertation research, Samek came upon the work of radical librarian Celeste West and was impressed with West's courage and the risks that she undertook. West may very well have been the prototypical radical librarian qua rabble-rouser to emerge from the heady stew of 1960s activism. Working as a reference librarian at San Francisco Public Library's Bay Area Reference Center (BARC), West was a feminist author and publisher of the award-winning *Synergy* magazine (1967–1973), an experimental publication that connected BARC with other libraries nationwide. *Synergy* only ceased publication following a directive from California Governor Ronald Reagan delivered by State Librarian Ethel S. Crockett. This would not, however, dissuade her from continuing to publish, and, if anything, it spurred her on to seek out other independent avenues for publishing. West, along with "Elizabeth Katz, and a few others" (Samek, 2006, p. 137), started Booklegger Press in 1972, the first American woman-owned independent library press. As collaborator-provocateurs, West et al. (1972) co-edited Booklegger Press's first book, *Revolting Librarians*, a landmark work in radical librarianship that,

> [...] took the field by storm with its diverse collection of library workers' free voices on a wide range of topics: the image of librarians, library schools and education, professionalism, mainstream bias and representation in Library of Congress subject headings, undemocratic library work practices, paraprofessional issues, homophobia, alternative libraries, alternative education, young adult services, libraries for migrant workers, and the library press.
>
> (Samek, 2001, p. 137)

In addition to West and Katz, essays appeared in the book by a Who's Who of early 1970s progressive librarians, including Sanford Berman, Steve Wolf, and

Joan Marshall. Samek first encountered *Revolting Librarians* during her graduate studies. The book had an immediate and lasting impact on her professional career and research and teaching agendas:

> In my reading of *Revolting Librarians*, I understood its authors as protagonists in library history. They were saying that the catalog reflected a rearview mirror. [Radical cataloger] Sanford Berman too was pushing for bibliographic reform and had us thinking about national bibliography and our knowledge and organization systems. You start to think more deeply about the omissions and the gaps and the negations and the rationalizations, and then you begin to ask questions like who is at library school and who is not? Like where do we publish? And what do we read and do not read?

One reason Samek was drawn to *Revolting Librarians* was that it included discussion of library labor, which got her thinking about the importance of bringing history and labor into library education. Samek sees many library school students who maintain a critical library worker identity as imagining their careers in terms of only front-line, entry-level positions that are typically oriented as anti-management and administration; many of these students do not necessarily ever want to take on a manager role. Samek, however, is quick to tell her students that if they want better collective agreement language but do not want to imagine themselves through time being on both sides of the labor bargaining table, they are not going to get that preferred language. The language comes from both sides of the table. That is, librarians cannot just make complaints; they must take on responsibility and support the people who do.

Samek feels that while *Revolting Librarians* has not become dated, it was certainly marginalized because of its authors and their politics. West was not what the ALA establishment would consider the poster child for the profession: she was a lesbian, an advocate for polyamory, a political protestor, lived and labored with difficult mental health challenges, and had been arrested for her advocacy work. Nevertheless, Samek said, she never won over the establishment, unlike prominent contemporaries such as civil rights activist E.J. Josey.

Samek learned valuable lessons from investigating the work of activist librarians. First and foremost, she said, activist librarians need to "keep it real," i.e., they need to be humble, honest, and as fearless as they possibly can:

> Do not self-censor. And I think consistency is important, not that we do not learn in life and change our minds, but consistency is important. I also think expressing one's opinion is key. I have said that so many times in the academy to colleagues that you are getting a paycheck from here, you are paid to express your opinion. Bring it!

The problem, however, is that librarian education is not adequately providing its graduates with the needed perspective that is only provided through learning about the past. New librarians, Samek said, are not getting enough library history when earning their master's degrees. These days, library and information science (LIS) graduate programs look more and more like the increasingly popular "ischool" model, with the typical faculty member or instructor likely not having a background in librarianship and likely knowing next to nothing about the history of librarianship. Samek is keen on getting back the history that was pushed out by technological and managerial topics. The typical contemporary LIS programs, she said, are not even at a point of amnesia concerning library history because people never knew that history in the first place:

> Like this whole library neutrality thing that we are seeing now in the literature. I am endlessly telling students that this is not new. There are new variations on it and new voices, but this goes back decades. It has been at least since the 1930's that we have been arguing about this stuff. That was when the Progressive Librarians Council was born, and they created their own newsletter because they were tired of a handful of venues (e.g., *Wilson Library Bulletin, Library Journal*) dominating library discourse. This is not new, but students do not know that. They think that they are the first generation to be arguing this stuff out. And that is a disservice to generations of colleagues before us.

It is part of Samek's teaching strategy to use voices like West's to disrupt students' comfortable identity with critical library work. The important figures of LIS, Samek said, must be studied and understood for their contributions—whether those contributions are positive or negative—to understand the historical trajectory of the LIS professions. If one does not study history in their library school program, how do they make sense of what they see coming out of the ALA? For the ALA to fully make sense, Samek said, librarians must go back to at least 1876 (the year the organization was founded) and then follow the journey to the present. One of Samek's own contributions to patching up these historical lacunae is the book she co-edited with K.R. Roberto and Moyra Lang, *She was a Booklegger: Remembering Celeste West* (Samek et al., 2010), which explored West's life and work.

Samek is critical of the now ubiquitous and diluted use of the phrase "critical librarianship" and feels we are in a new era of something akin to a "post critical librarianship." Public library plus X (e.g., makerspace), she asserts, does not automatically mean critical librarianship and social justice. But we see that approach too much:

> We need to express more clearly where critical librarianship can be going. I do not have it figured out yet, I am just sort of sensing it. I saw a job posting recently from the Faculty of Information Media Studies at Western University in London Ontario, here in Canada. It listed some of the areas that they are looking for, including the generic phrase 'critical

librarianship.' I do not know an LIS program in North America that is not teaching some elements of critical librarianship, my own School included. That might present in various ways in breadth, not necessarily depth. Then, I saw a posting from another institution a few days ago where I really liked one of the phrasings, which was 'epistemicide'. With this we can identify a clear call for a line of interest and expertise which could be interpreted to be under the umbrella of critical librarianship and beyond.

Samek said that she figured out early on in her career that the most radical library workers were teacher librarians and government librarians who did not identify as critical librarians but were "really taking shit on." Teacher librarians, e.g., were always ahead on technology, access to information, and multicultural issues. Historically, these librarians were doing heavy lifting but rarely getting any credit for it. They are also not the ones identifying as critical librarians. Government library workers, likewise, are doing incredible things but are rarely heard from in certain discourses because they must do their work in a certain way and under certain conditions:

> I do not want to take away from the work that people are doing with great intention. But, if you are going to put on your 'social justice angel badge,' then do not be a hypocrite. Define your terms and show some consistency and commit to something grassroots. Do not just show up and give another blurb about what is wrong with library neutrality. I mean, we have done that. I feel like there are people that are doing something very serious and committed with great risk. People who are in it for the long haul and maybe they are not getting as much credit because they are not card carrying for considered and serious reasons.

In other words, "keep it real."

When asked what the profession might focus on in its post-critical phase, Samek said that she is interested in connecting with people and engaging in conversation, which she has done already with colleagues in the Association for Library and Information Science Education's (ALISE) PIE group, which brings together people from ALISE's Information Ethics and Information Policy special interest groups, addressing questions like, what is post-critical librarianship? What does it mean? What does it look like? The post-critical librarian needs to identify what work is bearing fruit, why, and how: "There are some amazing people doing amazing things and we are advancing in the field. And that is exactly what Celeste West and E.J. Josey would have wanted." For Samek, it is all about the long haul: "I think we are on a continuum where we are heading into something interesting. We cannot quite understand it yet, but I am excited about it."

References

Samek, T. (2001). *Intellectual freedom and social responsibility in American librarianship, 1967–1974*. McFarland.

Samek, T. (2006). Unbossed and unbought: Booklegger Press, the first women-owned American library publisher. In J. P. Danky & W. A. Wiegand (Eds.), *Women in print: Essays on the print culture of American women from the nineteenth and twentieth centuries* (pp. 126–155). University of Wisconsin Press.

Samek, T. Roberto, K. R., & Lang, M. (Eds.). (2010). *She was a booklegger: Remembering Celeste. West*. Library Juice Press.

West, C., Katz, E. et al. (1972). *Revolting librarians*. Booklegger Press.

19 Gina Schlesselman-Tarango

Gina Schlesselman-Tarango is an Associate Professor and Science Librarian at Grinnell College Libraries, Iowa. Her route to critical librarianship has been a circuitous one. Schlesselman-Tarango grew up in rural Iowa in a conservative area and household, went to Drake University in Des Moines for her undergraduate degree in sociology and anthropology, and then joined the Peace Corps. After teaching English in Ukraine, she moved to Denver to pursue a master's degree in social science and a graduate certificate in women's and gender studies at the University of Colorado Denver, a decision that provided her with a firm grounding in critical theory as opposed to traditional social science methods, and her core courses focused on philosophers like Hegel and Marx, as well as Frankfurt School thinkers like Habermas, Horkheimer, and Adorno. Attending a program that was so keenly focused on critical theory had not been her primary intention, and,

> [...] in hindsight, I did not really know what I was doing. But what I think what drew me to it at the time was that the program appeared to be interdisciplinary, and I have always appreciated studying sociology because it borrows from a lot of different fields and traditions.

After graduation and during a short stint as a K-12 teacher, Schlesselman-Tarango took a part-time job as a personal care attendant for renowned poet, journalist, and disability rights advocate Laura Hershey (1962–2010) and her partner Robin Stephens. It was through this experience that she received an introduction to disability rights activism. A former poster child for Jerry Lewis's Muscular Dystrophy Association, Hershey would later protest that organization's depiction of people with disabilities while fighting for the civil rights of both people living with disabilities and members of the LGBTQIA2+ community:

> I do not think working for Hershey and Stephens directly informed my practice as a librarian, but it was cool being in their space and knowing them, not only what they were doing in the political sphere but knowing them very intimately because I was helping with their physical needs and

things like that. They certainly informed my idea of what it means to live a full and intentional life in service of the greater good.

Schlesselman-Tarango ultimately ended up leaving K-12 education to attend the University of Denver for library school, where she focused on academic librarianship. After graduating, she took her first professional library job coordinating the library instruction program at California State University, San Bernardino. As an introvert, Schlesselman-Tarango had found teaching K-12 exhausting, and academic library work allowed for a rewarding combination of face-to-face instruction with a reasonable amount of alone time. Eventually moving back to Iowa with her partner and new baby during the COVID-19 pandemic, she transitioned into health sciences librarianship and now works as a science librarian at Grinnell College.

Schlesselman-Tarango's library practice is grounded in her encounters with critical and feminist theory. While she is happy and eager to contribute at the workplace, she remains alert to the ways that exploitation or job creep may occur on the job:

> I am always attentive to making sure that work is distributed evenly and equitably as possible while also leaving room for all the different circumstances people bring with them to the workplace. I know this really comes back to my time at California State University in San Bernardino, because I was really involved with the union, and I was our union representative for the library. So, it is hard for me to take that lens off even now when I am at Grinnell College. We do not have a faculty union, but I am very attuned to issues like shared governance.

Schlesselman-Tarango's objective is to make library work more humane and sustainable, e.g., through promoting changes like moving meetings to an online format—doing so not only has an environmental impact and increases accessibility but also impacts quality of life. She has adopted the perspective of library work as a form of labor, as opposed to a "calling." She had encountered the latter viewpoint while working as a K-12 teacher, where the dominant narrative was that teachers were "there because they love it" and, as a result, should be content with low pay and long hours. That, Schlesselman-Tarango said, leads to burnout (see Chapter 8 for a profile of Fobazi Ettarh and more on "vocational awe").

In terms of pedagogy and library instruction, Schlesselman-Tarango tries to be attuned to how power is exercised within the library:

> I think that the biggest gift that critical theory and a feminist lens has given me, is that it attuned me to how power and resources are distributed. [...] When I teach, I use a teaching style that is not top down—active learning and creating classroom environments that are interesting and inclusive and things like that. But I do not think that is critical theory

necessarily. My pedagogical approach has probably been more informed by my experiences as a K-12 teacher. And I have had opportunities here and there to teach credit bearing courses that help provide more room than a one-shot library instruction session.

These semester-long, credit-bearing information literacy courses allow her to assign readings and discussion prompts informed by critical and feminist theory. For example, in 2025, Schlesselman-Tarango taught an introduction to science, medicine, and society course that allowed her to put what she knows as a librarian about publishing and scholarly communication in conversation with her interests in reproductive health, gender, and sexuality, among other things. Teaching such a course, she said, is a rare opportunity for an academic librarian, and she does not take it for granted:

> I wish for everyone to just have that space to really teach things that are interesting to them. I think that with librarianship, there is a lot we could say, especially those of us who are interested in critical librarianship or critical theory. But we just do not have the space or the time.

Of particular importance to Schlesselman-Tarango's development as both a critically oriented library worker and scholar is Carol J. Adams's (2015/1990) book *The Sexual Politics of Meat: A Feminist-Vegetarian Critical Theory*, which she discovered while researching her master's thesis on women's depictions in bridal magazines. *The Sexual Politics of Meat* is a highly influential and controversial ecofeminist exploration of the connections between the patriarchal oppression of women and the oppression of non-human animals as depicted in dominant cultural imagery (i.e., the depiction of women *as* meat). What Schlesselman-Tarango found particularly compelling about the book is Adams's politicization of Derrida's concept of the "absent referent":

> Behind every meal of meat is an absence: the death of the animal whose place the meat takes. The 'absent referent' is that which separates the meat eater from the animal and the animal from the end product. The function of the absent referent is to keep our 'meat' separated from any idea that she or he was once an animal, to keep the 'moo' or 'cluck' or 'baa' away from the meat, to keep *something* from being seen as having been someone.
>
> (Adams, n.d.)

With the absent referent, Adams named something that had long unsettled Schlesselman-Tarango; she articulated a link between women's bodies and non-human animals' bodies where the act of meat eating becomes "the re-inscription of male-power at every meal" (p. 241). When she first read *The Sexual Politics of Meat*, Schlesselman-Tarango was struck by Adams's bravery in writing it. The book was problematizing something—the association of women with meat—that had become normalized in the dominant culture. She appreciated how Adams talked about how techniques like repetition and erasure contribute to these normalizing practices. She was also impacted by the ways in which Adams also pointed out the limitations of feminism and the things that it had thus far missed:

> This might have been the first time that I was engaging with a text that did that. Certainly, other scholars had always been doing that, but at that time it struck me that you can still be a feminist and disagree with some corners of the feminist project.

It is not only the content of the book that is meaningful to Schlesselman-Tarango, but also the role *The Sexual Politics of Meat* played in her education and development as a researcher. She sees the book as the first text that she really engaged with on a deep level, diving into the footnotes and following references to explore related ideas (she still has her first physical copy covered with her marginalia). Adams points out that gender is everywhere, even in the meal that is on your plate, "and I think she would probably agree that the same could be said about class, race, and gender and other points of identity. So that is how I approach the world too." When Schlesselman-Tarango looks out at the world, she considers how metaphors work to produce certain sets of ideas and practices. While she does not owe all this sense of critical analysis to the *Sexual Politics of Meat*, it is something that she really values about the book.

Schlesselman-Tarango does have some criticisms of *The Sexual Politics of Meat*. She sees the writing style as trying at times and finds Adams's use of evidence sometimes questionable. Adams is a product of second-wave feminism and studied under radical feminist philosopher Mary Daly (1928–2010), who often gets included in the trans exclusionary radical feminist (TERF) camp. And while Schlesselman-Tarango thinks that Adams does engage in quite a bit of gender essentialism and does not give her a pass, the book is "is reflective of the tradition that she comes out of." She also questions Adams's insistence on obligatory moral vegetarianism. For example, she critiques Adams' fixation on food choices:

> I think one of the obvious problems around her argument is that not everyone has access to a healthy vegetarian diet. And there are not a lot of nuances there. She ultimately advocates for feminist rituals of eating, which to me is a very individual choice framework to a larger structural problem. And I do not love feminisms that are prescriptive about individual choices.

Schlesselman-Tarango's own research agenda has evolved and shifted over the years based upon her personal interests and experiences, but it remains broadly focused on the critical examination of gender and racial dynamics in library work (Schlesselman-Tarango, n.d.). Her earliest research projects investigated racial dynamics in libraries and information spaces. She had seen a lot of those same dynamics while in the Peace Corps and K-12 education, and this prior experience allowed her to identify something similar happening in the library environment. This led to the writing of the *Library Trends* article "The Legacy of Lady Bountiful: White Women in the Library" (Schlesselman-Tarango, 2016). In that article, she identified and critiqued the "Lady Bountiful" archetype, an idealized form of whiteness found in library and information science (LIS) that enables racism under a guise of feminine benevolence. She followed "Lady Bountiful" with an article that considered the feminized "cuteness" aesthetic found in library work and how that reinforces white supremacy through neutrality (Schlesselman-Tarango, 2017a). Seeing that people were excited about this work led to Schlesselman-Tarango's next project, *Topographies of Whiteness: Mapping Whiteness in Library and Information Science* (Schlesselman-Tarango, 2017b), a collection that she edited for Library Juice Press. Editing *Topographies* was a new and challenging experience, but an ultimately rewarding one that allowed Schlesselman-Tarango to connect with like-minded people and put their work in conversation. The book was well-received, coming at a time when people within library work were really wanting to talk about whiteness, white supremacy, and race more broadly. The book energized a lot of people in LIS, and Schlesselman-Tarango saw it as "giving folks permission to start – or in some cases, continue – talking about things that were often left unsaid."

Schlesselman-Tarango had a child in 2019, resulting in a shift in research emphasis:

> Prior to the birth of my daughter, I had experienced infertility and pregnancy loss, which compelled me to engage in some really intense information practices, both looking stuff up and figuring out how to address this problem and also creating lots of information, whether it be bio information – information about my body and what it was doing – or just like accumulating medical records and things like that. So, I started thinking about this idea of information work again, the question of labor and how people in certain circumstances or situations are doing a type of work that is perhaps unique, work that is certainly not really legible or visible.

Following this route, Schlesselman-Tarango wrote two pieces employing auto-ethnography, a qualitative method that begins with the researcher's personal experiences, systematically documenting and reflecting upon them to consider what is happening on a larger scale. Through this process, the auto-ethnographer puts their own experiences in conversation with structural or sociological critique. This methodology allowed Schlesselman-Tarango to look at her own experiences with health information while also dealing with infertility and pregnancy loss. This work also led to her current research project, a forthcoming co-edited collection for Library Juice Press titled *Information, Power, and Reproductive Health* (Schlesselman-Tarango, forthcoming).

When asked if she had advice for someone considering approaching a career in academic library work from a critical perspective, Schlesselman-Tarango said that one should not limit oneself to the LIS literature because there are many powerful ideas outside of that corpus that have not been considered when studying LIS work. Citing the "Lady Bountiful" article as an example, she said she looked heavily to the field of education to argue that particular subjects are put in educational roles and the implications of that, "but you could probably look to any field and find examples and theories and frameworks that make sense in librarianship." But just as important to one's professional development as what they read are the extraordinary *people* one encounters during their career trajectory. For Schlesselman-Tarango, one such person was a Peace Corps trainer who taught her how to create welcoming learning environments and provided her with substantive ideas for making connections with and among students: "And even the way she wrote lesson plans, I still use her formula to this day."

Schlesselman-Tarango said that she is currently in a good place. She remains excited about working with students in a small college in rural Iowa, which comes with its own opportunities and challenges. In the present, she plans to remain focused on the intersection of reproductive health and information and will be starting a PhD program in 2025 to explore these ideas further. The future, however, remains open.

References

Adams, C. J. (2015/1990). *The sexual politics of meat: A feminist-vegetarian critical theory*: Bloomsbury Academic.

Adams, C. J. (n.d.). The absent referent. Caroljadams.com. https://caroljadams.com/the-absent-referent

Schlesselman-Tarango, G. (2016). The legacy of lady bountiful: White women in the library. *Library Trends, 64*(4), 667–686.

Schlesselman-Tarango, G. (n.d.). *Gina-Schlesselman-Tarango*. https://www.grinnell.edu/user/schlesselman

Schlesselman-Tarango, G. (2017a). How cute! Race, gender, and neutrality in libraries. *Partnership: The Canadian Journal of Library and Information Practice and Research, 12*(1), 1–18. https://journal.lib.uoguelph.ca/index.php/perj/article/view/3850

Schlesselman-Tarango, G. (2017b). *Topographies of whiteness: Mapping whiteness in library and information science*. Library Juice Press.

Schlesselman-Tarango, G. (forthcoming). *Information, power, and reproductive health*. Library Juice Press.

20 April Sheppard

April Sheppard has worked in academic libraries for 25 years, starting as a student worker at the Dean B. Ellis Library at Arkansas State University (A-State), then later becoming paraprofessional staff before moving to a librarian position. Currently, Sheppard is the Associate Dean of the Library at A-State, where she is Chair of the University Diversity Affirmative & Action Committee. Sheppard was also the Coordinator of the American Library Association (ALA) Social Responsibilities Roundtable (SRRT) from 2022 to 2023 and Co-coordinator from 2023 to 2025. As such, she coordinated one of ALA's largest and longest-running round tables, and one that actively addresses issues of social justice and equity both within libraries themselves as well as broader society, both in the United States and internationally.

Sheppard said that she first became conscious of social justice issues during her teenage years. She had been interested in free speech issues as far back as her junior high school years: "one cannot read about First Amendment rights and free speech issues without being exposed to systemic injustice and racism." As a high school student, Sheppard had had many friends from diverse backgrounds. This all changed when her family moved from Illinois to Arkansas, and Sheppard got a taste of what it is like to be an outsider:

> I was in the 11th grade when my family moved to an all-white town in the South, and the welcome sign on the way into town had 'KKK' spray-painted on it. I did not know the KKK even still existed. I thought that was just something in history books. Just having that experience of going from such a diverse friend group and then being such an outsider. Where I grew up in Illinois, no one cared that I was a heavy metal chick. No one cared that I was into horror movies. I had all these friends from different backgrounds, but then I ended up in a place where everyone kept asking 'where are you from?'

It was not until Sheppard was working at her first professional position as an academic librarian that she began to pursue social justice activism. The delay, Sheppard said, was largely because she had suffered from imposter syndrome:

I thought to myself, who am I to say anything? Who am I, you know? I am just a person who struggled through college financially, who came from a white, poor family with lots of alcoholism, substance abuse. I did not feel like I was qualified to be that person [a social justice activist].

Sheppard credited Dr. George Grant, former Dean of Arkansas University Libraries, for providing her with the impetus to become a librarian *and* an activist. An African American man, Grant owned an independent publishing company, GrantHouse Publishers, for which Sheppard did side work editing books. Working with the authors, she listened to their stories about growing up in the 1950s and 1960s and the experiences that they had living through Jim Crow segregation and the civil rights movement. These conversations made things "more real" for Sheppard, who realized "I am having conversations with people who walked with Dr. King. That really opened up my world. I thought 'maybe this is something. Maybe I am qualified to have opinions on these types of things.'"

As a socially conscious librarian deeply invested in diversity issues, music has played an important role in Sheppard's development of critical consciousness. She has always been heavily influenced by music, and some recordings have proven especially inspiring to her work. Around 2013, while listening to tunes on YouTube, the site's algorithm queued up soul man Solomon Burke and The Blind Boys of Alabama's (2002) definitive rendition of Mann, Weil, and Russell's "None of Us Are Free." The song's lyrics stress collective humanity as well as the need for collective action:

> It's a simple truth we all need, just to hear and to see,
> None of us are free, one of us is chained.
> None of us are free.
> Now I swear your salvation isn't too hard to find,
> None of us can find it our own.
> We've got to join together in spirit, heart and mind.
> So that every soul who's suffering will know they're not alone.
> (Mann, Weil, & Russell, 1993)

Sheppard first heard the song when the Black Lives Matter movement was first starting up, and it provoked feelings in her of "what can I do" and "who am I." She has revisited the song many times since this first encounter, and the one lyric that really sticks with her is "If you don't say it's wrong, then that says it's right." This lyric, Sheppard said, was a call to action: "I have to do more. I have to actually speak up and put myself out there."

As noted above, heavy metal music has also been an important element of Sheppard's life. She said that even though there has been a fair bit of thrash metal (her favorite genre) on things like "we are gonna go get drunk and worship the devil," there is a certain awareness in the music beginning in the late

1980s and early 1990s, when bands began calling out social issues, including anti-capitalism and environmentalism:

> I remember growing up with a hole in the ozone and being told not to use hairspray. And then Metallica's song, 'Blackened,' comes out and it's talking about the nuclear holocaust and the destruction of the Earth. Around this time, Nuclear Assault also came out with 'Critical Mass,' a song on the destruction of the world due to climate change. This was my introduction to environmentalism. To this day, sustainability is still really high on my list, as well as injustice and intellectual freedom. Those are the things I started developing when I was listening to heavy metal in junior high and high school. Megadeth was a really big influence on me. Several of their songs still resonate with me. Unfortunately, many of the things these bands sung about back then, we have not made improvements on.

Another bit of pop culture that has impacted Sheppard's professional work is the television series *Impractical Jokers* (DeBevoise et al., 2011–), the long-running hidden camera practical joke reality show. Every week on *Impractical Jokers*, the Tenderloins, a comedy troupe, plays pranks on unsuspecting people, and oftentimes they adopt alternate personas in order to sell the gag. The comedians' improvisational abilities really struck a chord with Sheppard:

> I grew up this really poor kid. I came to college really poor. I did not have a ton of support. And I was a heavy metal kid in northeast Arkansas during the West Memphis Three trial, and that had a big impact. So, when I started college, I would have people call me a devil worshipper. I had someone put 'Die, witch die,' on my dorm door. So, I had this feeling that I did not belong. When I became a librarian, that feeling that I did not belong never really went away.

Because of this imposter syndrome, Sheppard felt uncomfortable taking on an advocacy role and addressing issues such as diversity, equity, and inclusion, even though she had a passion for these issues. But watching episodes of *Impractical Jokers* was revelatory:

> You know what? If they could go into a situation and convince people that they are, say a boss of a scientific company, it is not whether or not they had the credentials, it is how they carry themselves. I realized that *I do have the credentials*. I have four degrees. I am smart even if it is tough to admit it. But I have to carry myself with that authority to go and speak about things. It is really funny that improv comedy was what got me to do that.

When Sheppard speaks about social justice issues to a group or even just delivers a one-shot library instruction session to a class of undergraduates, she has learned to channel this authority, even if it might not have always felt completely authentic.

Even though Sheppard had previously felt powerless, experience had taught her that she had something to say. She became actively involved with SRRT following the rash of police brutality against African Americans in the 2010s and 2020s, which resulted in the death, among many other Black men and women, of Tamir Rice. According to its online mission statement, the SRRT:

> [...] works to make ALA more democratic and to establish progressive priorities not only for the Association but also for the entire profession. Concern for human and economic rights was an important element in the founding of SRRT and remains an urgent concern today. SRRT believes that libraries and librarians must recognize and help solve social problems and inequities in order to carry out their mandate to work for the common good and bolster democracy.
>
> (SRRT, n.d.)

In his book, *Progressive Library Organizations: A Worldwide History*, Alfred Kagan (2015) wrote that the SRRT has often been called "ALA's conscience" (p. 209) (See Chapter 12 for a profile of Kagan). Kagan said that, although the ALA had a history of addressing social issues, the SRRT was the first professional organization developed for the explicit purpose of addressing pressing social issues and advocating for social change (p. 153). Since its official recognition in 1969, the task force has adopted multiple resolutions to influence ALA policy. Round Table members shepherd resolutions, which are then brought to the organization's Action Council, i.e., their executive board. Such resolutions have included ones on LGBTQIA2+ rights, intellectual freedom, labor unionization, Nicaragua, South African apartheid, the destruction of libraries in Gaza, and the destruction of libraries in Ukraine.

Sheppard saw SRRT as an organization in which she could make some level of difference. At the time of the interview, Sheppard was still in a Co-coordinator role at SRRT. When asked if there was any project that she was particularly passionate about, she said that she had been working hard to "get SRRT moving":

> There is a lot of institutional knowledge. But there has been a lot of new blood coming in. So, we have really been working on what SRRT will look in 2024, 2025, you know, what the 2030 SRRT looks like. We just did a massive survey of all our members gauging what type of topics are important to our members, making sure that we are addressing those topics that are important to our members. Diversity and racial justice was the number one topic in the survey, and right now we are doing a lot with that. And that is my special interest too. I really hope after I am off the Action Council to start a task force on diversity.

Another recent SRRT accomplishment was a resolution on making membership meetings virtual because of the high cost of travel expenses: "Going to conferences is incredibly expensive and people who cannot physically go to a conference do not get take part in daily government." This commitment to membership inclusion led to a proliferation of virtual programming on a variety of topics, from native treaty rights to indigenous libraries to women and war and libraries. Sheppard was also the author of the SRRT's Resolution Calling for Student Loan Cancellation, which was unanimously passed by the ALA Council in 2022.

Sheppard said that anyone considering social justice-oriented librarianship must, before anything else, learn to separate themselves from criticism—and one should expect to be called unpleasant names because of their library work. Adopting a critical advocate approach to work must be constant; it cannot just be performative. One should not, Sheppard said, claim that they practice socially conscious librarianship and then hide behind closed doors. One should not clock off and then not continue that work. They must be willing to constantly speak out against injustice, racism, and systemic issues. And many times, Sheppard said, this fortitude can be hard:

> [...] especially for someone like me, because I am white. I am straight passing. If I do not want to deal with it, I could turn it off, you know, and go to the grocery store and pretend that I do not see things happening. But a person of color, they do not get that privilege. Or someone who is disable or LGBTQ, they do not get that privilege of turning things off because they do not want to deal with it anymore. So it takes effort to make sure that you are not turning off, at least for me. You have to have the energy, and you have to separate yourself from the criticism because [criticism] will come. You know, us librarians, 'groomers' and 'destroying the youth' and all that stuff.

Mindfulness and intentionality are watchwords for Sheppard. To effectively incorporate social justice into daily work, the library worker must remain mindful of the privilege and power associated with libraries throughout history. So, for example, when selecting books as part of your collection development work, you must make sure that you are really practicing diversity and providing well-rounded collections, not just picking something because it checks off a box on a diversity list. Or, when working with library instruction classes, the librarian should use diverse examples. Maintaining this dedication and vigilance, she said, may result in difficult situations not only with the public but in professional settings as well. Although Sheppard has not been called unkind things by colleagues, she has encountered tense situations on the job. A diversity advocate might, for example, walk into a room, and, all of a sudden, people might get quiet and stare at you. But, Sheppard said, the social justice-oriented library worker must not compromise on their values. "I have been," Sheppard said,

[...] in professional situations with other library workers where we go into a room for a class or meeting, and someone may say 'Oh gosh, thankfully it is just white people, we do not have to watch what we say.' And I will be 'yes, yes we do.'

For the most part, Sheppard sees the diversity and inclusion in libraries as improving, largely because there are more younger people who are willing to speak up when necessary. However, there is still a long way to go, especially when considering the current political climate. Arkansas has seen a recent spate of anti-diversity legislation happening in its school systems, and because of this, many library workers are hesitant to be noticed. The work, however, continues, and one cannot pretend that these things are not happening:

I think there is a whole lot of talk and not enough walking. I think librarians like to pretend like we do not have the '-isms.' The -isms, however, are very strong. Sexism, racism, homophobia, ageism, ableism, all of those things we take a gazillion classes on and we host a gazillion webinars that say, 'do better.' But over and over again, I see the actions of people saying that we really have not made that much improvement. I have been to some ALA events where there is definitely some unspoken racism, some off things, and really recently too. So, we know what we are supposed to do. We are just not doing it.

Sheppard's basic work philosophy is "do no harm," i.e., make a positive impact whenever possible, even when it may be uncomfortable making positive impacts. Academic library work appeals to Sheppard because of the variety of activities that one ends up engaging in, allowing her to teach in the classroom, provide customer service at the reference desk, and perform administrative duties. This variety also supports her professional goal as a library worker, which is to help as many people as she can to "make the world a little better, the university a little better when I leave it. When I retire, I want to leave a positive impact."

References

Burke, S., & The Blind Boys of Alabama. (2002). None of us are free [Song]. On *Don't give up on me*. Fat Possum Records.
DeBevoise, C., Hickman, M., Quinn, B., Murray, J., Vulcano, S., Gatto, J., McPartland, P., & Kustanowitz, S. [Executive Producers]. (2011–present). *Impractical jokers*. NorthSouth Productions.
Kagan, A. (2015). *Progressive library organizations: A worldwide history*. McFarland.
Mann, B., Weil, C., & Russell, B. (1993). None of us are free [Recorded by R. Charles]. On My world. Warner Brothers.
Social Responsibilities Round Table. (n.d.). *Our mission*. American Library Association. https://www.ala.org/srrt

21 Naomi Smith

When this interview was conducted, Naomi Smith, then an academic librarian and subject specialist for Global Black Studies at a London university, was "falling out of love with librarianship." A social justice advocate, Smith's initial excitement for library work had been tempered by her observation that the academic library is closely tied to oppressive bureaucratic and capitalist structures, and she found herself increasingly disillusioned with the institutional constraints that prevented her from fully engaging in social justice-oriented work. In 2024, Smith left academic librarianship to focus on her decolonial consultancy work, bringing with her "my lived experiences, theoretical expertise in Race and Resistance theories, and Decolonial Knowledge Systems to creatively reshape the future of Society by making decolonial ideas accessible, interesting and appealing to Gen-Z and Gen-Alpha especially" (Smith, n.d.).

Smith firmly believes that librarians can be powerful vehicles of social justice. But rather than acting as gatekeepers, they must embrace their role as knowledge facilitators that actively dismantle systemic barriers to information: "librarians are powerful teachers, and they have the potential and the capacity to be very powerful teachers in terms of social justice issues." To accomplish this task, she said that library practice must be shaped by critical theory and decolonial thinking:

> Without an underpinning of some type of critical theory, you may think that just because you are talking about an anti-hegemonic subject, that makes your classroom decolonial. No, the very fact that you are in a classroom makes it colonial. Librarians need to read and expand their knowledge. I appreciate that it can be difficult considering time constraints and the fact that many of these resources are not necessarily accessible. […] But I feel like librarians are the best people to get this knowledge out because they have experience teaching students and different people of the community who have different levels of knowledge, levels of learning, and levels of how they understand information.

Smith said that an important part of decolonial work is recognizing the biases and assumptions that one has grown up with since childhood, and she advocates for a continuous process of "unlearning and relearning" that challenges the colonial structures embedded in education. Undoing this conditioning is key to unlearning and relearning from a decolonized standpoint, and Smith pointed to Paulo Freire's (1970) *Pedagogy of the Oppressed* as particularly applicable to a liberatory library pedagogy in its argument for making education accessible and removing the teacher/pupil relationship reflective of colonialism. Critiquing the traditional "banking" model of education in which the teacher "deposits" information into the passive student, Freire advocated for a reciprocal relationship model between teacher and student where liberation is achieved through collaboration. In the learning process, students develop *conscientização*, or "learning to perceive social, political, and economic contradictions, and to take action against the oppressive elements of reality" (Freire, 1970, p. 35).

Freire's work has shaped Smith's viewpoints on community and the need to educate people about issues like systemic racism that have ripple effects across society. She hopes that people will become more conscious of and open to critical theory, and therefore more critically conscious, so that they will press politicians to create positive change or create that change on their own: "I am big on community and community power, for communities to come together and create the answers for themselves instead of relying on institutions for those answers." Adopting this idea of a participatory educational process where students co-create knowledge rather than passively receive it, Smith sought to create learning environments within her library that subverted traditional hierarchies, made the learning experience more equitable for students, and developed space in the classroom for critical inquiry. For example, instead of teaching at the front of the classroom, Smith had students sit in a circle where everyone could speak and engage with one another and herself during sessions. One of Smith's academic interests is the intersection of fashion and social justice. Having once been a library subject specialist for Fashion and Design, she worked extensively with students to explore topics such as cultural appropriation versus cultural appreciation within the fashion industry. Smith encouraged students to critically examine fashion through a historical lens to better understand the deep cultural significance of styles commodified by the fashion industry. For example, the class discussed the depiction of white models with cornrows and braids as a misinterpretation of these intricate hairstyles' usage during American slavery, where they were used to convey information regarding religion, ethnicity, age, and even escape routes for runaway slaves (Quampaha et al., 2023). Smith encouraged her students to go to the library and read the history of a fashion phenomenon to learn about stereotypes and the evolution and appropriation of culture.

Unfortunately, Smith said, the structure of modern neoliberal academic institutions often hinders Freirean approaches to learning:

> I found that because academic librarians are affiliated with the university, they must work within rigid constraints. There are a lot of things that

universities are doing in reflection of them being neoliberal/capitalist/colonial entities that I do not feel comfortable with. In terms of my values, I do not necessarily feel aligned with them, nor do I feel like I have and the freedom to do what I want to do within that type of structure.

In addition, modern neoliberal educational institutions circumscribe hegemonic boundaries around their employees, and particularly those from marginalized groups. As an academic librarian of color, Smith routinely encountered the disproportionate burden that academic institutions place on faculty and staff from these backgrounds to lead diversity, equity, and inclusion (DEI) initiatives. Being the only Black librarian on her work team, she found herself expected to lead the library's DEI efforts, a burden that was emotionally taxing and often left unacknowledged:

> I am expected to be the person to be at the forefront because I am politically and socially conscious. Issues, like regarding race, I am obviously very heavily and personally invested in these issues, but I just feel it is always me who is the person that is the one to go to, and there is very little regard about the kind of emotional labor. There is very little awareness or understanding about how that expectation is microaggression itself.

The performative nature of institutional DEI efforts was also disheartening. While universities emphasize diverse library collections to market themselves as inclusive spaces, they often fail to engage with real-world issues like racial justice movements or global crises. Smith supports the building of diverse collections for its constituencies but feels that libraries should do more than select books to check off DEI boxes to market to a diverse demographic. Although her academic library had the potential to be a site of activism and social change, Smith said that little work was being done there to discuss race or social justice issues. During the 2024 UK race riots, her library said nothing—Smith was not even asked if she was doing OK—illustrating a stark contrast between the institution's outward commitment to diversity and their inaction during a real crisis. This disconnection reinforced Smith's belief that libraries many times prioritize optics over meaningful change.

Belonging to a marginalized population, Smith also faced microaggressions in professional life. She related her experience participating in a six-week decolonial fashion course for European information professionals:

> That course was enlightening, but it was also very problematic. There were many microaggressions. There was this one class where a participant, I think she works for museums, was talking about how she was committing 'orientalism,' and how she 'got excited by that.' I said that I really objected to her use of the word 'excited' because it is basically saying that she was getting excited by something that has real life

implications for people in my ancestry. They told me that how I was talking was not conducive to everybody sharing knowledge. I felt like they were tone-policing me, and that I should not get upset about the comment.

Increasingly dissatisfied with working within the constraints of the institution, Smith has since left the academic library to focus on two full-time public relations projects that she has developed: Black and Gold Education (https://www.blackandgoldeducation.org/) and DIE4ART (https://www.die4artbynaomi.com/). She said that she is using her experience of being a critical librarian as a roadmap to provide education and advocacy through her consultancy work, and she pointed to Remi Joseph-Salisbury and Laura Connolly's concept of "reparative theft," the theoretical foundation of this application of academic library training and experiences to post-academic library work. In their book *Anti-Racist Scholar-Activism* (Joseph-Salisbury & Connolly, 2021), Joseph-Salisbury and Connolly describe strategies for working within universities to leverage resources as a means of resistance to oppression. In the book's chapter on reparative theft, i.e., liberating knowledge and ideas from academic institutions to create resistance in larger society, the authors argue that "the university holds a range of resources that scholar-activists can and do leverage for communities of resistance" (p. 113). Inspired by this notion, Smith described her own progression from academic librarian to social justice entrepreneur:

> I am taking these ideas outside of the university. That is where the idea for my public relations consultancies came from. [...] Black and Gold Education was in direct response to me just feeling that I cannot really teach the things I want to teach [at the university library], as well as my just viewing institutions as elitist. If you do not go to a university, then you do not really have access to this knowledge. It is behind paywalls. Or if you do have access, a lot of the information is written in elitist language that the everyday person, especially if they have not gone to university, is not going to understand.

With Black and Gold Education (an acronym for "Black Librarian Addressing Critical Knowledge gaps Aiming to start discussions & New ways of thinking for disadvantaged people"), Smith sees her work as an extension of her critical librarianship through the creation of accessible educational content for information professionals that bridges the gap between institutionally bound knowledge and marginalized communities. Through Black and Gold Education, Smith provides public speaking events, workshops, and webinars for academic libraries and decolonial consulting services for educational institutions, like reviewing their educational resources to see if they adequately reflect DEI perspectives and offering them transformative decolonial strategies. This work democratizes information by ensuring that critical information is not confined to universities that often confound marginalized communities with institutional barriers.

Smith's other current project, DIE4ART, is "Creative Activism. Empowering brands, creatives, and influencers to navigate industry and societal challenges with power by telling New Stories rooted in Equity, Imagination and Impact" (DIE4ART, n.d.). Recognizing the influence of popular culture on younger generations, she sees DIE4ART as a platform for engaging in fruitful collaborations with creatives and brands to amplify messages of social change:

> I want to work with brands and creatives to create a positive message related to liberation. I want to discuss with creatives some of the issues that I cannot really discuss in the academic library. I come from a creative background. My friends are in different areas of the music industry and the fashion industry. But as a librarian, I also saw just the influence popular culture has, especially on younger people. So, thinking about trying to create change, and seeing how not many people listen to politicians—maybe this is fortunate because I do not think a lot of politicians are for the people—but younger generations will listen to their favorite rapper, their favorite artist, or their favorite influencer.

Smith pointed to the New York-based organization, The Slow Factory, as an inspiration for her current work. The Slow Factory is dedicated to open-access education that distributes videos on multiple topics aimed at supporting systemic change (The Slow Factory, n.d.). She respects the organization's efforts to influence systematic change, noting that librarians should look at the organization's website and Instagram account (@theslowfactory) as examples of online platforms that provide accessible information in an aesthetically pleasing format:

> From a pedagogical perspective, The Slow Factory is really at the top of my personal inspirations for how I want to teach, the type of things I want to teach, and the intended outcome. I know their social media account has nearly 1 million followers, and that is despite it being very heavily shadow-banned for talking about political topics. I do not really know many purely educational platforms that are so popular.

Smith remains hopeful for the future. She views the post-pandemic period as a time where people question established systems and seek alternative ways to engage with knowledge. She sees change coming and emphasizes the importance of grassroots efforts and community power, believing that real change happens when individuals take action within their own spheres of influence: "everybody has to chip away in their own corner of the world and their own area, and it is all connected." As she moves forward, Smith envisions a future where librarianship, education, and activism interact in a holistic manner, and she is committed to ensuring that critical knowledge reaches those who need it most.

References

DIE4ART. (n.d.). Services. DIE4ART. Retrieved June 24, 2025 from https://www.die4artbynaomi.com/

Freire, P. (1970). *Pedagogy of the oppressed*. Continuum.

Joseph-Salisbury, R., & Connolly, L. (2021). *Anti-racist scholar-activism*. Manchester University Press.

Quampaha, B., Owusub, E., Aduc, V. N., Agyemang Opokud, N., Akyeremfoe, S., & Ahiabor, A. J. (2023). Cornrow: a medium for communicating escape strategies during the transatlantic slave trade era: Evidences from Elmina Castle and Centre for National Culture in Kumasi. *International Journal of Social Sciences: Current and Future Research Trends, 18*, 127–143.

Smith, N. (n.d.). *Healed people heal structures & heal others*. Blackandgoldeducation.org. https://www.blackandgoldeducation.org/

The Slow Factory. (n.d.). The slow factory. Retrieved March 24, 2025, from https://slowfactory.earth/

22 Raegan Swanson

As the Executive Director of The ArQuives: Canada's LGBTQ2+ Archives (https://arquives.ca/), Raegan Swanson negotiates the intersection of archival practice and community empowerment to preserve the voices and histories of marginalized people in the 2SLGBTQIA+ community. Her work is driven by both personal conviction and a profound sense of responsibility, and it challenges one to rethink what it means to collect, preserve, and share histories.

Swanson first encountered archival work during her undergraduate years at College universitaire de Saint-Boniface when she met two influential University of Manitoba archivists: Terry Cook and Tom Nesmith. Cook and Nesmith opened Swanson's eyes to the "wonders and joys of being an archivist." Nesmith's mentorship steered her first toward taking a volunteer position in a community archive and committing herself to preserving the histories of people and communities that are too often overlooked.

After moving to the University of Toronto to pursue a Master of Information degree, Swanson immersed herself in learning about community-driven archives and focused on bridging the gap between diversity-focused archival practices and grassroots initiatives. Upon graduating from UofT, Swanson started her career as a professional archivist. She first worked at Library and Archives Canada, which houses Canada's National Archive and serves to preserve and document Canada's history (Library and Archives Canada, 2025), and then for the Truth and Reconciliation Commission of Canada, an organization established by the Canadian government to identify and investigate the Indian Residential School System as part of the Indian Residential Schools Settlement Agreement (Government of Canada et al., 2024). Having experienced working for government and government-adjacent institutions, Swanson gravitated back to community archives, taking a job at a northern Quebec community archive, the Aanischaaukamikw Cree Cultural Institute (ACCI) in Oujé-Bougoumou, a town with a population of 737 people.

ACCI opened in 2011 with an institutional focus on *aanschaa* (cultural continuity) and the representation of nine Cree communities (Swanson & Graham, 2015, p. 244). When Swanson started at ACCI, her aim was to work *with* the community to build a vibrant archival collection *within* that community. Swanson's approach to archival collection centers on transparency and

DOI: 10.4324/9781003473640-23

community engagement, and she challenges traditional archival practices through her work. Swanson holds that the only places that are safe for marginalized groups are collections that are owned or operated by those communities, and that there cannot be archival autonomy or community building if the collections are not held in or accessible to the community itself. While Swanson recognized that there is a big push to diversify collections that exist in government and in universities and museums, she said that she does not think that those institutions are putting in the work to be upfront about why those collections do not presently exist in their collections.

Swanson cited Elizabeth Kaplan's (2000) article "We Are What We Collect, We Collect What We Are: Archives and the Construction of Identity" as having a particularly profound impact on her approach to managing community archives. In "We are What We Collect," Kaplan investigated the creation of the American Jewish Historical Society (AJHS), using the organization as a case study to explore how identity is constructed through archival collections. Kaplan argued that archivists make fundamental choices concerning how to describe and validate identities, and even though such work may be conducted under a veneer of objectivity or neutrality, "As archivists, we do not seem to recognize that ours is a subjective endeavor" (p. 147). In the article, Kaplan challenges archivists to be mindful in their role of constructing historical memory and identity. The process of appraising, selecting, and organizing archival material inherently carries political and social consequences, influencing how groups are perceived both internally and externally. Kaplan's article ends with a powerful summation of how identity can be misinterpreted or condensed, erasing nuance:

> History constantly reminds us that the reification of ethnic identity does not foster tolerance or acceptance; it constructs communities and then draws hard, arbitrary lines between them, creating differences and making them fixed, constricting the freedom of the individual to define or understand him or herself in multiple ways.
>
> (p. 151)

For Swanson, archival work is more than just organizing documents and artifacts; it is about constructing narratives that faithfully represent community identities, and her efforts to create policies that prioritize community narratives over rigid archival standards reflect this vision. By sharing collection reviews and engaging community members early in the archival process, Swanson reimagines how archives function in a society that is engaged in a process of continual redefinition.

The ACCI was successfully set up under Swanson's lead and has since made significant progress with the Cree communities it serves, ensuring the representation of all identities. The ACCI building accommodates research laboratories to conserve and protect valuable artifacts (Swanson & Graham, 2015, p. 248). Researchers who visit ACCI are asked to sign a research agreement acknowledging that the people of Eeyou Istchee hold the copyright to traditional knowledge and respect local customs (p. 255). Public programming includes tours, workshops, and exhibitions to invite visitors to learn about the Cree culture through storytelling, ancestral connections from past to present, and capturing the voices of Elders for future generations (p. 250). For the library materials, Swanson helped implement the Brian Deer Classification System, "a subject-based classification system that focuses on First Nations/Inuit/Métis and classifies relevant topics such as self-government, rights and title, Elders' stories, and traditional pursuits" (Swanson, 2015, p. 571). This system allowed for nuance in cataloging materials rather than classifying under one call number or mainstream library classification system, e.g., Library of Congress Classification.

Following her experience at ACCI, Swanson's determination to redefine community-driven archives led her in 2016 to her current role as Executive Director of The ArQuives: Canada's LGBTQ2+ Archives, in Toronto. Founded in 1973 by the Canadian Lesbian and Gay magazine *The Body Politic* as the Canadian Gay Liberation Movement Archives (later named the Canadian Gay Archives and Canadian Lesbian and Gay Archives), the community archive was run as a collective, with volunteers—most of whom were community members—putting in hundreds of hours of work to organize and describe collections and materials. At times, operating the archives had been difficult—with police raiding the offices and being called on the archive throughout the 1980s and even into the early 2000s as a means of harassment—but they have since been left relatively free of provocation by bigots with the exception of some online harassment. In 2018, under Swanson's directorship, the Canadian Lesbian and Gay Archives changed its name to The ArQuives and made it clear that it would work to include those silenced and persecuted communities that had previously been marginalized in its collections, collections that had centered primarily on the perspectives and experiences of white, cisgender, gay men (Swanson, 2015).

Swanson recognized the need to better represent those identities that had effectively been archivally erased, including "Black, Indigenous, people of colour, trans, non-binary, bisexual, women, and disabled LGBTQ2+ folks" (ArQuives, 2025). As is the case with many archival institutions, The ArQuives faces internal biases within the communities it serves, and Swanson said that such biases may impact both active and passive collecting and play a part in the construction of community narratives. For example, even within marginalized groups, issues such as transphobia and white supremacy can skew which stories are prioritized. When she first joined the organization, Swanson recognized the extent of diversity within the community it served, i.e., that there are "a bazillion different communities at a bazillion different intersections within that small group." Nevertheless, she saw a history of bias toward transgender and bisexual identities that had resulted in a lack of representation of those identities in the collections. Although Swanson has worked to include those groups that had been edged out of the collections in the past, she has encountered some resistance from white cis gay men—an identity that is well documented in The ArQuives' collections:

> Somehow the idea that engaging those communities [that have been systematically marginalized within The ArQuives] is somehow the exact same as ignoring the people that have been the focus for the last few years. The idea that different identities cannot exist in the same space is a huge part of the challenges that we now face. Getting white cis gay men to realize that their own systemic white supremacy and the colonial mindset that they inherited as part of the generation that they were brought up in and never had to question because they were in positions of privilege, is extremely challenging. Getting them to understand that even though they are gay, they also have privilege, has been tricky at best. They may respond, 'Oh, no, we are not the majority. We were marginalized ourselves.' And it is like, yeah, and then you marginalized other people. Just because you were marginalized does not mean that you are suddenly free of racism and misogyny. There are huge amounts of racism, misogyny, and transphobia. So, it has been and ongoing transition.

Swanson highlighted other challenges faced by The ArQuives, including the inadequacy of traditional organizational methods in supporting community-based projects:

> Rules for Archival Description are handy because the standard prescribes a narrative, and we can adapt it fairly easily for our descriptive practices in the archive. We struggle with our library and museum collections, we struggle because narratives is not standard description and classification style. We are forced to create our own systems and attempt to make our collection meet professional standards, so we do not get the rebuttal that we are not a serious institution while but still making material accessible.

Another obstacle faced by both The ArQuives and the 2SLGBTQIA+ communities it serves is the impact of Toronto's ongoing housing crisis, where even a one-bedroom condo now costs nearly a million dollars. The resulting instability experienced by many community members has directly affected The ArQuives' ability to collect and preserve their histories. With many of its members needing to constantly move due to eviction, the community has little stability to create robust collections of their lives and experiences. The ArQuives also faces a lack of funding when political climates impact the communities they serve and represent. The organization receives only project funding from the government and relies on community members and donors for its operating funds, with a small amount of additional funding coming from local organizations. A large part of Swanson's work involves keeping initiatives going to ensure the partnerships, programming, and day-to-day management are representative of the communities she serves, and Swanson and her team work to create partnerships with academic institutions like Canada's Social Sciences and Humanities Research Council (https://www.sshrc-crsh.gc.ca/home-accueil-eng.aspx) and historians and other scholars working on sexual diversity or historical studies to boost sustainability.

Reflecting on her career thus far, Swanson's story is one of navigating a complex professional landscape where archival standards, community involvement, and identities collide. Whether it is negotiating the delicate balance of inclusivity in archival collections or confronting the practical challenges of sustaining a diverse community archive, Swanson's work forges spaces that are representative of the communities she serves. Her commitment to transparency, community control, and ethical archival practices offers a blueprint for building archives that serve as living, breathing repositories of community memory. When asked about her professional goals, Swanson said:

> I feel weird saying it, but I have kind of met my professional goals. [...] when I started, my goals were clear. I wanted to work in a community space, I wanted to work in a human rights organization, and I wanted the chance to work in a community to build something from the ground up. I hit all those goals. [...] I am still currently in the process of figuring out what my new goals will be because I do not know if I just did not set lofty enough goals, or if I have just been very fortunate in what I have been able to have experience. It is a weird space to be in.

Even though Swanson may have achieved her professional goals, she continues to push forward, not only in terms of community archival practice but also in her research. Swanson recently completed a PhD in Archive and Information Studies at Scotland's University of Dundee, and she described the reason for pursuing the degree as originating from "pure anger and spite" after having discovered that not only are many of the communities served by community archives made up of marginalized groups, but the archives themselves are being marginalized in the professional literature. After starting her job at ACCI, one of Swanson's first steps was to look for case studies of similar Canadian Indigenous community archives for guidance. Unfortunately, she found "nothing, not a thing that was helpful [...] This made me angry. And so that is why I did a case study for my PhD on Indigenous community archives." Not only was there a lack of literature on Indigenous communities and their archival processes but also a dismissal of these community archives' professionalism and status as legitimate archival repositories:

> Community archives get dismissed as not professional, or they are like, 'Oh, that is a community project. It is not an archive.' And my reply is, 'Well, they have got an archivist on staff who is a trained archivist. So, which part is not professional? Is it just that it is not meeting your expectations of what you think professional is?' It has been interesting to dig into. So yeah, spite and anger.

Swanson remains steadfast in her belief that community archives are legitimate and necessary and that they must reflect the full spectrum of community life. Through her work, Swanson is redefining archival practice and empowering communities to reclaim their narratives—one record at a time.

References

ArQuives. (2025). *About us*. The ArQuives. https://arquives.ca/about/

Government of Canada, Relations, C.-I., & Northern Affairs Canada. (2024, December 12). Truth and reconciliation Commission of Canada. Rcaanc-Cirnac.Gc.Ca. https://www.rcaanc-cirnac.gc.ca/eng/1450124405592/1529106060525

Kaplan, E. (2000). We are what we collect, we collect what we are: Archives and the construction of identity. *American Archivist*, 63(1), 126–151.

Library and Archives Canada. (2025, February 17). Library and Archives Canada. Canada.Ca. https://library-archives.canada.ca/eng

Swanson, R. (2015). Adapting the Brian Deer classification system for Aanischaaukamikw Cree Cultural Institute. *Cataloging & Classification Quarterly*, 53(5–6), 568–579.

23 Eamon Tewell

While earning his bachelor's in English from the University of Denver with the hopes of pursuing a career as an author, Eamon Tewell found himself working part-time at the university library circulation desk. It was there that he realized that while "writing books is great, working in a library would be a viable career choice that came with a steady paycheck as well as the satisfaction of connecting people to information and helping them to interpret it." After receiving a master's degree in library and information science from Drexel University's College of Computing and Informatics, Tewell worked his first professional academic librarian jobs in reference and instruction at Sarah Lawrence College and Long Island University before moving into his current position as Head of Research Support and Outreach at Columbia University Libraries. Tewell approaches both library practice and research from a perspective rooted in the critical/cultural study of communication and media.

Tewell credits his drive to identify and challenge oppressive power structures to his upbringing. His mother, an advocate for people with disabilities, encouraged him to question authority and to view existing societal relations with a healthy amount of skepticism. He would later apply the general principles he learned from observing his mother's work to his own work in academic libraries:

> First, I am interested in advancing critical perspectives in libraries. I try and do that through my day-to-day work. It can be through simple things, like one-on-one meetings, looking for opportunities to think about what we are doing as library workers, looking for the assumptions we make as library workers. A lot of my coworkers are responsive to that, identifying oppressive functions of the library and university, situating ourselves within that, finding ways to pay attention to it, and working against it. This is something that I do day-to-day, but also through publishing and presenting. Second, I do whatever I can to support librarians, new librarians, and prospective librarians in the profession.

While Tewell sees academic libraries as sites of learning, he recognizes that they are also sites of oppression. He seeks to understand how libraries, and by extension, library workers, act as barriers through their institutional weight and gatekeeping functions, and he does this with the goal of providing workable interventions. Deeply invested in educating users to navigate the library and world of information, Tewell sees library instruction, whether it be in a classroom setting or individually through the reference interview, as a means for fostering critical perspectives in library patrons.

Prominent British Cultural Studies scholar and former director of the acclaimed University of Birmingham Centre for Contemporary Cultural Studies (CCCS), Stuart Hall (1932–2014), is a major influence on Tewell's approach to librarianship. Hall is known for his development of the encoding/decoding model of communication, which he explicated in a series of influential papers published in the 1970s. Tewell first read Hall's (1973) conference paper, "Encoding and Decoding in the Television Discourse," as a course reading while completing a second master's degree in media arts at Long Island University. The main concept of "Encoding and Decoding" is a simple one, i.e., that mass media messages of all sorts (although Hall focuses on television broadcasts in this paper) all communicate something, whether it is subtext or not. These highly produced messages are sent out to a mass audience and are then decoded by individual audience members. During this decoding, however, something interesting happens. According to Hall's analysis, the messages are not simply received and accepted as held by previous theories of communication transmission like Harold Lasswell's (1927) "hypodermic theory" of communication transmission, in which audience members passively accept the contents of media messages that are broadcast to them, or the Shannon-Weaver (1963) model of communication, in which a message is encoded, transmitted through a channel where it might be altered through encountering "noise," and then decoded. Taking the Shannon-Weaver model, Hall recognized audience member agency in the decoding process. He proposed three possible ways an audience member might react to a particular message: (1) accepting the hegemonic position as presented, (2) rejecting the message, or (3) assuming a negotiated position in relation to it that "accords the privileged [hegemonic] position to the dominant definition of events, whilst reserving the right to make a more negotiated application to 'local conditions'" (Hall, 1973, p. 17). Although Hall used broad strokes when developing these three possible outcomes, other communication and information researchers would explore the model in more detail. For example, Dick Hebdige's (1979) classic book on punk rock subculture, *Subculture: The Meaning of Style*, used Hall's encoding/decoding as a touchstone. Tewell recognized the possible applications of Hall's theory to his work in the academic library:

> Hall's encoding/decoding model is a model for thinking about learning in libraries, people's relationship to search engines, and other advertising platforms… that is, new forms of mass media that extend way beyond TV but still have this essential takeaway, which is that people may go with the dominant hegemonic narrative. They may say, 'sure, that sounds right

to me.' They may take a negotiated position, which is some elements of the message they agree with, and some they do not—kind of a mixed bag. Or they may take a resistant and oppositional approach to it. They are hearing, learning, encountering. So yeah, I apply this approach to libraries, information literacy, and how we engage students in these resistant and oppositional ways of understanding information whether it is the library, whether it is a search engine, whatever it is. So, cultivating a third type oppositional reading.

For Tewell, this might mean taking a text that his library instruction class is working with, or possibly a particular database, and interrogating what is going on behind the scenes with it. For example, investigating questions with the class like, where did the library get a certain database? What other business ventures might the database's publishers be involved with, which, by default, the academic library supports as well? The reference desk also serves as a site for teaching and providing students with oppositional readings of concepts that they—as well as many educators—might not have thought much about or had taken for granted. Tewell offered the traditional scholarly peer-review process as one example:

> One area that has been productive for critical pedagogy is peer review. Students are always asked to find five, seven, possibly ten peer-reviewed articles for the research paper. That continues to be the default. Because of that, it has been a great way to problematize the scholarly process and explain what happens when an article is published, i.e., what goes into that. Like it is typically someone who is doing research as part of their job, maybe in a graduate assistant position. Whatever it is, they are doing it for free for the journal in a concrete sense. So, this might mean the reference librarian explaining what peer review means to some amount and then just having that sort of conversation with students because they are scandalized when they hear about it, 'Really? They do that for free, and the journal publishes it, and the libraries pay for it? That makes no sense.'

Tewell thinks that Hall's encoding/decoding model still holds up today, more than 50 years since he introduced it. This fortitude is likely because the model leaves room for communication researchers to consider how things might play out in different communities and contexts, allowing them to expand beyond Hall's three decoding categories and develop a spectrum of ideological decisions. While Hall dealt with polished media messages and television broadcasts, today's social media platforms and networks of communication that allow push-pull communication exchange open interesting avenues for reconsideration of Hall's work.

Tewell said that critical/cultural communication theories like those of Hall and other CCCS luminaries like Raymond Williams and Richard Hoggart do not often show up much in the library and information science (LIS) research literature. Nevertheless, he said that there are many sources for inspiration outside of the library literature that apply well to the work being done by critical library workers today, including queer theory, anti-racism, and critical race theory. Critical pedagogy has been one that really provided a different direction and knowledge base for teaching in libraries. Tewell suggested the work of author Django Paris as an important source of thinking on the topic of culturally responsive pedagogy. Through books like *Culturally Sustaining Pedagogies: Teaching and Learning for Justice in a Changing World* (Paris, 2017), Paris draws on existing sources of knowledge for students, avoiding as much as possible imposing value judgments about what type of information is useful and what is not. Through his work, Tewell said, Paris really gets to the source of issues faced by libraries, such as why there are hetero-male-oriented collections in every library across North America, and considers why, if you are not actively working on them or at least surfacing these issues, then you are perpetuating the status quo.

The critically conscious and communication-centered approach Tewell has taken in the classroom has led him to extend his research to issues of librarian labor within the library classroom and the library as a whole:

> When you are working with students as a librarian in a classroom setting, there is only so much you can do in that period of time. That got me thinking about time as an issue. Are the faculty and instructors interested in giving up their own class time for our librarians as guest lecturer? It made me realize that, instead of being a time issue, it is more of a broader labor issue in general. So, my time spent at my job doing instruction or otherwise, is my labor. […] I began thinking about it in that context and asking questions like: Okay, if this is the time that I am spending in the classroom, how do I really want to prioritize? How do I choose to spend it? Does that mean teaching dozens of one-hour sessions every semester? And that just leads to burnout. Does that mean saying no to requests if that is even possible?

Tewell's current research explores the implications of the usage of buzzwords and popular concepts in the context of library labor. The word "Resilience" is an example of one such buzzword that has seen increasing use in the academic library. Resilience is used to describe the ability to bounce back from an obstacle or adverse effect that comes in an employee's way, denoting the ability to respond to a challenge, rise above it, and overcome it. Tewell pointed to the COVID-19 pandemic as a catalyst for an uptick in the word's usage in the workplace and the underlying structural issues that are revealed by such buzzwords' usage for human resource management:

> The problem is not the specific buzzword. It is not like if you swap out this buzzword out for another one that everything will be OK.

The buzzword points to these foundational issues of transferring blame and responsibility onto the individual library worker. So, it becomes not the fact that the university made these decisions or that the government made this decision that is the problem, it becomes the way that an individual chooses to respond to the decisions that is really the problem: 'If you just found a way to *be Resilient*, then great, you are on the right track.'

Words like Resilience, Tewell said, draw attention away from systemic issues in the academic library and higher education, such as changes that should be happening within the institutions at a deeper level. So instead of facing such fundamental issues, employees might instead "get weekly emails from human resources to do things like 'join our Mindfulness session and learn how to boost your personal resilience.'" Resilience becomes a means to shift blame elsewhere, i.e., from the systemic issue to the individual who is not being sufficiently Resilient. Tewell pointed to another buzzword used in education: "Grit," a term he investigated thoroughly in a recent article for the journal *portal: Libraries and the Academy* (Tewell, 2020). The library employee is expected to develop their Grittiness and, if they work harder, they will persevere and be successful at their labor: "It is just kind of this cottage industry that aligns well with the use of buzzwords like Resilience and Mindfulness and everything else."

Considering issues like this, insidious institutional coercion, Tewell said that it is important for critical library workers to remain vigilant and to push back as much as they are able to in the positions that they find themselves in, for incorporating change in the most radical way that they can:

> Honestly, I think it leads a lot of the time organizing with colleagues, labor organizing, or just identifying concerns that we need to have addressed as workers. So, it comes down to labor issues. If it is critical librarianship without teeth, then what is the point. But what the teeth look like is very dependent on lens, context, and institution. You know, if you are precariously employed, whatever it is, what you can do really differs.

Tewell noted critical librarianship's increasing popularity among today's library workers. But, although popularity might be a good problem to have, it runs the risks of becoming window dressing, clever yet superficial, and a buzzword:

> Institutions will be like 'Nice! You go have fun in your little class and teach them all about critical perspectives and knock yourself out.' A lot of that has happened. We will continue to have diversity and racism initiatives—which for many US states at this point are not even able to happen under that same language. Just kind of that whole 'encapture,' for lack of a better word, of the critical approach. Institutions will love to just say 'Oh, look at this innovative stuff that we are doing! Good for us!

Keep doing it! We are going to support you in any meaningful way, but we are going to make it so it does not question any of our actual structures or foundations and reflect and change what we are doing. But as long as it does not really change anything, go for it!'

The point then—and this is what Tewell strives to accomplish as an academic librarian—is to get library workers to recognize that they do indeed have teeth. Furthermore, they must put those teeth to good use, transforming not only the realities of their patrons but their own realities as well.

References

Hall, S. (1973). Encoding and decoding in the television discourse. *Council of Europe Colloquy on Training in the Critical Reading of Televisual Language.* http://epapers.bham.ac.uk/2962/

Hebdige, D. (1979). *Subculture: The meaning of style.* Routledge.

Lasswell, H. (1927). *Propaganda technique in world war.* A.A. Knopf.

Paris, D. (2017). *Culturally sustaining pedagogies: Teaching and learning for justice in a changing world.* Teachers College Press.

Tewell, E. (2020). The problem with Grit: Dismantling deficit thinking in information literacy instruction. *Portal: Libraries and the Academy, 20*(1), 137–159.

Weaver, W. (1963). *The mathematical theory of communication.* University of Illinois Press.

24 Jessamyn West

A long-time public librarian, Jessamyn West is a seasoned information technologist dedicated to improving digital literacy and bridging the digital divide through active civic engagement. Currently, she juggles multiple roles; among other things, she engages in frequent public speaking engagements at libraries and on technology, writes a column for the magazine *Information Advisor's Guide to Internet Research*, is a community manager for the Flickr Foundation, and assists patrons with technology at her local public library.

West's commitment to community involvement was inspired by the example of her mother, who worked from home and was always deeply involved in the local community. Her father was a technologist, which meant that she was exposed to computers and digital tools from an early age. Because of this, she sees herself as a bridge connecting community and technology—an advocate for accessibility and inclusivity:

> The main thing that makes me good at what I do is, I understand technology. But I can also explain technology to somebody who does not understand it, and I understand community values and library values. I share them. I can explain them to tech people who often are not necessarily geared that way. They just want to build a thing that does the thing they want done. And you must remind them to think about accessibility, think about how people can use this tool for abuse. Think about the community aspects if you have got people as part of your community. So, I bring the human side to tech and the tech side to people.

West said that for libraries to remain effective, they must adapt in response to technological shifts, community needs, and larger systemic challenges. She also sees the role of the activist librarian as extending beyond the walls of the library itself. A long-time advocate for social justice, West has been bringing information out to the people for years. She is responsible, e.g., for initiating mobile reference services at the 1999 World Trade Organization (WTO) protests in Seattle. Living in Seattle at the time of the protests, West said that she was planning on going to the action just like everyone else:

> But when I went to WTO, I showed up in a sort of community space where a whole bunch of people were getting together. I walked in and there is this kind of triage table where somebody asked me whether I would like to be part of this group or that group and what would I like to help with as part of this big protest going down. I told them that what I really wanted to do was their job. They said 'great!' and got out from behind the table and put me behind it. That is my joy, figuring out what is going on and figuring out what people need. In this case, it was a lot of directing people to housing or transportation. It was not rocket science, and there was no technology involved beyond pieces of paper.

On protest day, West joined the "green coalition," which provided support services to frontline protesters. She scrawled "Ask Me" across her chest and picked up a flag, becoming a "street librarian" and providing necessary information to protesters. The next day she left for Massachusetts to spend Thanksgiving with her family:

> I feel like we accomplished some of what we wanted to accomplish. Sometimes people look at protests like Occupy Wall Street and they are like, 'Yeah, but did it work?' But there are a lot of conflicting goals. What does 'worked' mean in the case of the WTO protests? It worked for a time like Hakim Bey's (1991) idea of temporary autonomous zones, where you are in a place that is temporal in addition to spatial that can become a period of profound activity and change. And it does not have to last forever.

West later initiated a similar street reference service at the Burning Man arts festival. Her efforts at the WTO and Burning Man did not go unnoticed, and they would later serve as a model for other street-level library advocacy groups, including Radical Reference (see Chapter 9 for more on Radical Reference). West sees being in the community and answering questions as at the core of library workers' heart of hearts, but said that most librarians end up practicing librarianship,

> in this weird artificial way, where they do it when they go to work and stop doing it when they leave work. I do not want to be a vocational awe weirdo and be like 'it is my calling.' It is certainly not my calling, but it is something that I cannot not do.
> (see Chapter 8 for more on the concept of vocational awe)

West's drive to get information out to those who need it is also reflected in her continuing efforts to bridge the digital divide, a topic about which she has frequently written and presented. In 2011, West published the book *Without a Net: Librarians Bridging the Digital Divide*, which presents the concept to library workers in an easily digestible way while providing them with workable strategies (West, 2011). She said that much of what was happening in 2011 with the digital divide is still going on today. For example, companies are still telling consumers that they have one neat trick to solve the digital divide or that it is just the people who do not have access to technology who do not want it:

> I think that it is denigrating to people who are not able to get online or get broadband, who may have food instability or cell phone instability or whatever. And meanwhile, what we really have seen happen, is the rapid acceleration in certain places of things like ubiquitous broadband, 5g, and mobile. […] When I go to bigger cities that have much more technology imbued in much more parts of their life, and seeing just how it is different, but how also people just they think about the world differently, because they have different technological affordances. And I feel like that slowly changes culture.

While large urban centers are reaping the benefits of new communication technologies, places like the small Vermont town where West resides are not keeping pace. She said that the disparity she currently sees is because this difference in the acceleration of technological change is resulting in the creation of different classes of people in a society that was once more homogenous. In addition to library users, library workers are facing their own digital divide. Librarians are not necessarily on the cutting edge of technological knowledge, but, in many ways, technology has "become the job." They are constantly faced with increasingly sophisticated technology problems, both when helping library patrons navigate their technology problems and when facing their own knowledge gaps. Navigating this terrain to do things like combat rampant online misinformation and predation requires an immense amount of knowledge on the librarian's part. Because of this, library professionals with advanced technological skills and credentials tend to move to urban areas to take advantage of higher-paying jobs:

> Where I live, I am pretty much the only person who works at the library with what I would perceive to be a sophisticated understanding of these technological issues. The other people that I work with have more sophisticated understandings about other things. I do not know the Dewey Decimal System, and we use that every day.

This disparity often leaves rural areas in a lurch, making it tricky for librarians in large swaths of the US to adequately provide their communities with service.

West has witnessed the digital divide firsthand in her small-town public library, where many patrons, particularly older patrons, are unfamiliar with information and communication technology and struggle with using it. She said that she feels that it is her responsibility not only to provide information but also to foster digital literacy to narrow these technology-based knowledge gaps.

In a way, this community-level work reminds West of former Library of Congress reference librarian Thomas Mann's (1987) championing of open stacks library shelving systems versus keeping information behind locked doors. Similar to closed stacks, information and communication technology often renders resources hidden or inaccessible to novice learners:

> A lot of what I do is kind of report almost sociologically on the problems people have, why I think they are having them, what I think might fix them, because my audience, such as it is, is sort of a combination of library people and technology people. And I think for library people, it is helpful to know what is going to come up, and for tech people, it is helpful to know what people have problems with.

A core element of West's philosophy is that libraries should serve as spaces where people feel comfortable learning. She approaches technological instruction with patience, recognizing that many barriers to learning are not technical but psychologically rooted in anxiety, lack of confidence, or previous negative experiences with technology. She recounted stories of patrons struggling with fundamental computer skills, such as saving documents, and highlighted the importance of non-judgmental guidance. When asked for an influential work that impacted her work, West pointed to a pamphlet by American computer scientist Phil Agre (1996), "How to Help Someone Use a Computer." Agre's pamphlet lists 30 helpful points on assisting and reflecting on novice computer users' perspectives. West believes that library workers see themselves as do-gooders, but that attitude can come with implicit judgments. People can become pitted against technology and feel like they are in a losing battle. Because of this, being a non-judgmental ally is one of the most important parts of helping people with technology, and Agre provides helpful tips to create solidarity with technology-challenged patrons:

> There are a lot of pieces of Agre's advice that I bring up. One of them is when they blame themselves, blame the computer, you know, if they, if they say that they are bad at this, you say it is the computer's fault. And then it is like you and the person against the computer, not them feeling like they are fighting a robot, and they are losing. There are a lot of concepts there that are really helpful. But the other one that I bring up time and time again is that knowledge lives in communities.

The 14th point on Agre's list is "Knowledge lives in communities, not individuals. A computer user who's part of a community of computer users will have an easier time than one who isn't" (Agre, 1996). West told librarians that they must always keep this in mind and think deeply about where people and communities get their information. As her public library's "computer lady," West always tries to challenge her patrons to develop their skills rather than do everything for them; it is gratifying to help people evolve with technology, and she wants to show people how to solve problems, whether it is through constructing Google queries or demonstrating how to use software.

Since the start of her career, West's commitment to information activism has also long been deeply connected to her professional service. During the early days of her career, West became involved with the American Library Association's (ALA) Social Responsibility Roundtable (SRRT) (see Chapter 20 on April Sheppard for more on SRRT), providing her with the opportunity to work with many old-guard progressive librarians like Herb Biblo, E.J. Josie, Mark Rosenzweig, and Al Kagan (see Chapter 12 for more on Kagan). Having previously read *Revolting Librarians* (West & Katz, 1972), the classic anthology of essays on radical librarianship edited by Celeste West and Elizabeth Katz, West was able to match the names appearing in the book to many of the people she met through ALA and SRRT. From this meeting of old and new, West and critical cataloger K.R. Roberto (2003) determined to publish a follow-up to *Revolting Librarians*—*Revolting Librarians Redux: Radical Librarians Speak Out*:

> We got this idea that with all the legends still around—Celeste was still around—we can probably talk to them and see how it went for them. What happened? Would you be willing to write some stuff? It was not supposed to be a retrospective, but talking to them as well as talking to the next generation of people who espoused similar values.

For (Jessamyn) West, it was a great experience assembling all of these people, the old guard and the new, and West was thrilled that the book got picked up by early-career librarians who read it, realized that there were other people like themselves out there, and went on to build their own networks and communities of progressive librarians. When asked if it is time for a third *Revolting Librarians*, West said that she would leave that up to some other young librarian. She remains, however, excited about the state of critical librarianship today, which she sees as now being at a high level within the profession:

> People of my era have influenced a younger generation of librarians who feel like critical librarianship is one of the essential parts of librarianship. It makes me happy, because we have made an effect. I think people know about it in library school. I think that they meet people who are not afraid to talk about it out loud.

West has also seen how advances in information and communication technology have allowed her library colleagues to create things like Homosaurus (https://homosaurus.org/), a cataloging language that is incredibly inclusive of all sorts of LGBTQIA2+ terms. These advances, West said, have come just in time: "This stupid government administration and all the stupid people in it, they have got their weird programs, and part of their programs is trying to keep people from being able to educate themselves." The creation of distributed, slightly underground ways to get information to people is refreshing and will likely be effective "if we do not shy away from the fact that now is our time, and this is what we have been training for."

West's career is a testament to the adaptability required of modern librarians, reinforcing the profession's role in shaping access to information in an increasingly digital world and the evolving nature of librarianship. No longer confined to physical collections, librarians now serve as digital navigators, community advocates, and policy influencers. West's insights underscore the importance of adaptability, clear communication, and a commitment to equity. As libraries adapt to technological advancements and shifting societal needs, professionals like West remind us that librarianship is not merely about information management—it is about empowerment, advocacy, and lifelong learning. By embracing technology while maintaining a strong commitment to human-centered values, librarians can ensure their relevance in the digital age.

References

Agre, P. (1996). *How to help someone use a computer*. Retrieved February 20, 2025, from https://pages.gseis.ucla.edu/faculty/agre/how-to-help.html

Bey, H. (1991). *T.A.Z: The temporary autonomous zone, ontological anarchy, poetic terrorism*. Wiretap.

Mann, T. (1987). *A guide to library research methods*. Oxford University Press.

West, C. & Katz, E. (Eds). (1972). *Revolting librarians*. Booklegger Press.

West, J. C. (2011). *Without a net: Librarians bridging the digital divide*. Libraries Unlimited.

West, J. C. & Roberto, K. R. (Eds.). (2003). *Revolting librarians redux: Radical librarians speak out*. McFarland.

25 Baharak Yousefi

Whether conscious of it or not, library professionals must navigate the broader social and political implications of their roles. Baharak Yousefi, an academic librarian and PhD candidate in geography at Simon Fraser University, recognizes this complex reality and epitomizes critically conscious practice. With a background in psychology, women's studies, and library and information studies, she brings an interdisciplinary approach to library work that is unapologetically activist and challenges traditional disciplinary boundaries.

Born in Shiraz, Iran, Yousefi immigrated to Canada as a teenager. After completing a bachelor's degree in psychology and a master's in women's studies at Simon Fraser University, she pursued a master's degree in library and information studies at the University of British Columbia after being drawn by library work's potential for both intellectual inquiry and community engagement. Her first job out of library school, however, was not in a library but for a Canadian software company beta-testing an online public access catalog with several library systems across the country. Even though she found this work to be an interesting experience that provided her insight into the technological aspects of library work, Yousefi ultimately wanted to work in libraries themselves:

> I ended up working in a large public library system here in Vancouver. I began as an on-call librarian and ended up being a teen librarian, which was just an incredibly rewarding position. I loved it. I worked with really great people. It was my first real librarian job, and I learned a ton. I just loved a lot of the aspects of public librarianship, especially, the variety of it. You never know what question you are going to be asked, and I enjoyed the ability to be able to help folks immediately. I also had the opportunity in that job to work with a few colleagues that were at the forefront of this community-led librarianship movement that was emerging in the 2000s in Canada, which ended up being just a fantastic experience for me personally.

Yousefi's experience in public librarianship provided her with a strong foundation in community-centered library services. However, the appeal of academic freedom and research eventually led her to transition into academic librarianship. She has spent the past 14 years at Simon Fraser University Libraries in various roles, including as a middle manager and as a subject liaison in humanities and social sciences.

In her current position as a librarian for history, political science, international studies, and graduate liberal studies, Yousefi fits into a "Jill of All Trades" practitioner model, providing instruction, research consultations, and collection development. She is deeply interested in information literacy work and advocates for an engaged literacy program as an alternative to the traditional model, where the librarian provides a single instructional session to students as part of a semester-length course:

> I do not see the 'one-shot' model, which is the norm at my institution, as working for learners. I do not think folks are learning. That has been a struggle and a great source of frustration for me. Ultimately, it is frustrating to see undergraduate education and a lot of our universities not being a priority, to put it bluntly. Doing advocacy work in that has been a goal.

Yousefi described the aggravation of conducting a fifty-minute one-shot instruction session that does not resonate with students. She goes into many of these sessions knowing little about students' backgrounds and what they already know or do not know about library research, making it difficult to assess prior knowledge or build meaningful research skills. Furthermore, it is challenging to create a connection with students when the librarian will likely never see many of them again. Yousefi said that it is impossible to ensure that students leaving one-shots feel confident in their research skills, but that such barriers can be eliminated. If students are not truly learning how to critically engage with the research process—something difficult to achieve using the "one-shot" model—there needs to be a broader commitment to a model of undergraduate education that integrates research skills more comprehensively into the educational process. She envisions a model where information professionals are embedded into curricula, supporting students throughout their academic careers rather than showing up as one-time guest lecturers. Recognizing the barriers within current instructional models, Yousefi sees an opportunity for librarians to push for systemic change by developing deeper collaborations with teaching faculty to improve research literacy and create a more sustainable model for information instruction.

Considering that Yousefi's ideas concerning library instruction place an emphasis on the development and maintenance of relationships, it makes sense that her work is informed by both feminist theory and labor-organizing principles. As a unionized library worker, she has been actively involved in advocacy efforts surrounding librarianship and professionalization, de-professionalization trends that threaten the field, and the value of the master of library and information science (MLIS) degree. In the past, she has served on her library worker union's executive board and remains vocal about labor issues, particularly the need for library workers to play a more significant role in institutional decision-making processes. She sees library work as a continual process of study and advocacy that requires information workers to develop their critical consciousness concerning institutional power dynamics for them to be able to actively shape the field:

> I define myself when the opportunity comes up as part of the critical librarianship movement, which to me, means understanding that things can be different, and also understanding that we are the folks who are going to have to make the difference. It is just not going to come down from anywhere. I always say I am interested in libraries as sites of study, solidarity, and struggle, and those three things really go hand in hand for me. I think we are just going to keep having to learn, if that makes sense, and we have to set up things that can help us do that.

Yousefi has no interest in library impartiality or neutrality and believes that librarianship is inherently political, particularly considering that it is a terrain facing issues like censorship and the weaponization of information. She does not think that librarians should "keep their heads down," even though she understands why many library workers just want to clock in and out without making waves. She said that the torpor resulting from willful inaction is just as impactful as socially conscious advocacy, but negatively so. Ultimately, Yousefi said, making a positive impact through library work must center on the belief that libraries, "despite all the issues we have with them, are worth our time, efforts, and lives." Because of this, she remains deeply committed to creating spaces for librarians to engage in professional learning and critical discourse; she is not interested in traditional professional learning models but in conspiring with fellow librarians to understand institutional structures and structures of power.

Yousefi said that the *Combahee River Collective Statement* (Combahee River Collective, 1977), a bedrock text of Black feminism and identity politics, greatly influenced her development as a critical library worker, and she considers it foundational to both her professional praxis and identity as a feminist:

> I am a feminist. It is my training. I would say it is my politics. And specifically, I would define myself more as an anti-colonial, anti-imperialist, anti-capitalist, internationalist feminist, so very broad description of feminism. The *Combahee River Collective Statement* is something that has been particularly formative and grounding for me throughout the years. What it has helped me do, over and over again, is help me remember that we are part of each other's struggle [...]

The Combahee River Collective was a Black feminist and lesbian organization operating from 1974 to 1980 that challenged capitalism, racism, and sexism (Anders, 2012). Published in 1977, the *Statement* analyzes the struggles of Black women under capitalist patriarchy, shining a light on "racial, sexual, heterosexual, and class oppression" (Combahee River Collective, 1977). The *Statement* demands Black women's right to be recognized as human, positing that the only way to achieve liberation is through the destruction of capitalism, imperialism, and patriarchy. In the process, the *Statement* provides one of the first examinations of identity politics and what would later be termed intersectionality (Crenshaw, 1989):

> We believe that sexual politics under patriarchy is as pervasive in Black women's lives as are the politics of class and race. We also often find it difficult to separate race from class from sex oppression because in our lives they are most often experienced simultaneously. We know that there is such a thing as racial-sexual oppression which is neither solely racial nor solely sexual, e.g., the history of rape of Black women by white men as a weapon of political repression.
> (Combahee River Collective, 1977)

The *Statement*, Yousefi said, could be viewed by library workers as a tool for better understanding the relationship of librarianship qua feminized profession to the power held by the patriarchy. In a broader sense, she said, the *Statement* can be examined in the context of power struggles in librarianship as a profession, and it has helped her believe in and advocate for the notion of self-determination in a hierarchically structured institution:

> One thing that I really believe in is that libraries need to be run by library workers. I think our libraries should be collegially run, democratically run. I am honestly under no illusion that that kind of setup, or whatever library workers decide for ourselves, will be easy or it will solve our problems. But I do think it is a very reasonable alternative to this top-down hierarchical library leadership that is very prevalent here in libraries. The library, in the public library sphere, for sure, and in academic libraries as well, does not have the same collegial governance structures that our colleagues in the departments do. And again, I am not saying departments are run with no dysfunction at all, but we need to have more say in how our libraries are run and we need to understand why things are the way things are. So, these are some of the ways that this statement and these philosophies have influenced me.

Librarians must examine their work within these hierarchical structures and reflect on how these institutions are constructed to place limits on them. Yousefi questioned whether library administration, a small group of people, can truly solve libraries' problems. Instead, she called on librarians to assert their own expertise in shaping the profession's future.

In addition to the *Combahee River Collective Statement*, Yousefi is inspired by several other scholars and writers who analyze and challenge dominant power structures. One of these scholars is Ruth Wilson Gilmore, a geographer, social theorist, prison abolitionist, and currently a Professor of Earth and Environmental Sciences, Africana Studies, and American Studies and Director of the Center for Place, Culture and Politics at CUNY Graduate Center. The author of multiple influential books, including *Golden Gulag: Prisons, Surplus, Crisis, and Opposition in Globalizing California* (Gilmore, 2007) and *Abolition Geography: Essays Towards Liberation* (Gilmore, 2022), Gilmore said,

> Being a good geographer means going to look and see, and then to challenge oneself in one's description of what one is seeing. But politically, it is giving all the attention you have to the thing so you understand how it works.
>
> (Card, 2020)

Yousefi sees Gilmore's philosophy as foundational to her own approach to library work, urging librarians to critically analyze the forces shaping their work rather than passively accepting institutional norms. Librarians cannot simply observe from a distance but must get into the nitty-gritty nuance of why things are happening the way that they are.

Yousefi also looks to the work of feminist political activist Angela Davis as a guide to resisting dominant power structures. Although librarianship may be described as a feminized profession—women overwhelmingly dominate the library science field (Statistics Canada, 2022)—Yousefi agrees with Davis's understanding of feminism as "not as something grounded in gendered bodies, but as an approach—as a way of conceptualizing, as a methodology, as a guide to strategies for struggle" (Davis, 2016, p. 33).

In addition to Gilmore and Davis, Yousefi cited Arundhati Roy and Sara Ahmed as important influences. Roy is best known for her book, *The God of Small Things* (Roy, 1997), winner of the 1997 Booker Prize for Fiction. In *The God of Small Things*, Roy follows the lives of fraternal twins in India to examine colonialism, social injustice, and the Indian caste system. Ahmed, a British-Australian feminist scholar and the author of *The Cultural Politics of Emotion* (Ahmed, 2014), theorizes emotions as a social presence that circulates between persons, creating "surfaces and boundaries" as they respond to objects and others.

Grounded in these critical perspectives, Yousefi applies her understanding of power, resistance, and social justice to librarianship, particularly in her exploration of feminist advocacy and leadership within library spaces. Yousefi's 2017 co-edited book, *Feminists Among Us: Resistance and Advocacy in Library Leadership* (Lew & Yousefi, 2017), grounds professional praxis and library leadership in feminist theory. The book's various chapters explore the intersections of gender, race, sexuality, and class within information and library settings, examining phenomena like the feminization of librarianship and exploring the conversations surrounding community and leadership in libraries.

The challenges faced by libraries signal a turning point for a profession in an increasingly precarious position. As library professionals navigate a world marked by the proliferation of misinformation, censorship, and the corporate control of knowledge, Yousefi sees an urgent need for library workers to advocate for access and equity—and she sees feminist theory as invaluable to achieving these goals. While Yousefi said that she has a hard time at this historical moment picturing the future of the library, she remains committed to it as a site of both scholarship and activism. She will continue to advocate for a profession that prioritizes justice, freedom, and self-determination for library workers and their communities. Through research, advocacy, and direct engagement with students and colleagues, Yousefi embodies a librarianship that is both intellectually rigorous and unapologetically political—neutrality is not an option.

References

Ahmed, S. (2014). *The cultural politics of emotion* (2nd ed.). Routledge.

Anders, T. (2012). Combahee River Collective (1974–1980). *BlackPast.org*. https://www.blackpast.org/african-american-history/combahee-river-collective-1974-1980/

Card, K. (2020, May 29). Geographies of racial capitalism with Ruth Wilson Gilmore. *Antipode Online*. https://antipodeonline.org/geographies-of-racial-capitalism/ Accessed March 14, 2025.

Combahee River Collective. (1977). *The Combahee River Collective Statement*. https://www.blackpast.org/african-american-history/combahee-river-collective-statement-1977/ Accessed March 14, 2025.

Crenshaw, K. (1989). Demarginalizing the intersection of race and sex: A Black feminist critique of antidiscrimination doctrine, feminist theory, and antiracist politics. *University of Chicago Legal Forum*, 1989(1), 139–167. http://chicagounbound.uchicago.edu/uclf/vol1989/iss1/8

Davis, A. Y. (2016). *Freedom is a constant struggle: Ferguson, Palestine, and the foundations of a movement*. Haymarket Books.

Gilmore, R. G. (2007). *Golden gulag: Prisons, surplus, crisis, and opposition in globalizing California*. University of California Press.

Gilmore, R. G. (2022). *Abolition geography: Essays towards liberation*. University of California Press.

Lew, S. & Yousefi, B. (2017). *Feminists among us: Resistance and advocacy in library leadership*. Library Juice Press.

Roy, A. (1997). *The god of small things*. HarperCollins.

Statistics Canada. (2022, November 30). *2021 Census and the LIS Community*. Librarianship.Ca. https://librarianship.ca/features/2021-census-and-the-lis-community/

Epilogue

We would like to conclude this book with a few brief observations concerning the project as well as an annotated bibliography, the #critbib, which collects the inspirational sources discussed by participants in their interviews.

First off, counter-hegemony is alive and well in libraries of all types, which is testament to both that library workers have for social justice and related issues as well as the good work happening in library schools. Only 26 library and information science professionals were interviewed for this book, but there are many more out there. Although academic librarians and library school professors seem more likely to speak about their critical library work openly, resistance is happening in public and school libraries, even if the library workers engaging in it may be more prone to flying under the radar for their own professional welfare. Although we were only able to get a few public and school librarians to agree to take part in interviews, we learned about many more during these conversations who are also fighting the good fight, particularly concerning intellectual freedom issues like book banning.

We learned that inspiration for one's professional work comes in many different forms, whether that be a massive tome like *Capital, Volume 1*, a punk record like *The Shape of Punk to Come*, or an organization like Radical Reference. We will never be able to watch the hidden camera television show *Impractical Jokers* in the same way again.

Many of the participants pinpointed significant scholars who oppose racism and colonial-neoliberal institutions prevalent in society today, and intentional reflexive engagement within critical liberatory frameworks prevailed. Libraries and archives are places to build community, as well as to find refuge and one's identity in a book. The participants recognized that their activism infused their professional praxis and strengthened their support of marginalized communities through material action relating to social justice. Consistently, they demanded equity for the constituencies served by libraries and archives, and they stressed the need to actively resist the hegemony of the dominant culture, whether through building upon the ideas contained within a journal article like "*Demarginalizing the Intersection of Race and Sex*" or championing a pamphlet on "How to Help Someone Use a Computer." Our participants made it clear that this work is rewarding but also difficult. Balancing labor and the work that librarians do cannot be overlooked; empathy and care are vital for information workers' emotional and political well-being.

Finally, even though we engaged in interviews with individuals, we were struck by just how closely connected the community of *critical voices* is. Participants constantly referenced each other's work. We also made it a practice to ask participants during the interviews to suggest other people that we might contact to chat with (the well-tested "snowball" technique). Many times, the suggestions that we received were for people whom we had already agreed to interview or whom we had tried to contact for an interview. This may have something to do with the large number of academic librarians in our sample, but we discovered that the public and school librarians all seemed to know about each other's work or have collaborated with each other on projects. If we are, as Toni Samek suggested in her interview, on the cusp of a "post-critical" library work, the community basis for such a movement appears to be well on the way to being in place, and the mutual respect and willingness to collaborate that we observed suggests that Samek's hope for something that is clearly defined, rigorous, and focused does indeed appear to be possible.

The #critbib

We have compiled this list of inspirations discussed by this book project's participants and present it below in the form of an annotated bibliography. We have cleverly (at least we thought it was clever at the time) titled the list #critbib as a play on the #critlib hashtag that was popular several years ago, before Elon Musk's takeover of Facebook (now X). The reader will note that the list contains more than 26 entries (the number of participants). Although we asked participants to come prepared to talk about a particular intellectual or artistic work that had made an impact on their professional development, work, or identity, some were unable to decide on just one. While nobody specifically selected Fobazi Ettarh's article on "vocational awe," we decided to include it because so many participants spoke about vocational awe in their interviews.

It is our hope that the #critbib will not only provide insight into these *critical voices'* motivations and professional identities but that it will also point budding activist library workers to valuable resources, no matter how unconventional some of them may be.

Bibliography

Adams, C. J. (1990). *The sexual politics of meat: A feminist-vegetarian critical theory*. Bloomsbury Academic.
First published in 1990, Carol J. Adams's *Sexual Politics of Meat* is an eco-feminist critique of the patriarchal conflation of women with cooked animals. Adams employs Derrida's concept of "the absent referent" to articulate a link between the bodies of females and animals, alienating them both from their identities and rendering them non-existent objects. Following upon her analysis, Adams advocates for a feminist veganism.

Agre, P. (1996). *How to help someone use a computer.* https://pages.gseis.ucla.edu/faculty/agre/how-to-help.html Accessed February 20, 2025.
Phil Agre created this helpful guide for people advising beginners about computers. Considering that only the last couple of generations were born digital natives, this thoughtful list of suggestions combines empathy with positive reinforcement to navigate technology. Agre encourages community-centered learning.

Ahmed, Samira. (2019, August 14). Internment author Samira Ahmed at SLJ Teen Live. *LB School & Library Podcast.* https://podcasts.apple.com/us/podcast/internment-author-samira-ahmed-at-slj-teen-live/id1019181903?i=1000446913428
The LB School & Library Podcast presents author Samira Ahmed's 2019 keynote address at the *School Library Journal* Teen Live! virtual event. The author of popular young adult books, including the *New York Times* bestseller *Internment*, Ahmed spoke about the need for diversity in young adult literature and how attendees should use their power and privilege to empower marginalized groups.

Ahmed, Sara. (2014). *The cultural politics of emotion.* Routledge.
In this book, feminist scholar Sara Ahmed explores how emotions form identities and systems of power. Ahmed examined how emotions are often associated with women's bodies, providing an in-depth accounting of "cultural politics." She considers fear, hate, and love in the context of performativity and analyzes how emotions impact both community and individualized identity. A key text in the emerging field of affect theory.

Alcott, L. M. (1869). *Little women.* Roberts Brothers.
Louisa May Alcott's *Little Women* is a classic coming-of-age novel that follows the lives of the four March sisters as they grow up in Civil War-era New England. The novel explores the dynamics between four sisters as they navigate family, maturity, love, and sisterhood. Remarkable for the time, *Little Women* challenges conventional expectations of femininity.

Anderson, L. H. (1999). *Speak.* Penguin.
Laurie Halse Anderson's bestselling young adult novel is the story of Melinda, a teenage rape survivor who has withdrawn into herself. Over the course of the novel, Melinda finds her voice. Despite winning multiple awards and honors, including being named a 1999 National Book Award Finalist, *Speak* was controversial at the time of its publication and remains a target for book banners. Later versions of the book include an afterword by Anderson in which she discusses her anti-censorship position and activism.

Bishop, R. S. (1990). Mirrors, windows, and sliding glass doors. *Perspectives: Choosing and Using Books for the Classroom, 6*(3), 1–2.
In this brief essay, educator Rudine Sims Bishop describes books as entry points into fantastic worlds, inviting their readers to enter. Sims Bishop notes that books can also be seen as mirrors, reflecting identity and representation through stories that capture diverse experiences. She emphasizes the importance of diverse representation in children's literature, championing inclusive storytelling rather than ethnocentrism.

Bowker, G. C., & Star, S. L. (1999). *Sorting things out: Classification and its consequences.* MIT Press.
Geoffrey C. Bowker and Susan Leigh Star's *Sorting Things Out* explores the political and social consequences of classification systems through their largely hidden role in shaping modern information infrastructure. Using multiple examples ranging from comprehensive medical classification to simple desktop organization, the authors demonstrate how categories structure resource access while scaffolding systems of power. Bowker and Star explore the moral and ethical implications of classification

work, revealing how even mundane organization systems marginalize individuals and endanger communities.

Burke, S., & The Blind Boys of Alabama. (2002). None of us are free [Song]. On *Don't give up on me*. Fat Possum Records.
This is soul man Solomon Burke (1940–2010) and the Blind Boys of Alabama's definitive rendition of the 1993 protest song penned by Barry Mann, Cynthia Weil, and Brenda Russell and originally sung by Ray Charles. The track appeared on Burke's late-career comeback album, *Don't Give Up on Me*. A rhythm and blues song with strong influences from gospel music, None of Us Are Free's lyrics call for solidarity and mutual care in the struggle for human and civil rights.

Combahee River Collective. (1977). *The Combahee River Collective Statement*. https://www.blackpast.org/african-american-history/combahee-river-collective-statement-1977/ Accessed March 14, 2025.
This is a foundational text in Black feminist sociopolitical thought. Authored by the Combahee River Collective, a Black lesbian feminist collective, the *Statement* argues that the intersection of racism, sexism, heterosexism, and classism act as interlocking systems of oppression. It critiques the exclusion of Black women by white feminists who do not recognize their own racism. The *Statement* calls for the liberation of Black women and the dismantling of capitalism, imperialism, and patriarchy.

Coville, B. (1994). "Am I blue?" In M. D. Bauer (Ed.), *Am I blue?: Coming out from the silence* (pp. 1–16). Harper Collins.
Bruce Coville's LGBTQIA2+ oriented young adult short story "Am I Blue" is the humorous tale of protagonist Vince, who faces bullying while coming to terms with their sexuality. Receiving three wishes from their fairy godfather, Vince decides to make it so that all gay people are temporarily turned the color. The story is a frequent target of book-banning attempts. "Am Blue" was included in the Marion Dane Bauer-edited short story collection of the same name, which was awarded the American Library Association's 1995 Gay, Lesbian, and Bisexual Book Award.

Crenshaw, K. (1989). Demarginalizing the intersection of race and sex: A Black feminist critique of antidiscrimination doctrine, feminist theory and antiracist politics. *University of Chicago Legal Forum, 1989*(1), 139–167. http://chicagounbound.uchicago.edu/uclf/vol1989/iss1/8
In this highly influential law review article, Kimberlé Crenshaw argues that current critical theoretical frameworks like feminism do not adequately address the intersections of class, race, and gender with women of color. Historically, Black women as a category have been defined within white patriarchal society, which has resulted in a distorted analysis of racism and sexism. Instead, Crenshaw argues for a critical analysis that takes the "intersectionality" of identity into account and one that centers the most marginalized groups.

DeBevoise, C., Hickman, M., Quinn, B., Murray, J., Vulcano, S., Gatto, J., McPartland, P., & Kustanowitz, S. [Executive Producers]. (2011–present). *Impractical jokers*. NorthSouth Productions.
A long-running and immensely popular hidden camera reality show. Members of the Tenderloins comedy troupe play practical jokes on unsuspecting victims.

Engel, M. (1976). *Bear*. Atheneum.
This controversial novel by Canadian author Marian Engel (1933–1985) tells the story of archivist Lou's journey of self-discovery while archiving a deceased author's donated collection on a remote island. Over the course of the summer project, Lou befriends and then becomes sexually involved with a tame bear. The book explores themes including loneliness, solitude, and humanity's relationship with nature. The

frequent target of book banning and censorship attempts, *Bear* is the recipient of multiple literary awards, including the prestigious Governor General's Literary Award for English-Language Fiction, presented by the Canada Council for the Arts.

Ettarh, F. (2018, January 10). Vocational awe and librarianship: The lies we tell ourselves. *In the Library with the Lead Pipe*. https://www.inthelibrarywiththeleadpipe.org/2018/vocational-awe/
This is the paper in which Fobazi Ettarh first presents the concept of "vocational awe." Through attributing to librarianship a sort of religious or spiritual value, it becomes a "calling" as opposed to simply being a job. Vocational awe, however, is not benign but becomes a tool for exploiting the labor of library workers who, feeling beholden to the cult of the profession, sacrifice things like equitable pay and work-life balance in the service of something "higher."

Freire, P. (1970). *Pedagogy of the oppressed*. Continuum.
Written by Brazilian philosopher of education Paolo Freire, *Pedagogy of the Oppressed* is a landmark text in critical pedagogy. In the book, Freire advocates for a collaborative learning model that subverts the traditional teacher/student hierarchical and oppressive "banking model of education," where the learner is a *tabula rasa*. The book introduces Freire's concept of *conscientização*, or critical consciousness, developed through collaborative education. Freire elaborated on the *Pedagogy of the Oppressed* with 1992's *Pedagogy of Hope*. A search of Google Scholar by the present authors indicates that the *Pedagogy of the Oppressed* had been cited 130,607 times as of June 24, 2025.

Grain, K. (2022). *Critical hope: How to grapple with complexity, lead with purpose, and cultivate transformative social change*. North Atlantic Books.
In this book, University of British Columbia professor Kari Grain connects the concept of hope directly with critical praxis as a tool for realizing transformational change. The book presents real-world examples as well as Grain's own personal reflections to illustrate its points. Grain's ability to explain complex critical theory through clever metaphor and easily digestible language is unmatched.

Hall, S. (1973). Encoding and decoding in the television discourse. *Council of Europe Colloquy on Training in the Critical Reading of Televisual Language*. http://epapers.bham.ac.uk/2962/
In this conference paper, Stuart Hall, a renowned cultural theorist and founding member of the Birmingham School of Cultural Studies, outlines his encoding/decoding communication model. With encoding/decoding, the target of a message is no longer seen as a wholly passive receiver of information. Instead, the receiver actively interprets the message during the decoding process. This results in three possible outcomes: accepting the dominant message/narrative, modifying it through a process of negotiated reading that considers the receiver's experiences and beliefs, or an oppositional position that rejects the dominant understanding of the message.

Harris, M. H. (1986). State, class, and cultural reproduction: Toward a theory of library service in the United States. *Advances in Librarianship*, *14*, 211–225.
In this journal article, library historian Michael H. Harris makes the case that library and information science researchers should look beyond positivism to consider critical approaches to understanding the institution and profession. This article is considered seminal because it introduced Gramscian hegemonic analysis into library and information science and inspired a generation of researchers to look beyond the discipline's artificially imposed theoretical and methodological limitations.

Jewison, N. (Director). (1973). *Jesus Christ superstar* [Film]. Norman Jewison; Robert Stigwood [Executive Producers]. Universal Pictures.
Directed by Norman Jewison, this is the film version of Andrew Lloyd Webber and Tim Rice's popular rock opera, depicting Jesus Christ's (played by Ted Neeley) final days

and crucifixion. Mirroring the counterculture of the late 1960s and early 1970s, Jesus was portrayed as something of an activist. The film was a hit.

Joseph-Salisbury, R., & Connelly, L. (2021). *Anti-racist scholar-activism*. Manchester University Press.
Joseph-Salisbury and Connelly explore the university as a site of oppression and a resource for anti-racist resistance. Universities are deeply neoliberal and continue to practice institutional racism and colonial hierarchical structures. However, the authors contend that universities have gaps that scholar-activists can exploit. Their foundational concept of "reparative theft" argues that scholar-activism is reframed as praxis to divert resources to marginalized communities and radical movements.

Kaplan, E. (2000). We are what we collect, we collect what we are: Archives and the construction of identity. *The American Archivist, 63*(1), 126–151.
Elisabeth Kaplan's article, "We are what we collect," considers how archival collections are shaped and the impact of things like collector and archivist bias on selection and description. Kaplan argues that identity is a social convention used to craft communities via identity politics and cautions archivists that they are not neutral, but that they actively define and create historical narratives.

King, M. L., Jr. (1967, October 26). What is your life's blueprint? *The Seattle Times*. https://projects.seattletimes.com/mlk/words-blueprint.html
In this 1967 address to Barrett Junior High School students in Philadelphia, M. L. King encourages the students to persevere and strive for excellence, to face challenges head-on, and to seek better opportunities.

Marx, K. (1990/1867). *Capital volume 1*. (B. Fowkes, Trans.) Penguin Books.
First published in 1867, *Capital Volume 1* represents the most mature exposition of Marx's analysis of capitalism and the only one of the three volumes of *Capital* to be published during his lifetime. Among the many topics covered in *Capital* are the commodity, labor and its alienation, the labor theory of value, the transformation of surplus value into capital, and primitive accumulation. The effects of Marx's magnum opus cannot be overstated, both in terms of its impact on the political revolutions of the 20th century and its role as fertile soil for the many critical and cultural theorists to develop their thought.

McAdam, S. (2019). *Nationhood interrupted: Revitalizing Nêhiyaw legal systems*. Purich Publishing.
Sylvia McAdam details the Cree nêhiyaw legal system, which the nêhiyaw kêhtê-ayak, Cree Elders have been hesitant to write down. McAdam explains how nêhiyaw laws are intertwined in kinship (wâhkôhtowin), songs, ceremonies, and sacred sites. Through a historical investigation of nêhiyaw laws, McAdam explores the land, language, and culture of the nêhiyaw Nation.

Radford, M. L., & Radford, G. P. (2003). Librarians and party girls: Cultural studies and the meaning of the librarian. *Library Quarterly, 73*(1), 54–69.
Marie L. Radford and Gary P. Radford examine the librarian stereotype as seen in popular media through an analysis of the 1995 movie *Party Girl*. In the movie, hipster Mary, played by Parker Posey, is forced to take a job as a library assistant. Over the course of the film, Mary transforms from a party girl to a staid (if still pretty cool) librarian. Radford and Radford use a cultural studies analysis—at the time, a novel approach for LIS research—to parse the film's representation of library workers.

Radical Reference. (2017, October 4). Info. *Radical Reference*. http://www.radicalreference.info/
Originating in New York City to support protestors of the 2004 Republican National Convention, Radical Reference was a grassroots, on-the-ground reference service for

activists, journalists, and researchers. Reference services were provided in real time and included help with maps, legal information, and logistical support. Although Radical Reference is now dormant, at its height, it included many national and international chapters.

Ranganathan, S. R. (1931). *The five laws of library science*. Madras Library Association.

LIS philosopher S. R. Ranganathan may have written *The Five Laws of Library Science* in 1931, but the principles found in this book remain relevant today: (1) Books are for use, (2) Every Reader his/her book, (3) Every Book Its Reader, (4) Save The Time Of The Reader, and (5) The Library Is A Growing Organism.

Refused. (1998). *The shape of punk to come: A chimerical bombination in 12 bursts*. Burning Heart Records.

The fourth studio album by highly influential Swedish anarcho-punk band Refused, *The Shape of Punk to Come*, hits very differently than the pop punk records that were so popular in the 1990s. This was a hardcore punk record that held no punches in either its delivery or the left-wing political content of its song lyrics. Songs like "The Refused Party Program," "Protest Song '68," and "Refused Are Fuckin' Dead" offer loud critiques of modern capitalism while, in the same instance, suggesting that anything is possible. Refused would have many albums, but this is considered their magnum opus.

Roy, A. (1997). *The god of small things*. HarperCollins.

In this novel, Arundhati Roy tells the harrowing tale of Rahel and Estha, twins who endure loss, psychological separation, and illicit love affairs in post-colonial India. The rigid caste system shapes the twins' family dynamic and burdens them with oppressive societal expectations.

Slow Factory. (n.d.). Slow factory. https://slowfactory.earth/ Accessed March 24, 2025

The Slow Factory is a New York City-based environmental and social justice organization with the mission to promote education, culture, responsible media, and transformative policies to address human rights and encourage systemic change. Slow Factory argues that to transform society, activists must build a culture of solidarity over a culture of pity, and it engages in community-driven campaigns to challenge dominant societal narratives. The Slow Factory website provides free tools for activists, including open-source educational material and curricula.

Spade, D. (2011). *Normal life: Administrative violence, critical trans politics, and the limits of life*. Duke University Press.

Dean Spade, law professor and founder of the Sylvia Rivera Law Project, critiques the US legal justice system through the lens of critical trans theory, arguing that dominant legal models support the oppression of marginalized groups through propping up the dominant culture and the status quo. *Normal Life* advocates instead for dismantling the legal system in lieu of reforming it. This is a visionary work that refutes the legitimacy of the normative legal apparatus while challenging the reader to consider radical alternatives.

Stookey, N. P. (1986). El Salvador. *On No easy walk to freedom*. WEA.

Formed in 1961 by Peter Yarrow, Noel Paul Stookey, and Mary Travers, the American folk group Peter, Paul, and Mary released multiple hits over their five decades of existence, including "Puff, the Magic Dragon," and "Leaving on a Jet Plane." Included in their 1986 studio album *No Easy Walk to Freedom*, the track "El Salvador" protests the United States's backing of the Salvadoran government in that country's Civil War (1979–1992). Widespread human rights abuses were reported, which were primarily attributed to government forces.

West, C., & Katz, E. (Eds.). (1972). *Revolting librarians*. Booklegger Press.

The brainchild of radical librarians Celeste West and Elizabeth Katz, *Revolting Librarians* is the first book to be published by the world's first female-owned independent press, Booklegger Press (founded by West and her colleagues). Following an introduction penned by West, *Revolting Librarians* collects the essays and poems of progressive and radical library workers on a wide array of political and social topics, including homophobia, sexism, and the library as a democratic institution. Although the book was marginalized in its time, it was highly influential among library workers who prioritized social justice issues, and many of its authors would go on to be recognized as leading voices in progressive and radical librarianship. The book inspired a follow-up volume, 2001's *Revolting Librarians Redux: Radical Librarians Speak Out*, edited by Jessamyn West and K. R. Roberto.

Zinn, H. (1980). *A people's history of the United States: 1492–present*. Routledge.

In this wide-ranging historical survey, radical historian and lightning rod Howard Zinn provided a history of the American colonial period and the United States from the perspective of ordinary people as opposed to traditional histories that privilege the views of elites. This was a radical telling of US history that made no pretensions to objectivity. This, of course, upset traditional historians and *really* upset the right wing, resulting in efforts to exclude it as a textbook in high schools. *A People's History* would, nonetheless, sneak its way into many classrooms. Zinn continuously updated the book through later editions, with the final "present" being the first decade of the 21st century and the Global War on Terror.

Index

Aanischaaukamikw Cree Cultural Institute (ACCI) 138
ableism 131
Accardi, Maria: feminist pedagogy 8; *Feminist Pedagogy* and *The Feminist Reference Desk* 10; liberation theology 7
Adams, Carol J. 122
Adler, Liam: critical pedagogy 13
Adler, Melissa: *Cruising the Library* 18–19; gender and sexuality 18; Jefferson's classification 19; sexuality studies 20
ageism 131
Agre, Phil 153
Ahmed, Samira 71
Ahmed, Sara 160
Alcott, Louisa May 34
Alfino, Mark 113
American Jewish Historical Society (AJHS) 139
American Library Association (ALA) 26, 43, 56, 62, 73, 77, 109, 114, 126, 154; conscience 129
American Library Association Intellectual Freedom Manual 72
anarcho-punk 82, 168
Anderson, Laurie Halse 64
anti-censorship: activism 62; advocacy 33, 68; efforts 3, 65; fight 34; groups 65
anti-communism 2
anti-critical race theory 63
Anti-Racist Scholar-Activism 135
A People's History of the United States: 1492– Present 61
The ArQuives 140–141
artificial intelligence (AI) 28, 97, 102
Association for Library and Information Science Education's (ALISE) 118
Atwood, Margaret 20, 64

Bale, Carolina 25
Banned Books: 2007 Resource Book 63
Barthes, Roland 112
Baughman, James L. 114
Bay Area Reference Center (BARC) 115
Berman, Sandy 18
Berman, Sanford 115
Bey, Hakim 151
Bhaskar, Roy 112
Bishop, Rudine Sims 26
Black and Gold Education 135
Black, Indigenous, and People of Color (BIPOC) 59
Black Lives Matter movement 127
blockheaded awareness 108
The Bluest Eye 111
Bourdieu, Pierre 112
Bowker, G. C. 44
Brian Deer Classification System 140
Brown, Alex: collection development policy 27; *Hidden History of Napa Valley* 25; *Lost Restaurants of Napa Valley and Their Recipes* 25; Punk-Ass Book Jockey 28
Budd, John 106
Burning Man 56, 151
Buschman, John 106
Butler, Judith 36

Calzada, Becky: anti-censorship advocate 34; *Prepared Libraries, Empowered Teams: A Workbook for Navigating Intellectual Freedom Challenges Together* 34; race, gender, and sexuality 31
Canada's Social Sciences and Humanities Research Council 142
Canadian Gay Liberation Movement Archives 140
Capital, Volume 1 162

Cary, Jocelyn 20
Centre for Contemporary Cultural Studies (CCCS) 145
Christine Jorgensen: A Personal Autobiography 45
City University of New York (CUNY) 43
Coleman, Ornette 83
Coltusky, Laura 113
Combahee River Collective Statement 157
Connolly, Laura 135
Cook, Terry 138
Cooperrider, David 40
COVID-19 pandemic 10, 37, 121, 147
Coville, Bruce 49
Creeping Meatball 1
Crenshaw, Kimberlé 4, 36, 50, 53; intersectionality 51
critical consciousness 2, 4, 36, 39, 48, 52, 112, 127, 158
Critical Feminist Pedagogy in Library Instruction 9
Critical Hope: How to Grapple with Complexity, Lead with Purpose, and Cultivate Transformative Social Change 39
critical librarians 97, 103, 118
critical librarianship 2, 22, 102, 112–113, 118; state of 41
Critical Librarianship and Pedagogy Symposium (CLAPS) 97
critical theory 2, 8, 12–13, 18, 36, 39, 94, 100, 103, 106–107, 112, 120–122, 132–133
Critical Theory for Library and Information Science: Exploring the Social from Across the Discipline 112
#critlib 2, 163
Crockett, Ethel S. 115

Daly, Mary 123
Damasco, Ione: *Critical Hope* 39–40; marginalized library 39; personal reflection 37
Dance of the Happy Shades 20
Day, Ronald 106
Decolonial Knowledge Systems 132
Demarginalizing the Intersection of Race and Sex 162
DIE4ART 135, 136
diversity, equity, and inclusion (DEI) 27, 134–135
Do It Yourself (DIY) 82
Doyle, Robert 63

Drabinski, Emily 8–9, 16, 21–22; *Christine Jorgensen: A Personal Autobiography* 45; LGBTQIA2+ 46; *Sorting Things Out* 44–45
Dunn, K. 82
Dzodan, Flavia 52

Encoding and Decoding in the Television Discourse 145
Engels, Friedrich 101
Engel, Marian 20, 21
Equity, Diversity, and Inclusion (EDI) 59, 85
Ettarh, Fobazi 3; *Chicken Soup for the Teenage Soul* 49; developing critical consciousness 52; LGBTQIA2+ 50; *In the Library with Lead Pipe* 52; vocational awe 48, 52

Floyd, George 59
Foote, Carolyn: *Five Laws of Librarianship* 33–34; parental rights 33; race, gender, and sexuality 31
Foucault, Michel 94, 112
Freire, Paolo 8, 13, 39, 133
Friedman, Lia: *Bitch Magazine* 57

Given, Lisa 106
Graduate Record Examination 6
Grain, Kari 39
Gramsci, Antonio 102, 108
Grant, George 127
Grassroots Media Coalition (GMC) 57
Grimes, Nikki 72
Grinnell College Libraries 120

Hall, Stuart 95, 102, 145
Harris, Michael H. 106
Hebdige, Dick 145
Heinrich, Michael 103
Hershey, Laura 120
Hoggart, Richard 146
homophobia 2, 115, 131
Honma, Todd 97
hypodermic theory of communication 145

inclusion, diversity, equity, and access (IDEA) 27
Indiana University Southeast Library 6
Indian Residential Schools Settlement Agreement 138
Information, Power, and Reproductive Health 124

Informed Agitation: Library and Information Skills in Social Justice Movements and Beyond 59
intellectual freedom 30, 33–35, 72, 100, 101, 109, 113, 115, 129; advocated for 33; book banning 162; educational equity and 35; ethos of 114; injustice and 128; in school and public libraries 70; workshops and webinars on 31
Intellectual Freedom and Social Responsibility in American librarianship, 1967–1974 115
Intellectual Freedom Committee 32
International Indigenous Librarians Forum (IILF) 91
Israel-Palestine conflict 104

Jacobs, Heidi L. M. 9
Jefferson, Thomas 19
Jensen, Kelly 3; anti-censorship activism 62; book-banning efforts 63, 65; *Speak* 66–67
Johnson, Boris 103
Jones, Amanda: LGBTQIA2+ rights 73; student-centered learning 70; *That Librarian: The Fight Against Book Banning in America* 74–75
Joseph-Salisbury, Remi 135
Josey, E.J. 116, 118
Journal of Radical Librarianship (JRL) 84

K-12 education 121, 124
K-12 teacher 120–121
Kagan, Alfred 3, 129; *Progressive Library Organizations: A Worldwide History* 79
Karl Marx 4
Kendrick, Kaetrena D. 38
Knowledge Justice: Disrupting Library and Information Studies through Critical Race Theory 41
Knox, Emily 72
Kumbier, Alana 9
Kwasnik, Barbara 45

Ladenson, Sharon 9
Lang, Moyra 117
Lasswell, Harold 145
Lawson, Stuart: Liberation Frequency 83; Research Repository Advisor 81; *The Shape of Punk to Come* 83
Lee, Deborah 89

Leung, Sophia Y. 40
LGBTQ 63
LGBTQ2+ 138, 140
LGBTQIA2+ 26–27, 64, 73, 120, 129, 154
liberation theology 7
Librarians and Party Girls 95–96
Librarianship and Legitimacy: The Ideology of the Public Library Inquiry 109
library and information science (LIS) 43, 94, 105, 117, 124, 147
Library Community Collective (LCC) 44, 46, 59–60
Library Juice Press Handbook of Academic Freedom 113
library neutrality 2, 26, 28, 117–118
Library of Congress Classification system (LCC) 44, 46, 59–60
Library of Congress Subject Headings (LCSH) 17, 44, 115
Library Quarterly 46
Library School Journal 71
Litwin, Rory 18
Lopez-McKnight, Jorge R. 40
Loyer, Jessie: Indigenous librarianship 91; Indigenous language revitalization 91

Make America Great Again (MAGA) 2
Makoare, Bernard 92
Mandelbaum, David 90
Mann, Thomas 152
Marshall, Joan 115
Marx, Karl 101
master of library and information science (MLIS) 105, 157
master of science in library and information science (MSLIS) 55
McAdam, Sylvia 88
McCann, H. 46
McClure, Charles R. 110
Metropolitan College of New York 12
Miami Workers Center's (MWC) 14
Monaghan, W. 46
Morrison, Toni 111
Morrone, Melissa 59
Munro, Alice 20
Musk, Elon 163

Napa County Historical Society 24, 26
National Association of Independent Schools (NAIS) 26

Nationhood Interrupted: Revitalizing nêhiyaw Legal Systems, describes how *wâhkôhtowin* 88
Nesmith, Tom 138
The New Yorker Magazine 55
Nicholson, Karen 103
Normal Life: Administrative Violence, Critical Trans Politics, and the Limits of Life 13
Nursing Interventions Classification (NIC) 44

Olson, Hope 18

Pedagogy of the Oppressed 8, 39
performative theory of gender 36
Pho, Annie: critical theory 94; Librarians and Party Girls 94–95
The Plains Cree: An Ethnographic, Historical, and Comparative Study 90
The Politics of Theory and the Practice of Critical Librarianship 103
Popowich, Sam: *Capital, Volume 1* 102; *Communist Manifesto* 99; critical librarianship 103; Marxism 100–102
professional praxis 8, 92, 101, 158, 160, 162
Progressive Librarians Guild (PLG) 56, 79
Progressive Library Organizations: A Worldwide History 129
Punk-Ass Book Jockey 28

Queering the Catalog: Queer Theory and the Politics of Correction 46
queer theory-oriented analysis 46

Raber, Doug 3
Raber, Douglas: incorporation of critical theory 105
Race and Resistance theories 132
racial-sexual oppression 159
racism 2, 36, 39, 50, 59, 78, 126, 128, 130–131, 133, 141, 147–148, 158, 162
Radford, Gary P. 94
Radford, Marie L. 94
radical history 78
Radical Librarians Collective (RLC) 81; ethos 82
Radical Reference (RR) 55, 151, 162
Radical Research Center (RRC) 114
reparative theft 135
Revolting Librarians 1, 116
Rice, Aaron 24

Rice, William 24
Riddle, John S. 9
Roberto, K.R. 117, 154
Roy, Arundhati 64, 160

Salisbury, Remi Joseph- 135
Salvadoran Civil War 7
Samek, Toni 163; ethos of intellectual freedom 114; information ethics 114; *Revolting Librarians* 116
Sancho, Ignatius 19
Sarah Lawrence College 8
Schlesselman-Tarango, Gina: critically oriented library 122; feminist theory 121; K-12 education 121; *The Sexual Politics of Meat* 123
Seale, Maura 9, 103
sexism 2, 9, 10, 50–51, 131, 158
sexuality 12, 17–21, 31, 48–49, 122, 160
The Sexual Politics of Meat 122
The Sexual Politics of Meat: A Feminist-Vegetarian Critical Theory 122
The Shape of Jazz to Come 83
The Shape of Punk to Come 82, 162
Sheppard, April 4; anti-capitalism and environmentalism 128; social justice issues 128
She was a Booklegger: Remembering Celeste West 117
Smith, Naomi 3; microaggressions in professional life 134; neoliberal academic institutions 133–134; The Slow Factory 136
social justice 12, 26–27, 56, 85, 133, 150, 160, 162, 168; activism 80, 126; advocacy 24, 132; critical librarianship and 117; education 38; entrepreneur 135; and equity 126; four pillars of 14–16; issues 3, 97, 128, 132, 134, 169; oriented librarian 7; -oriented librarians 60, 130; -oriented library worker 130; -oriented work 132; powerful vehicles of 132; -related issues 47
Social Responsibilities Round Table (SRRT) 56, 77, 114, 126, 129, 154
Sorino, Melinda 66
Sorting Things Out 44
Sorting Things Out: Classification and Its Consequences 43
Southern Poverty Law Center 63
Spade, Dean 13

Srivastva, Suresh 40
Star, S. L. 44
Stephens, Robin 120
Subculture: The Meaning of Style 145
Swanson, Raegan: The ArQuives' collections 141; community-driven archives 140

Tewell, Eamon: critical/cultural communication theories 146–147; encoding/decoding model 146; library instruction 146; oppressive power structures 144
theory of intersectionality 36
Tokumitsu, Miya 52
trans exclusionary radical feminist (TERF) 123
Trump, Donald 3, 103
Truth and Reconciliation Commission of Canada 138
2SLGBTQIA+ communities 141
2004 Republican National Convention (RNC) 56

University of Chicago Legal Forum 50
University of Delaware 50
University of Michigan 37
University of Pittsburgh 7

University of Western Ontario (UWO) 17–18

value-laden historiography 78
vocational awe 3, 48, 52–54, 107, 151, 163

Wallace, David Foster 43
Ways of Knowing: Oral Histories on the Worlds We Create 46
West, Celeste 1, 114–115, 117, 118, 154
West, Jessamyn: acceleration of technological change 152; digital divide 152; *Without a Net: Librarians Bridging the Digital Divide* 151
Wheatley, Phillis 19
Wiegand, Wayne A. 114
Williams, Raymond 146
Wolf, Steve 115
Women's Talent Corp 12
World Trade Organization (WTO) 150–151

Yousefi, Baharak: *Feminists Among Us: Resistance and Advocacy in Library Leadership* 160; power struggles in librarianship 159; sexual politics 159

Zinn, Howard 61, 77–78

For Product Safety Concerns and Information please contact our EU representative GPSR@taylorandfrancis.com
Taylor & Francis Verlag GmbH, Kaufingerstraße 24, 80331 München, Germany

www.ingramcontent.com/pod-product-compliance
Lightning Source LLC
Chambersburg PA
CBHW061349300426
44116CB00011B/2054